Tage Frid Teaches Woodworking

Book 3: Furnituremaking

Tage Frid Teaches Woodworking

Book 3: Furnituremaking

The Taunton Press

Cover illustration: To avoid mistakes in designing a chair, it's a
good idea to make a drawing of three superimposed views—side,
front and top. This dining chair is explained on pp. 124-133.

First printing: September 1985
International Standard Book Number 0-918804-40-X
Library of Congress Catalog Card Number 78-65178
Printed in the United States of America

FINE WOODWORKING® is a trademark of The Taunton Press, Inc.,
registered in the U.S. Patent and Trademark Office.

The Taunton Press, Inc.
63 South Main Street
Box 355
Newtown, Connecticut 06470

Acknowledgments

I finally finished Book 3. This was by far the most difficult: making all the pieces and photographing many of them in different stages of construction. The working drawings had to be accurate, and I spent a lot of time making samples of various construction details and, if necessary, full-scale mock-ups.

I am especially grateful to Seth Stem for doing the working drawings, to John Dunnigan for helping to edit the text, to Roger Birn for the photography, to my wife, Emma, and to Jamey Hutchinson for helping me build the furniture.

Contents

Introduction
Chapter 1

People are practical when they buy furniture. They want a chair they can sit in, a table they can eat at and a bed they can sleep on. After 55 years as a furniture designer, craftsman and teacher, I believe that furniture should be functional, designed around the construction and the proportions and shapes of the environment and the users.

Every piece of furniture carves out the space in which it is situated. This is especially true for chairs and bentwood or sculpted furniture. The object becomes a positive element; the empty space around it is a negative factor. The relationship between these positive and negative elements must be considered when a piece is designed. Another thing to keep in mind is the shadow left on the furniture by any three-dimensional details, such as a rabbet or an edge chamfer.

When I came to this country from Denmark in 1948, most North American homes were furnished with heavy, upholstered furniture. My furniture was light, with uncomplicated lines and natural finishes: the tops of my tables and the seats of my chairs appeared to be floating; the construction was solid, but my joinery was often exposed, rather than hidden beneath folds of fabric or layers of stain and finishes. Most furniture back then was mass-produced and there were very few craftspeople, so I had a hard time selling my work. Later, I started a gallery in Rochester, New York, with three other craftspeople. This was a great success and gave me a chance to expose my furniture and educate people. After that, I never had any trouble selling my work. At about the same time, Scandinavian furniture, mostly from Denmark, became very popular in the North American market and that had a great influence on popular taste and design.

Maybe because furniture is functional, it has never been accepted as art—at least not until the designer has been dead for several years. But this is beginning to change. Today, galleries are beginning to show furniture, and museums and art collectors are buying it. This may be due, at least in part, to the influence of the Italian Memphis group, which claims that furniture does not have to be serious or functional. Much of the furniture that is being designed and built in this style is completely different from anything that has been made before and disregards some of the most basic properties of the material. If the wood's natural tendency to move is not taken into consideration, there is a good chance that a piece will fall apart, especially if it is moved to an area with a very different humidity.

A lot of this contemporary furniture is painted brilliant colors that make the wood look like plastic or metal. Some of the work is good, but I have always felt that if wood is made to look like plastic, the piece should be made out of plastic. Wood is a warm, living material and should be used to emphasize those qualities. I do not feel comfortable with furniture that screams at me when I come home to relax. I have a hard time understanding tables that were not meant to hold objects, or chairs that were not made to carry weight.

How long these design concepts of the 1980s will last I don't know, but I don't think that much of this furniture will become classic. I think that, ultimately, furniture will be judged by how well it meets those criteria I've mentioned. It also helps if the maker has a good knowledge of the material and the techniques of construction. The more experience you have, the better—I don't know of any shortcuts. There is nothing wrong with making art and getting well paid for it, but when furniture is finally accepted as art, it must not be at the expense of its fine tradition of craftsmanship and respect for the material. □

Designing for People
Chapter 2

1

2

When you get a commission to design the furniture and layout for a specific room, there are many things to consider. First, what is the function of the room? Then, what is the traffic flow—the invisible paths from one door to another, or between furniture and appliances? These paths should always be clear, with no objects blocking the way, or people will have to make detours.

Another important thing to consider is the height and size of the people you are designing for. People don't buy houses or furniture for their guests as much as for themselves. The furniture designer should scale the furniture to present its owner in a nice setting according to his or her size. Heavy people look ridiculous in furniture that is too delicate, and small people look lost in heavy, overbuilt furniture. Of course, if there is a great difference in the sizes of the people you are designing for and they will be sharing the furniture, you will have to compromise somewhere.

People differ most in height in the length of their legs; when they are seated, the difference is not that great. Here **(1)** you can see the difference between people when they are standing. Jim is 81½ in. tall, I am 67 in. and Vivian is 60½ in. Seated **(2)**, Jim is 40 in., I am 36 in. and Vivian is 33½ in., the difference between us being much less than when we are standing. Of course, I am a little better upholstered than Jim or Vivian, which helps somewhat when I am seated.

The average height from the floor for a dining-room chair seat is 17 in. to 18 in.; for the top of a dining table or a desk it is 29 in. to 31 in. The distance from the floor to the bottom of the table apron is usually about 24 in., and that is where a person like Jim has a problem. When he is sitting in a chair of average height, the distance from the floor to the top of Jim's legs is 27 in. So he is the one who ends up carrying the table. When working for a person of that height, I would design a dining table without an apron, such as a pedestal or trestle table.

Sometimes, an average size is best for all. For example, the two chairs shown here **(3)** were adjusted to fit Jim and myself. Jim's chair was raised to its full height and mine lowered as far as it would go, with the result that the top of Jim's legs ended up much higher. If we were both going to sit at the same dining table in these chairs, Jim would have to bend over to eat and I would not be able to see what was on my plate. If I were served soup in a tall pot, I would have to stand up to get at it. So usually an average-height dining chair (18 in.) is the best compromise for comfortably seating people of a wide variety of heights.

Another big problem arises when you are designing furniture, especially work tables, where a person will be standing. Most kitchen appliances are made for 36-in.-high counters, which are fine for a person of average height (68 in.), but are too low for a taller person and too high for a shorter person. The small person has the greatest problem in reaching things, especially on a countertop range. With the height of a burner on the stove at 36 in., add an 8-in.-deep pot on the back burner and it could be dangerous, especially if the front burners are in use. If I were designing a kitchen for a person about 60 in. tall, I would try to lower the stove by about 3 in. or 4 in.

If I were building only one small piece of furniture for someone who didn't live near me, I might send them a drawing for approval. But I would never take a major commission unless I could meet with the people to get their opinion and could see the space where the work was to go.

When you first meet with a customer, listen to what he or she wants and take notes. After listening for a few minutes, you might get a great idea and really want to talk about it. Don't do it or you may regret it later. By the time the customer gets used to that idea, you might have come up with a better one. And you might have a hard time convincing him or her that your new design is better.

Once you are satisfied with your design, bring only the one design that you are convinced is the best to show the customer. If you bring more than one, most

people get confused. Remember, you were called in because this client had seen your work and believes in your judgment.

Before you start the job, write an agreement with all the specifications, such as the woods that will be used, the hardware and the type of finish. Be sure to include the price and the terms of payment. I bill my customers in three installments: one-third when the design is accepted but before I order materials, one-third when the woodwork is complete and the piece is ready to be finished, and one-third upon delivery. Make two copies of the agreement for both of you to sign, one for you and one for the customer.

When the agreement is signed and you've gotten the first installment, order the materials if you don't have them in stock. I always tell my students to buy or make their hardware first, before they build the furniture. It's very frustrating to design and build a piece of furniture only to find out when it's too late that the hardware you wanted is no longer available.

3

Planning your work   Before starting the job, plan your work and make a cutting list so you can cut out all the pieces at the same time. It's quicker, you'll make fewer mistakes and there will be very little waste. I like to lay out the job on sticks, in full scale of the top and front views with all the details (see p. 192). From the sticks, I take the exact measurements of each piece and write them down on a cutting list. If I am doing a big job, I make one cutting list, then make another one the next day to make sure I have it right. When making my first rough cuts, I always add 1 in. to the length and about ¼ in. or more to the width, depending on the width of the piece. When all the stock has been rough-milled to these oversize dimensions, I joint and thickness-plane all the pieces to their finished measurements at the same time. (If boards are to be glued together, I leave them a little thicker so they can be resurfaced.) Then I cut every piece to its exact width and length and cut all the joints. If you are working in solid wood, make all the joints and assemble the piece as quickly as possible, before the wood has a chance to warp. But if you have to store the wood for a while until glue-up, stack it and cover it with a piece of plywood or Masonite, or leave the wood standing on end and separated so air can circulate around it.

Many people make scale models. I never do, because if you simply multiply your measurements up from the smaller model, the proportions always seem to change. I prefer to draw the piece in full scale. Then I hang the drawing on the wall to see if the relationships between the various elements are right. I'll live with it there for a while until I finalize the design and actually begin cutting.

Mock-ups   For tables and most casework, I usually work right from the drawing and make any changes on paper before I start cutting. But I do chairs a bit differently. I make a full-scale drawing of the side view, and of half the front and top views (see p. 125). If I want to experiment with a detail, such as the arm of a chair, I'll carve it out of a piece of styrofoam, which is easy to work with. When I've settled on a chair design that is more or less what I'm looking for, I al-ways make a full-scale mock-up out of scrapwood, screwed together, so I can try the chair out for comfort and have other people sit in it and criticize it, too (see p. 135). It helps to have people of various shapes and sizes try out the mock-up to see if it is going to work.

The drawings that accompany the designs in this book will give you all the essential information you'll need for each piece of furniture. But don't feel restricted to copying my designs exactly. They may have to be changed to fit the room or the people you are building for. Just remember that if you change the dimensions, the proportions will also change.

I have detailed only the most complicated steps of the construction of each piece. Where I refer to technical details or methods that are described in my earlier books (*Book 1: Joinery* and *Book 2: Shaping, Veneering, Finishing*), I have noted the book and page numbers in brackets. If a drawing doesn't give the precise measurement for something, it is probably because the part should be custom-fit (like the drawer in the drawing table in chapter 3).

A final note   Many students wonder how people will see their work when they're just starting out. The best way to expose your work is to send it to shows and galleries and try to get write-ups in magazines and newspapers.

The furniture and built-in cabinets included in the Gallery (pp. 224-231) represent a sampling of my own work over more than 30 years. Unfortunately, I made many more pieces of which I have no record. There's a lesson here: Don't forget to photograph everything you make. I never did and it was a great mistake. Most of my furniture was commissioned and I was always busy, so I never had the time. Plus I'm a lousy photographer.

With any luck, your most difficult job will be getting your first customer. If your design and craftsmanship are good, you will get a lot of work by word of mouth.   □

Furniture to Make Furniture

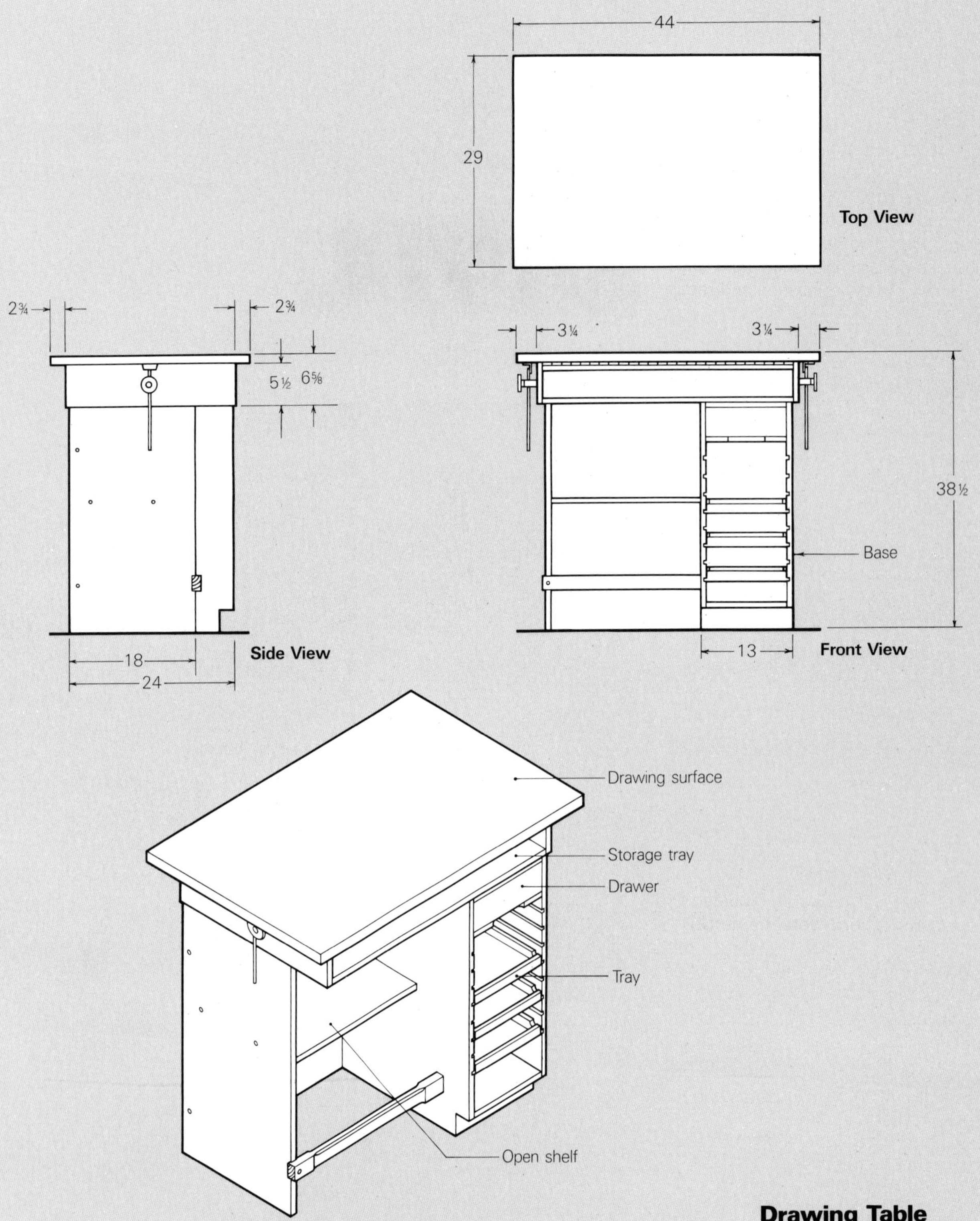

Chapter 3

44

29

Top View

2¾   2¾

5½ 6⅝

18

24

Side View

3¼   3¼

38½

Base

13

Front View

Drawing surface

Storage tray

Drawer

Tray

Open shelf

Drawing Table
Scale: ³⁄₆₄ in. = 1 in.

Drawing Table

About twenty years ago, I was commissioned to design the drawing tables for the dormitories at the Rhode Island School of Design. I ended up making about three hundred of them. I was asked to make them plain, simple and inexpensive, but able to withstand abuse.

Because dormitory rooms are small, the tables had to be compact and space-efficient. They also had to be easy to assemble and disassemble, with interchangeable parts for easy installation and repair.

I thought there should be a storage tray below the drawing surface to hold paper, and also one drawer for drawing tools and an open shelf to hold books. The dimensions of the top, and therefore the overall size of the piece, were based on standard paper and parallel-rule sizes. These specifications, and the large, adjustable, flat surface required for drawing, made me naturally start thinking about designing in plywood with some kind of knockdown hardware.

Recently I made a new drawing table for myself that is similar to the earlier ones. The overall dimensions are the same, but this one has sliding trays instead of stationary shelves in the cabinet **(1)**.

The cabinet and top sections are glued together. All the other parts are bolted together for easier installation. The carcase is made of ¾-in. veneer-core plywood, which is thick enough to resist flexing. The top is plywood, rabbeted and screwed into a solid-wood frame **(2)**.

The joints in the cabinet and top sections are ¼-in.-thick by ¼-in.-deep tongue-and-groove, which are strong enough in this case because the veneer core provides a gluing surface that is 50% long-grain to long-grain. Also there is very little stress put on these joints once the whole table is bolted together.

In this type of construction, the tongues close to the corners should be offset so the corresponding grooves will not be too close to the plywood's outside edge, which would weaken the joint (see p. 19). The other tongues can be centered.

1

2

As with all projects, a cutting list should be made first and all materials and hardware collected before any cutting proceeds, as described on pp. 5-6. I got myself into a lot of trouble by forgetting that when I built this table and discovered that the parallel rules we'd used before were no longer available.

The carcase   I used a router to cut all the grooves on the sides of the carcase first [*Book 1,* pp. 128-130]. With the grooves made, I cut the tongues on the corresponding pieces with a dado blade on the tablesaw. Use a spacer with the dado that will give you the right-size tongue.

3

After you have cut the tongues, lay the pieces flat and cut the shoulders. Be sure to change to a hollow-ground blade that will give a smooth cut without tearing out the veneer.

Once the joints are cut, glue a ¼-in.-thick facing on the front edges of the carcase so the rabbets won't show. Plane and sand the facings flush with the sides of the cabinet.

Next the grooves for the sliding trays are made. These should be cut before the carcase is assembled. I decided to make lots of grooves relatively close together so I would have maximum flexibility in the arrangement of the trays.

Like the carcase joints, the grooves for the trays could be made using a dado head in a tablesaw, but that would mean resetting the fence for each pair of grooves. In this case the distance between the grooves is constant, so I found the hand router, used with a jig, to be faster and more accurate.

To make the jig, attach a scrap of plywood to the base of the router with a 3-in. hole in it to clear the shavings. Screw a strip of hardwood that fits snugly in the groove to the bottom of the plywood so the bit lines up on the groove to be cut **(3)**. To correctly position the strip, cut a groove in a piece of scrap plywood, then measure and mark the desired distance from that groove to the next one.

For the first groove on each piece, you'll have to use a fence. But for the rest of the grooves, the jig works off the previous groove **(4)**. Place the router on the work so that the strip is in the first groove and cut the next groove. Continue until all the grooves on both sides of the carcase have been cut.

There are many ways to do this, including making more flexible jigs with adjustable slots, and jigs could be easily fashioned from aluminum or another more durable material, but the jig I have used here worked just fine for me on this table.

4

When all the grooves have been cut and the joints made, you can assemble the carcase. Don't put too much pressure on the clamps, and make sure that the grooves are clean. I eased the sharp edges of the grooves and tongues with a piece of sandpaper.

It is very important that the cabinet be square when you glue it together. If it isn't, the drawer won't work. Sometimes one of the sides bends temporarily from even slight clamp pressure, so the most accurate of squares won't always tell you if the cabinet is square. I always measure diagonally from corner to corner to avoid this problem. If the two diagonals measure the same, everything is okay.

Now that the cabinet is together, you can put in the drawer runners **(5)**. First make four drawer runners out of solid hardwood, and cut a ¼-in. by ¼-in. tongue on them to match the grooves in the side. Because the sides of the cabinet are plywood, they will not shrink or swell with changes in humidity, so you can glue the runners right in all the way across. If the sides had been solid wood, the same type of runners could have been used if they were glued only on the front 2 in. As long as the runners fit tightly, this system is easier and more accurate than runners that are screwed in place.

5

6

The drawer Making a drawer that works as though it were running on ball bearings is not difficult if you take the time to do it right. But you won't do it by following precise measurements from a drawing in a book. That is why I haven't drawn out the drawer's exact dimensions. It must be custom-fit to the carcase. Here's how.

First mill all the drawer parts slightly longer and wider than the space provided on the drawings on pp. 19 and 22.

The drawer front should be fitted first. Begin by hand-planing the top edge so that it will just about go in **(6)**.

7

Now fit the drawer front lengthwise. Insert one end and mark the other end from the back with a scriber **(7)**. Then cut the piece to fit on the tablesaw. Cut it a little bit long at first and then trim it with a hand plane.

In a situation where you can't mark the drawer front from the back, you can mark the top and bottom with a pencil **(8,9)**, draw a line between the points, and then cut and fit as before.

8

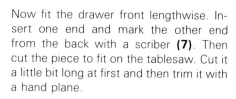

9

The drawer-front piece should fit snugly, so that it can be just pushed in halfway with your fist **(10)**.

Mark and cut the back of the drawer to the exact same length as the front. Cut the width smaller, leaving space for the bottom to slide in and also a little space at the top to make fitting easier later.

Mark the front and back pieces of the drawer so you will know how they fit back in the carcase **(11)**.

Fit the drawer-side pieces the same way; cut and plane the width until the sides fit very snugly.

Crosscut the back ends of the drawer sides square and push them back as far as you want them to go **(12)**. Then scribe the front ends where they extend beyond the face of the carcase and cut them to fit. Remember to make the sides shorter if half-blind dovetails are used on the drawer front, and allow for shrinkage if solid wood is used for the carcase.

When done, mark the drawer sides so you'll know where they belong.

10

11

12

13

14

After all the pieces have been fitted individually, the drawer is ready for assembly.

Join the drawer together with dovetails [*Book 1,* pp. 64-88]. This is the traditional joint for the job because it is mechanically strong against all the pushing and pulling that happens to a drawer. I used half-blind dovetails in the drawer front because I didn't want to see the ends of the tails. Through dovetails are fine in the back because they are easier to cut and you don't see them unless the drawer is pulled out all the way.

I like to hammer together dovetail joints instead of pulling them together with clamps because it is simpler and more controllable. If the joint fits right, you shouldn't need clamps anyway.

It is critically important to glue the drawer together absolutely square. Measure diagonally between corners, as I described before.

To keep the bottoms of the drawer sides from wearing out, I glued strips of wood to the bottom edges of the drawer. The strips are also grooved to hold the drawer bottom **(13,14)**. The ⅜-in.-thick drawer side plus the ⅜-in.-thick strip provides a good sliding surface on the bottom. This technique also allows you to work with thinner drawer sides, which look better, and still get a substantial surface for the drawer to slide on. On this drawer I also attached a strip to the bottom of the front, mostly to make the inside look consistent.

When the glue was dry, I sanded the sides and back with a belt sander to flush up the joints and remove any extra glue. If you don't feel comfortable using a belt sander, you'd better do this part by hand. After this, I planed and hand-sanded the tops and bottoms until the drawer slid right in. I moved the drawer in and out a few times and then removed it. I sanded down the spots that were shiny from rubbing until the drawer fit perfectly. This didn't take long, though, because each part had been fitted before assembly.

There is nothing more frustrating than working on a drawer that won't fit and you don't know where to begin to fix it. Usually the end result is that the drawer will be too loose and will wobble or bind instead of slide. The time spent fitting each part individually at the beginning is made up for many times over when fitting the drawer into the cabinet.

I did not want a handle to stick out on this drawer front, so I routed a shallow, ¾-in.-wide groove on the bottom of the front. Then I removed a section of the front stretcher below the drawer **(15)** to allow fingers to reach under and find the finger groove.

When everything slides perfectly, rub paraffin on all the sliding parts. Cover the drawer sides—bottom and top—as well as the inside of the cabinet around the drawer.

Now cut the plywood bottom to size and slide it in place **(16)**. If for some reason the drawer front is not flush with the front of the cabinet, plane the front of the bottom to correct the problem. Then screw the back of the bottom to the back of the drawer—do not glue it.

Never put any finish other than wax on the outside of a drawer or the inside of a cabinet where there will be drawers. The finish will gum up the works and might get tacky in the summertime, causing the drawer to stick.

15

16

The trays A sliding tray is more of a shelf with a lip around the edges than it is a drawer. It doesn't keep dust and dirt out, but it's much better than a plain shelf because you can pull it out for easy access to the contents. The frame prevents things from falling out, and is usually cut lower in the front so you can reach inside better. The frame pieces can be kept small in dimension because they are glued and screwed to the plywood bottom for stability.

Trays are a lot easier to make than drawers. Because the plywood bottom actually slides in grooves in the cabinet sides, it controls the way the tray works. Make the frame a little smaller than the opening so that after assembly and installation there will be a ⅟₃₂-in. to ⅟₁₆-in. space between the sides of the cabinet and the frame of the tray. The plywood should stick out about ⁵⁄₁₆ in. on each side to fit snugly in the bottom of the grooves in the cabinet.

To make the sliding trays, first cut out several pieces of ¼-in. plywood for the bottoms and fit them in the grooves in the cabinet.

Next prepare the fronts, backs and sides of the tray frames. Rabbet the bottom of each front piece to accept the plywood tray bottom, and make the curved cutouts on the leading corners of the side pieces. Then cut the joints on all the pieces. I used dovetails here for the same reasons I used them on the drawer, but almost any other joint would work.

Glue and square the frames and then sand. Line up each frame on one of the pieces of plywood already cut and then glue and screw it in place. Be very careful to make sure the frame is centered on the plywood.

When this is done, complete the final fitting by testing the trays in the grooves and sanding lightly if necessary.

When everything fits perfectly and the trays are finished, rub paraffin on the sliding parts, just as you did on the drawer.

T-nuts For furniture that has to be repeatedly assembled and disassembled, a good and inexpensive method is to use T-nuts. There are many kinds of more expensive knockdown hardware being manufactured today, but a T-nut inserted in a dowel works just fine.

To assemble this table, I used ³⁄₁₆-in. bolts and T-nuts inserted into the end of ½-in. dowels glued into ½-in. holes. The T-nut sits in the bottom of the hole. When used in veneer-core plywood, the dowel and the surrounding hole have at least 50% long-grain to long-grain gluing surface. In solid wood, the dowel would be surrounded by long grain and the joint would be even stronger. This is a good, strong knockdown joint that is also hidden.

Here's how to work with the T-nuts. I used a jig to hold the dowel on the drill press while I drilled the hole in the center **(17)**.

I bolted the left side of the jig to the table, but I hinged the right side so I could squeeze the handles together to hold the dowel firmly in place.

I used a small-center drill first to be sure that the hole was centered. After the holes were centered in all the dowels, I drilled them again with a ¼-in. bit **(18)**. If the dowel had been too long for the bit, I could have turned it over and drilled from both ends.

After all the dowels were drilled, I put a T-nut in one end and tapped it lightly to allow the prongs to mark the dowel **(19)**.

I then made little cuts on each mark, the length of the points, using a fine dovetail saw **(20)**. This keeps the dowel from splitting when the T-nut is hammered in **(21)**.

The dowel is now ready to be glued in place **(22)**. Of course, the holes in all the carcase pieces should have been drilled right after the final milling and before the cabinet was assembled, but double-check them now to be sure they are deep enough. Be sure that they are deeper than the bolt or dowel is long, so that even if the bolt is longer than the dowel, it won't force the dowel out as it is tightened. Also remember to keep the T-nut in the bottom of the hole.

Here's something else to watch out for. When gluing in the dowels, use just enough glue to secure them—don't use too much. And don't turn the piece upside down until the glue has dried enough that it won't run into the threads of the T-nuts. If glue gets into the threads, you'll have trouble assembling the thing. It happened to me once when I was making 100 drawing tables. The people working for me at the time glued the dowels in just the way I told them, but then they turned the pieces upside down and glue ran into the threads. Later, when we were installing the cabinets, we had to redrill a lot of holes and insert new dowels. Those poor guys; if they had never before seen a Great Dane get mad, they sure found out what it was like that day!

17

18

19

20

21

22

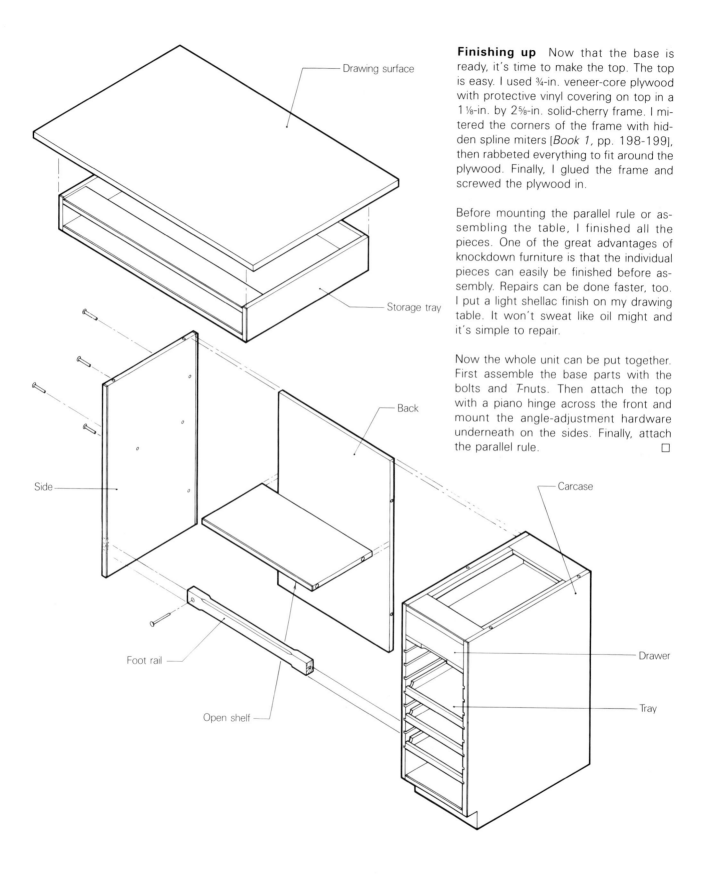

Drawing surface

Storage tray

Side

Back

Foot rail

Open shelf

Carcase

Drawer

Tray

Finishing up   Now that the base is ready, it's time to make the top. The top is easy. I used ¾-in. veneer-core plywood with protective vinyl covering on top in a 1⅛-in. by 2⅝-in. solid-cherry frame. I mitered the corners of the frame with hidden spline miters [*Book 1*, pp. 198-199], then rabbeted everything to fit around the plywood. Finally, I glued the frame and screwed the plywood in.

Before mounting the parallel rule or assembling the table, I finished all the pieces. One of the great advantages of knockdown furniture is that the individual pieces can easily be finished before assembly. Repairs can be done faster, too. I put a light shellac finish on my drawing table. It won't sweat like oil might and it's simple to repair.

Now the whole unit can be put together. First assemble the base parts with the bolts and T-nuts. Then attach the top with a piano hinge across the front and mount the angle-adjustment hardware underneath on the sides. Finally, attach the parallel rule.   □

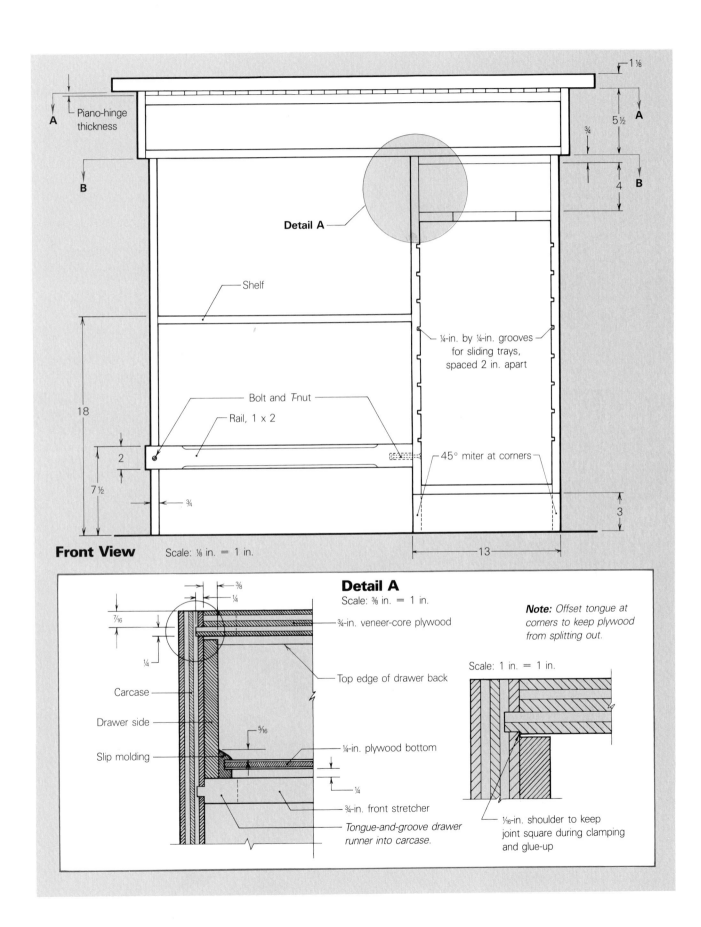

1⅛

Piano-hinge
thickness

A

B

5½

¾

A

4

B

Detail A

Shelf

18

Bolt and T-nut

Rail, 1 x 2

¼-in. by ¼-in. grooves
for sliding trays,
spaced 2 in. apart

2

45° miter at corners

7½

¾

3

13

Front View   Scale: ⅛ in. = 1 in.

Detail A

Scale: ⅜ in. = 1 in.

⅜

¼

7⁄16

Note: Offset tongue at
corners to keep plywood
from splitting out.

¾-in. veneer-core plywood

¼

Top edge of drawer back

Carcase

Scale: 1 in. = 1 in.

Drawer side

5⁄16

Slip molding

¼-in. plywood bottom

¼

¾-in. front stretcher

1⁄16-in. shoulder to keep
joint square during clamping
and glue-up

*Tongue-and-groove drawer
runner into carcase.*

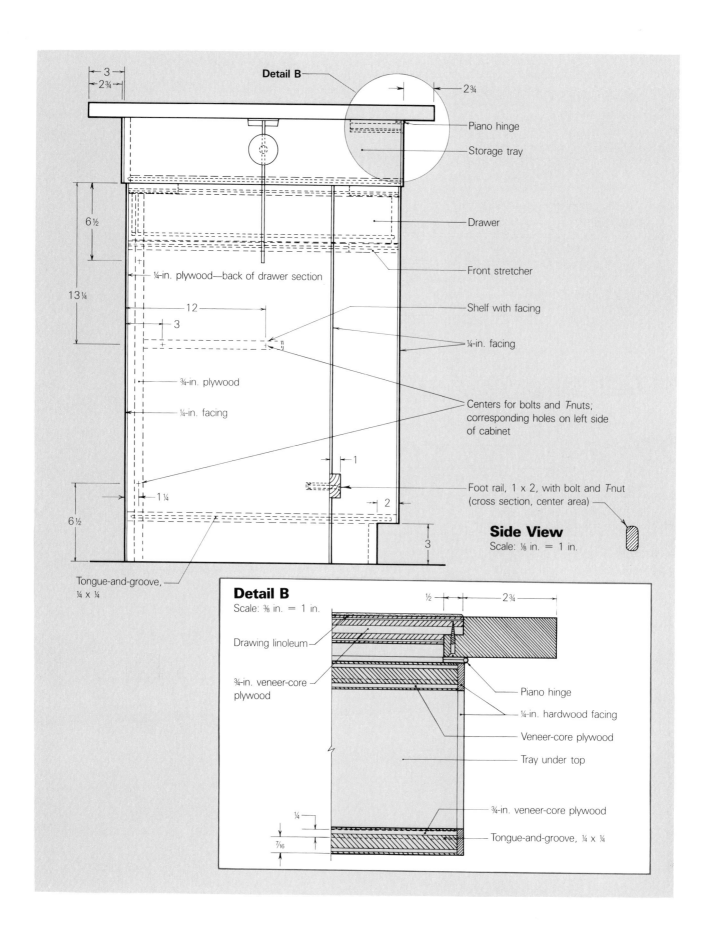

Detail B

2¾

Piano hinge

Storage tray

Drawer

Front stretcher

¼-in. plywood—back of drawer section

6½

13¼

12

3

Shelf with facing

¼-in. facing

¾-in. plywood

¼-in. facing

Centers for bolts and T-nuts; corresponding holes on left side of cabinet

1

6½

1¼

2

3

Foot rail, 1 x 2, with bolt and T-nut (cross section, center area)

Side View
Scale: ⅛ in. = 1 in.

Tongue-and-groove, ¼ x ¼

3
2¾

Detail B
Scale: ⅜ in. = 1 in.

½ 2¾

Drawing linoleum

¾-in. veneer-core plywood

Piano hinge

¼-in. hardwood facing

Veneer-core plywood

Tray under top

¾-in. veneer-core plywood

Tongue-and-groove, ¼ x ¼

¼

7/16

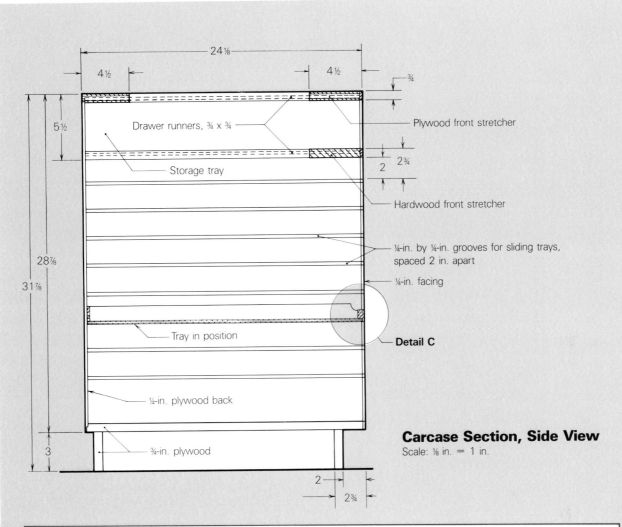

24 ⅛

4 ½   4 ½   ¾

5 ½

Drawer runners, ¾ x ¾ —

Plywood front stretcher

Storage tray

2   2¾

Hardwood front stretcher

¼-in. by ¼-in. grooves for sliding trays, spaced 2 in. apart

28 ⅞

31 ⅞

¼-in. facing

Tray in position

Detail C

¼-in. plywood back

3   ¾-in. plywood

Carcase Section, Side View
Scale: ⅛ in. = 1 in.

2

2 ¾

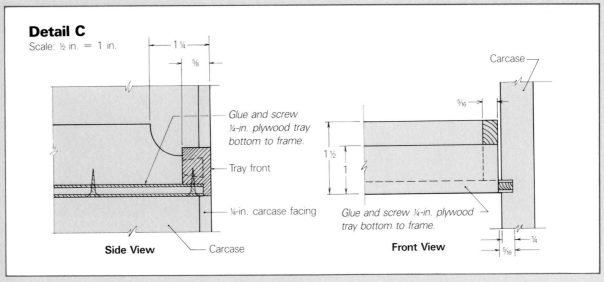

Detail C
Scale: ½ in. = 1 in.

1 ¼

⅝

Carcase

Glue and screw ¼-in. plywood tray bottom to frame.

Tray front

5⁄16

1 ½

1

¼-in. carcase facing

Glue and screw ¼-in. plywood tray bottom to frame.

¼

5⁄16

Side View   Carcase

Front View

Section A-A
Scale: ⅛ in. = 1 in.

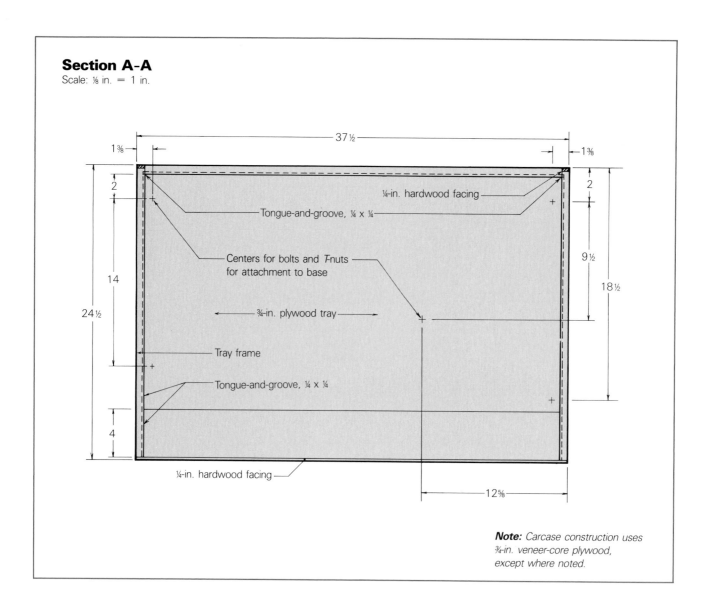

¼-in. hardwood facing

Tongue-and-groove, ¼ x ¼

Centers for bolts and T-nuts
for attachment to base

¾-in. plywood tray

Tray frame

Tongue-and-groove, ¼ x ¼

¼-in. hardwood facing

37½

1⅜

2

9½

18½

14

24½

4

12⅝

Note: *Carcase construction uses ¾-in. veneer-core plywood, except where noted.*

Section B-B
Scale: ⅛ in. = 1 in.

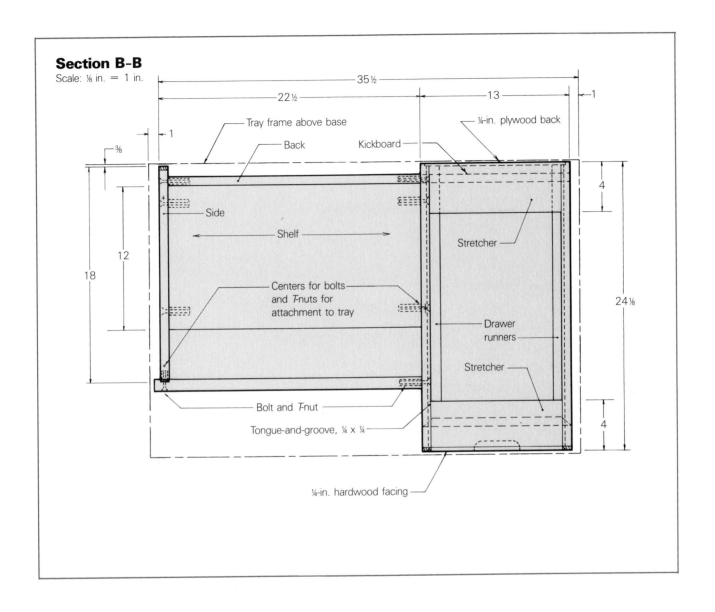

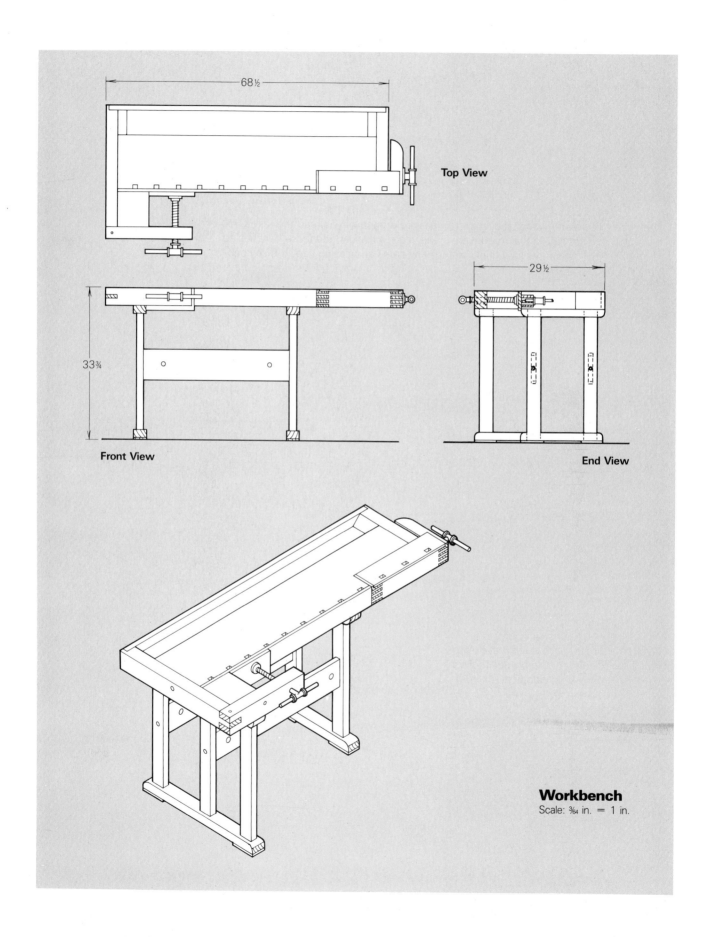

68½

Top View

33¾

Front View

29½

End View

Workbench
Scale: ³⁄₆₄ in. = 1 in.

Workbench

When I came to this country in 1948, I was given a tour of the school where I was to teach. I was guided to a large room and introduced to the teacher with whom I was to work. He did most of the talking because my vocabulary didn't go much beyond "yes" and "no," but using my arms and legs I finally conveyed to him that I wanted to see the woodshop. When I was told that I was standing in it, I just about passed out. In this room were a huge thickness planer, which I think Columbus' father must have brought over, and a few small power tools. I was really flabbergasted when I saw the students' workbenches. These were large, two-person tables with a vise at each end. Most of the time the students had to hold the work with one hand and use the tool with the other, which is a good way to get hurt. Some of the students had taken a lot of time to make special contraptions to hold the work so they could use both hands—which I'm sure was the Lord's intention when He designed us with two. (Of course, the Japanese use their feet to secure the work, which also leaves both hands free.)

After being at the school for several months, I realized that the bench I wanted was not available in this country, so I designed my first workbench. It was quite similar to the one I had been taught on.

Eventually we made a bench for each graduate student. Since then, we have been making these workbenches every two years so the students each have their own. This gives them the proper tool for holding their work. In addition, the process of building the benches is a good exercise in learning how to set up machines for mass production and how to work together as a production team. The last time, we made a run of fifteen benches, and it took us three days from rough lumber to having all the parts ready to fit or assemble, with the benchtops glued together.

Although you will probably be making only one bench at a time, I feel it is important to say something about limited production runs, so I am going to explain how to build the workbench the way we did it. I will give you some general information about the sequence of the operations, and some specific tips on how to make the difficult parts. I have labeled every part of the bench with a letter in the drawings and the cutting list to make for easy reference as you read the text. Over the years, having made these benches so many times and having had so many people use them and criticize them, I have arrived at these dimensions as the ones best suited for cabinetmakers.

My bench is about 6 ft. long **(1)**, but if you wish to lengthen it you can easily do so by extending the benchtop (pieces **a,b,c** on the plans) and tool tray **(h,i)** at the center and the two stretchers between the legs **(s)** by the same amount. You can shorten the bench in the same way. I advise making any dimensional changes to the length in 5-in. increments, so that the distance between the dogholes in the top will remain the same.

The bench can be made wider, too, in which case pieces **d,e,v,w,y** will have to be extended. This is a right-hand bench, but can be converted to a left-hand one by reversing the plans. If additional storage space is needed, you can attach a piece of plywood between the two stretchers in the base **(s)** and insert sides to form a large compartment. Not being a neat person myself, I found this to be a great place for collecting dirt and pieces of wood that I should have thrown out in the first place. If you wish, you can attach a rack on **h** to hold chisels and screwdrivers, but I think this, too, is more of a bother than a help because you have to keep removing the tools so they won't interfere every time you are working on a piece that is wider than the benchtop.

With the bench's two vises, there are four ways you can hold the work: two in the right vise, one in the left vise and one between the benchdogs. Each vise is tightened with one screw, and there aren't any guide rods to interfere with the work. A piece can be clamped all the way to the floor if necessary, and the left vise can hold an irregularly shaped object. With only six bolts, the bench is easy to assemble and disassemble and requires minimum storage space. The only glued-up parts are the benchtop, the right vise and the leg sections. Everything else is bolted or screwed together so that any damaged parts can easily be replaced.

This reminds me of when I was an apprentice. At that time, the master was the master—especially in a remote area. In one shop, the master charged 1 krone for every cut a journeyman made in a benchtop by mistake. A young journeyman was going into the army, so on his last day when he got paid he told the master that he had made a sawcut in his bench. The master thanked him for being so honest and deducted the 1 krone from his final pay. The master was very surprised when he came out into the shop and found that the one cut had sawn the bench into two halves.

1

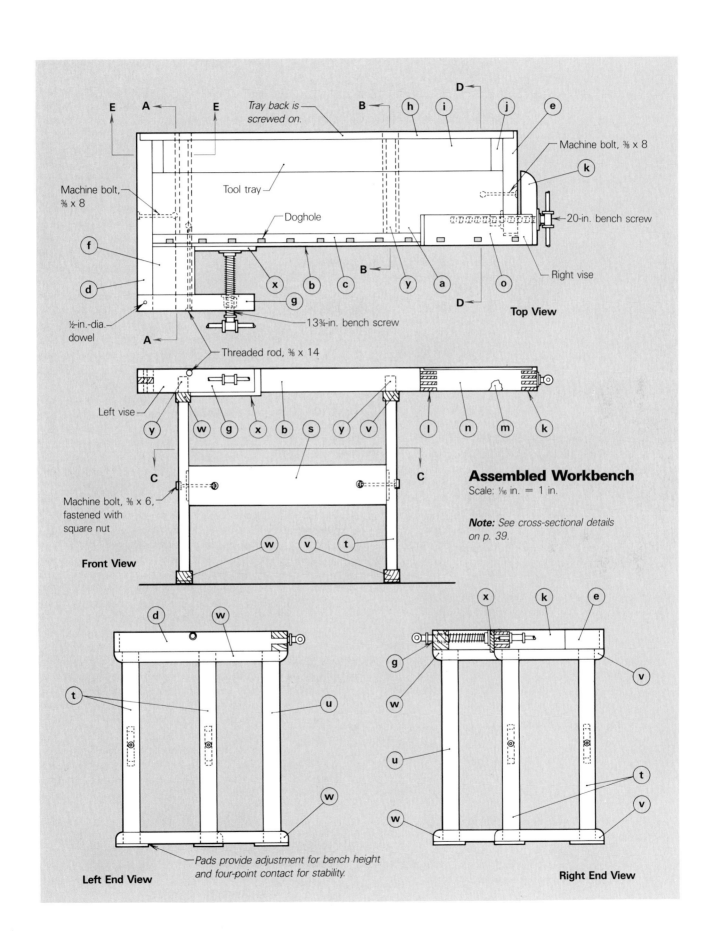

E   A   E   Tray back is screwed on.   B   h   i   j   e

Machine bolt, ⅜ x 8

D

Machine bolt, ⅜ x 8

k

Tool tray

20-in. bench screw

Doghole

Right vise

f

x   b   c   y   a   o

d

B

D

½-in.-dia. dowel

g

13¾-in. bench screw

Top View

A

Threaded rod, ⅜ x 14

Left vise

y   w   g   x   b   s   y   v   l   n   m   k

C   C   **Assembled Workbench**

Scale: ⅟₁₆ in. = 1 in.

Machine bolt, ⅜ x 6, fastened with square nut

Note: See cross-sectional details on p. 39.

w   v   t

Front View

d   w   x   k   e

t   g

u   w

u

t

w   v

Pads provide adjustment for bench height and four-point contact for stability.

Left End View   **Right End View**

Cutting List for Workbench

Quantity	Part	Finished sizes	Description
1	a	1¾ x 9¾ x 60¼	Benchtop
1	b	⅝ x 4 x 46	Cap piece
1	c	1⅞ x 4 x 46	Doghole strip
1	d	2¾ x 4 x 29½	Left end cap
1	e	2¾ x 4 x 16⅜	Right end cap
1	f	1¾ x 7⅜ x 8¾	Left vise filler
1	g	2¾ x 4 x 20	Left vise
1	h	1 x 4 x 63½	Back apron
1	i	½ x 7 x 59½	Tool tray, plywood
2	j	1¾ x 1¾ x 5½	Corner block
1	k	2¾ x 4 x 12	Right vise jaw
1	l	2¾ x 4 x 11	Right vise
1	m	1⅞ x 3½ x 20	Right vise
1	n	⅝ x 3½ x 20	Right vise
1	o	½ x 5 x 18½	Right vise
1	p	¾ x 1¼ x 18¾	Right vise guide
1	q	1 x 2¾ x 5½	Right vise guide
1	r	½ x 1½ x 15	Right vise guide
2	s	1 x 6½ x 35¼	Stretcher
4	t	1⅞ x 2⅞ x 31¼	Leg with mortise
1	u	1⅞ x 2⅞ x 31¼	Leg without mortise
2	v	1¾ x 2¾ x 18¾	Base right
2	w	1¾ x 2¾ x 29½	Base left
1	x	¾ x 5 x 16	Left vise jaw
2	y	1¾ x 2¼ x 14½	Filler

Note: *Finished sizes are expressed in thickness x width x length.*

Lumber: *Approximately 60 bd. ft. of ⁸⁄₄ maple, 10 bd. ft. of ⁵⁄₄ maple and one ½ x 8 x 60 piece of Baltic birch plywood.*

Hardware: *Four ⅜ x 6 machine bolts; two ⅜ x 8 machine bolts. One ⅜ x 14 threaded rod or bolt. Two ⅜ x 5 lag bolts. Two 7-in. benchdogs with heavy springs (1 x ⅝ knurled face and ⅞ x ⅝ shank). One 1¼-in.-dia. by 20-in.-long (overall length) bench screw, cut to fit; one 1¼-in.-dia. by 13¾-in.-long bench screw with swivel end.*

Before you begin work, study the drawings and the cutting list carefully. Don't forget to note any dimensional changes you've made both on the drawings and in the cutting list. The next thing you should do is get all your hardware. That way, if you wish to make a substitution or if some of the hardware you wanted to use isn't available, you can make your dimensional changes before any wood is cut. We had difficulty finding 14-in.-long bolts, so we made our own by brazing a nut to some ⅜-in. threaded rod that we cut to length.

For other specialized hardware, you will also need two 1¼-in.-dia. bench screws, one 20 in. in overall length and the other 13¾ in. long with a swivel end. We had trouble finding the right-length bench screw for the right vise, so we bought these screws a little longer and cut them to length. We also purchased one pair of 7-in. benchdogs with heavy springs for each bench. We used Ulmia dogs, which have a 1-in. by ⅝-in. knurled face and a ⅞-in. by ⅝-in. shank, but you could easily make your own benchdogs out of hardwood. The rest of the hardware and materials listed in the cutting list is fairly standard.

We used maple for all the parts of the workbench except the bottom of the tool tray, where we used ½-in. Baltic-birch plywood. Maple is hard and durable and is one of the least expensive woods in the area where I live. When choosing your wood, make sure to select a dense hardwood and be certain that it is dry. It is best to buy rough lumber and mill it yourself, because you can maintain control over the flatness of the stock. If you don't have a thickness planer available, buy the lumber already planed, but be extra careful to align the boards properly during glue-up. I suggest that you not use pieces wider than 4 in. in the top, to ensure that the top will stay flat. We used ⁸⁄₄ stock for everything except pieces **b,h,s,x**, which are made out of ⁵⁄₄ stock. For the very heavy pieces, we glued together ⁸⁄₄ and ⁵⁄₄ pieces because it's just about impossible to find such thick lumber that has been properly dried. Several parts of the bench are made up of short pieces of wood left over from the milling of the top.

With all the materials gathered, you are ready to start. Make a cutting list from your updated drawing, starting with the largest pieces. When you mill the lumber, always cut the longest pieces first.

When making more than one bench, it pays to have template sticks for each piece. If you use a ruler for each measurement, there are too many opportunities to make a mistake, but if the stick is measured correctly the first time, each piece will be the same. Each stick should be at least 1 in. longer than the final dimension of the piece because you should always rough-cut the pieces a little long and wide at first. The template sticks should have a letter corresponding to the drawing and the cutting list so you can easily keep track of how many of each have been cut.

After you have cut all the pieces to their approximate lengths and widths, they are ready to be jointed and thickness-planed. Pieces will be measured individually and cut to their final lengths and widths afterward, as needed. (Use the dimensions indicated in the cutting list.)

The top   We began with the top for two reasons: it is the largest piece, and it needs to be glued up before anything else can be done to it. We tried to get all the tops milled and glued together right away to keep a smooth flow to the production. While the glue was drying, we worked on the other parts. It is a good idea to use splines between the pieces of the top **(a)** to make alignment easier, and it isn't a bad idea for strength, either, because of all the hammering that will take place on the top. We used a dado head on the tablesaw to cut the grooves for the ½-in. by ¾-in. splines, but this could also be done with a shaper, hand router or plow plane. Remember, the grain of the splines and the boards in the top must go in the same direction. Make the grooves, mill the splines out of scrap from the top, and glue up the boards to get piece **a** [*Book 1*, pp. 54-57]. After the glue has dried, **a** is jointed and thickness-planed again before **c** is added. When you are laying out the dogholes in **c**, remember that the piece is a little longer than its final dimension, and that you will make the final cuts after it has been glued on.

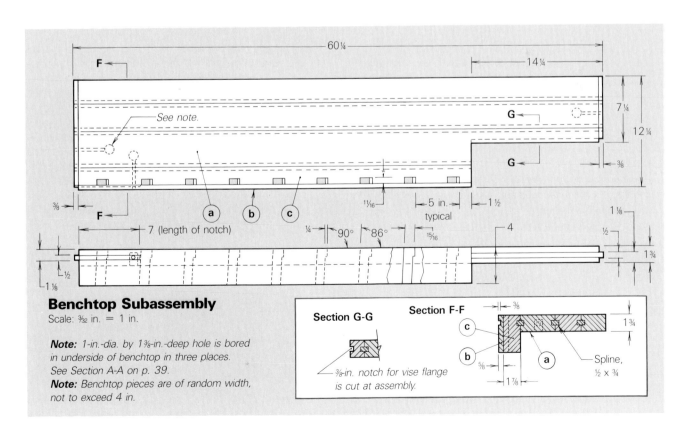

Benchtop Subassembly
Scale: ³⁄₃₂ in. = 1 in.

Note: *1-in.-dia. by 1³⁄₈-in.-deep hole is bored in underside of benchtop in three places. See Section A-A on p. 39.*
Note: *Benchtop pieces are of random width, not to exceed 4 in.*

Section G-G

³⁄₈-in. notch for vise flange is cut at assembly.

Section F-F

Spline, ½ x ¾

2

3

We also used the dado head to cut the dogholes, but since we didn't have a set that was wide enough, we had to make two cuts for each slot. In order to make the first doghole in each piece, if you have the same problem with your dado set, attach a long wooden fence to the miter gauge and clamp on two stop blocks—one on each end. Remember to set the fence at the correct angle to make the dogholes. Make the first cut with one end of **c** pushed against one block, and the second cut with the other end of **c** against the other block **(2)**.

After you have made the first slot in **c**, make a jig similar to a finger-joint jig [*Book 1*, pp. 90-91] to cut the rest **(3)**. If you are making two cuts for each slot, the pin on your jig should be the width of a single cut of the dado head, rather than the full width of the slot, so the jig will give you slots of the correct width.

Make one cut with the first doghole sitting over the pin and pushed up against one side of it **(4)**.

Slide the piece over so that the pin contacts the other side of the slot and make the second cut **(5)**. When this cut is complete, move the piece over so that the slot you just cut covers the pin, then repeat the process until all the dogholes have been cut. While you are set up for this operation, you might as well cut the dogholes in **m**, too, so you won't have to set up the jig twice. Don't forget that the slots in **m** must be angled in the opposite direction, so cut the piece from the other face.

4

5

After you have cut all the dogholes, glue on cap pieces **b,n**. Put glue on just the slotted pieces, and don't use too much of it because cleaning it out of the slots later is difficult. It is also a good idea to put a small brad in each end of the cap pieces so that they won't slide when clamped on **(6)**. It is preferable to put the brad near the end of the cap piece if it's long enough so the brad won't get cut by the saw later. When gluing up a number of benchtops, you can clamp two or more of these assemblies at the same time for efficiency. By the way, you will have to chisel a shallow shelf in all the dogholes in the benchtop and the right vise before the benchdogs will fit in, but wait to do this until the top is all done. Be sure to clean the glue out of the dogholes as soon as they are glued up. Push a wet rag through each slot with a stick and then follow with a dry rag.

6

When the glue has dried, joint the top surface of both pieces flush and rip them to final width. (Allow a bit extra for removing the sawmarks.) Set aside **m** for later. Crosscut the left end of **c** for a good square end to line up **c** with the benchtop **(a)**. My drawing on p. 29 shows the cut at 7⅜ in. from the back of the second doghole from the end, but use this measurement only if your dogholes are the same size and are spaced the same as mine.

Now cut the top to length and width and cut grooves for splines in **a** and **c**. Make the groove in **c** about ½₂ in. lower than the groove in **a** so that when **c** is glued on, it will stick up just a little and can easily be planed flush by hand. When you glue these two pieces together, make sure the ends are lined up flush.

7

When the glue has dried and the top has been planed flat, cut a ½-in. by ⅜-in. tongue on both ends of the top **(7)**. We used a shaper with two cutters to cut each tongue in one pass. You could also stand the top on end and cut the tongue using a dado head on the tablesaw. If you use the tablesaw, make a jig to hold the top [*Book 1*, p. 183] and proceed carefully. This operation requires two people. While you are set up for this, cut the tongue on **f**, too. Cut corresponding grooves in **d,e,g** and then set these aside for the moment.

8

9

10

The right vise The most difficult part of making this bench is the right vise. The lengthwise cut for the vise must be parallel to the front edge of the benchtop. The cleanest and most accurate way to do this is to use the tablesaw. Run the front face of the benchtop against the fence and set a stop to control the length of the cut **(8)**. If you must, you can do this with a bandsaw or handsaw and smooth the cut with a router.

The crosscut for the vise has to be precisely square and this, too, is best done on the tablesaw **(9)**.

If the blade on your tablesaw cannot be raised high enough for this cut, finish the cut with a handsaw **(10)**. Clean the corner with a chisel.

Finally, make the groove in **a** for the tongue on **l** to ride in. The accuracy of this groove is very important because it will largely determine how smoothly the vise will work. Once again we used the shaper, but a router will do just fine. In either case, the cutter won't be able to reach all the way into the corner, so you will have to clean it out with a chisel afterward. Now, except for the bolt holes, you have completed machining the body of the top.

Return to **k,l,m**, which make up the right vise. Cut the joints that will hold them together. We used finger joints on the corners because they are strong and easy to mass-produce, but dovetails might be faster and better if you are making only one bench. The accuracy of these and all other joints and grooves made in the right vise is critical, so take your time.

With the joints done, make the rest of the cuts on these pieces. Cut an accurate groove, ½ in. by ½ in., in **m**. Then drill the hole in **k**. Piece **l** looks complicated, but it isn't. Lay out the lines according to the drawings first. Most of the cuts on **l** can be made on the bandsaw. Make the tongue that rides in the groove in **a** slightly oversize.

Cut the grooves for the guides on the tablesaw. The first cut is easy and straightforward, as you can see **(11)**.

But on the second cut, be sure to clamp a block to the fence so that both ends of **m** have something to rest on **(12)**.

Make sure that everything fits together and that the vise is square **(13)**. Double-check with a ruler to ensure that the front and back of the vise opening both measure the same.

When you glue the vise together, it is very helpful to cut a piece of plywood to the exact dimension of the inside of the vise. If you clamp the vise pieces around this piece of plywood, the vise will come out square.

11

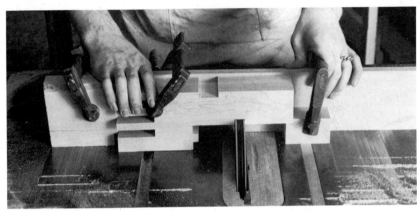

12

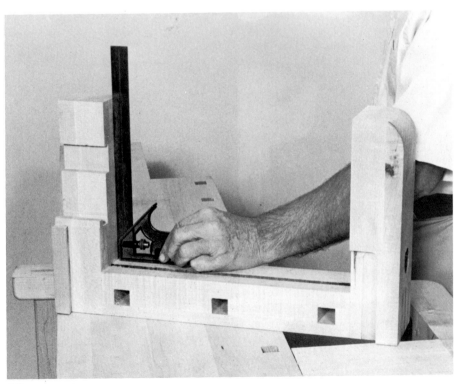

13

14

15

16

17

After the glue has dried, fit the tongue on **l** (which you left oversize before) into the groove in the benchtop so that it fits snugly **(14)**, but still slides. Then position the end cap **(e)**. Of course, this also involves fitting the tongue on **e** to the groove in **m (15)**.

When the tongues at both ends fit the groove, slide the vise into the closed position and cut a piece of scrapwood to fit tightly between the edge of the bench and **m**. In **(16)**, the scrap piece is dark for clarification.

Now move the scrap piece to the end of the bench and use it to position **e**. The vise has been removed for **(17)**.

With **e** clamped in position, drill a ⅜-in.-dia. hole through it into **a**, using a long bit. The hole in **e** should be drilled first on the drill press to make sure that it is square, so it can guide the long bit. Drill the countersunk hole in **e** first and make it big enough for the socket wrench to fit the bolt head. On the bottom of benchtop piece **a**, drill a 1-in.-dia. hole about 1⅛ in. deep to hold the nut. Use a Forstner bit and don't go too deep.

The final cut on top of **e** for **o** to slide against is not made until the vise has been fitted to the bench and is moving smoothly. When that's done, clamp the vise to the benchtop and mark on **e** the center for the bench screw. Remove **e** and drill the hole on the drill press, then bolt the flange (nut) on. It might be necessary to chisel a notch into the benchtop to make room for the flange, depending on which type you buy. Install the screw.

Flip the benchtop upside down to fit the guides **(18)**. Countersink all the screws so they won't interfere with the vise's travel. Piece **r** should be screwed down first and then **p** set in place. Take the time to make all these fit right. Fitting the vise will drive you crazy at times, but be patient and take care of one section at a time—eventually it will all fit just right. Then you can breathe a sigh of relief, because the hard part is done.

When the vise is working properly, **o** is added. It is set into **k** and **l**, so they must be routed or chiseled out. If you want to get a little fancy, you can undercut the ends so that the effect is like one large dovetail **(19)**. Just cut a complementary angle on the ends of **o**.

18

Glue **o** to the moving parts of the vise but not to the benchtop. Afterward, drill up from the bottom through the dogholes to locate the corners of the holes, then finish them by chiseling from the top.

When everything has been fitted and is working smoothly, all the places where wood runs against wood should be coated with melted paraffin that has been thinned slightly with turpentine (about one tablespoon to a 2-oz. block of paraffin). First melt the paraffin in a can or pot, then add the turpentine only after you have removed the container from the heat source. Liberally brush on this mixture in its warm, liquid state. It will protect the wood while helping to make the moving parts slide freely. Do not use oil on any of these pieces.

19

20

21

The left vise   The left vise is a lot easier to make than the right vise, and the drawings are self-explanatory. But I will give you a few tips that might speed it up a little. First, drill the hole for the bench screw in **g** and inlay the flange flush with the inside. Next, clamp **d,f,g** in place and drill the bolt holes the same way you did for **e**. Before drilling the hole for the 14-in.-long bolt, be sure that it does not run through one of the dogholes. Bolt these pieces in place. Do not glue the corner joint between **d** and **g**, in case you ever need to get it apart. Instead, pin the joint together with a ½-in. dowel.

The left vise has no guides, so to move it you often have to help it with one hand **(20)**. This is not a serious disadvantage when you consider the vise's flexibility. Because the clamping board swivels, you can hold wedge-shaped or irregular work **(21)**. If the vise were not flexible, a special jig would have to be made for this job.

When screwing the swivel end of the bench screw to the clamping board **(x)**, place it so it can be removed.

Finishing up the top   To make the tool tray, simply screw **h** onto the back of the benchtop after it has been grooved. The plywood is set in the groove and then screwed directly to the underside of the benchtop. It is further supported by filler pieces **y**, which also stabilize the top and are connected to the base. Screw in the two corner blocks **(j)** from the bottom to make it easier to sweep out the tray.

The top should be hand-planed or belt-sanded level if it is not perfect. All corners and edges should be chamfered slightly to minimize chipping out when banged.

After the benchtop has been planed and sanded, the dogholes have to be chiseled out so the benchdogs will rest flush with, or a little below, the surface of the benchtop when they are inserted. That way, they can be stored so you won't risk nicking them with a plane or chisel. Set the dog in the slot and make a pencil mark where the shoulder must be removed **(22)**. Then use a chisel to chop out the wood to the depth of the dog's face **(23)**. That takes care of the benchtop.

22

23

24

The base The leg assemblies in the base are held together by through-wedged mortise-and-tenon joints [*Book 1*, p. 162]. Cut all the joints as shown in the drawings. If you wish, you may round over the edges of the base pieces and radius the ends of the feet. This type of detail, along with the vise joinery and handles, can give your bench a personal touch with very little effort. Sand all the base pieces and drill all the bolt holes on the drill press before gluing up the base. When you glue up the tenons, be sure to hammer evenly on both wedges, and don't overdo it. When gluing up the base assembly with three legs, make sure the mortises for the stretchers **(s)** are made on the insides of the four vertical legs **(t)**, not in **u**. The width of the mortise is the thickness of **s**. A shoulder has been added top and bottom to stabilize the base. After the wedges are in, check each section for squareness. You can remove the clamps if you wish, because the wedges will hold everything in place. Clean off all excess glue while it is still wet and you will have very little finishing work. After the glue has dried, saw off the excess of the wedges and plane the tops and bottoms of the leg assemblies flat. Clamp the base together and drill holes for the hardware in the two stretchers **(s)**. The holes you drilled in the legs will guide your drill bit here. The holes for the nuts in the stretchers are also drilled on the drill press. Add the bolts, washers and nuts to complete the base.

Four small blocks of wood should be screwed onto the bottoms of the feet **(v,w)**, so that the bench rests on four points and won't rock. The thickness of the blocks can be varied to adjust the final bench height. Bolt the top to the base and the bench is ready to be finished.

Using the bench The entire bench, excluding the moving parts of the right vise, which have already been coated with paraffin, should be completely saturated with oil. We put several hearty coats of raw linseed oil on the work surface and a few on the rest of the bench. Once a year you should resurface the top by scraping it down, leveling it with a hand plane, if necessary, and reoiling it.

Now your bench is completed, and it looks so beautiful that you hate to use it. If you take good care of it, working on it but not into it, it should stay beautiful for years.

Although this workbench is a good, sturdy, all-purpose tool for holding work, there are many little accessories you can make to increase the versatility of this bench in your shop. Here's one of my favorites.

If you are working on long boards or panels, you can make a simple device to support the other end of the board. Cut a sturdy piece of wood, such as a 2x4, to the height of the benchtop. Drill a series of holes at least ¾ in. in diameter in a straight line down the length of the piece, about 1 in. apart. By clamping this piece into the right vise and placing a dowel in the hole just below the work, you can easily add support to a long piece **(24)**. □

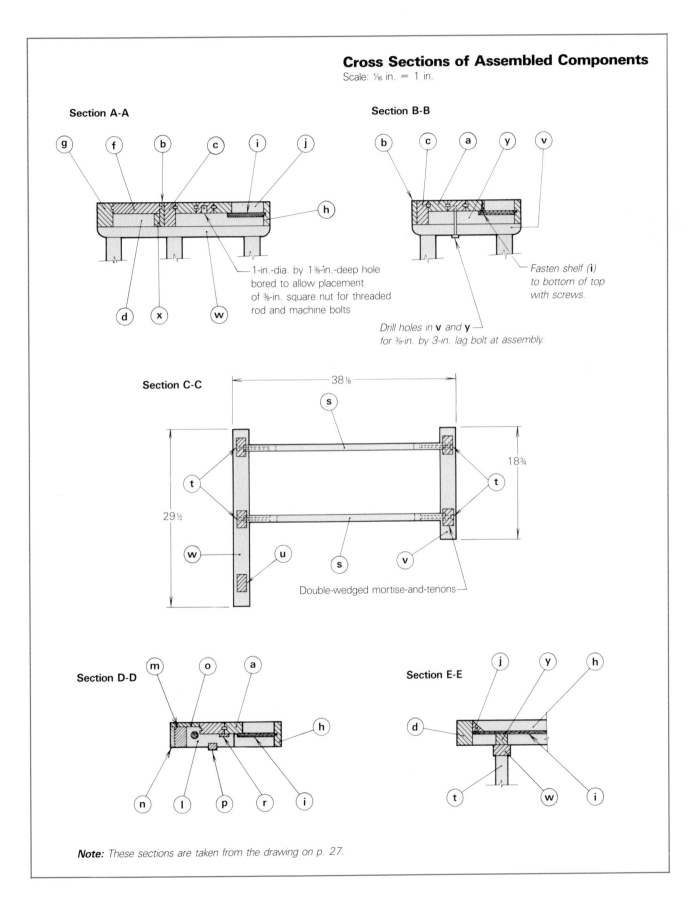

Cross Sections of Assembled Components

Scale: ¹⁄₁₆ in. = 1 in.

Section A-A

1-in.-dia. by 1⅜-in.-deep hole bored to allow placement of ⅜-in. square nut for threaded rod and machine bolts

Section B-B

Fasten shelf (**i**) to bottom of top with screws.

Drill holes in **v** and **y** for ⅜-in. by 3-in. lag bolt at assembly.

Section C-C

38⅛

18¾

29½

Double-wedged mortise-and-tenons

Section D-D

Section E-E

Note: These sections are taken from the drawing on p. 27.

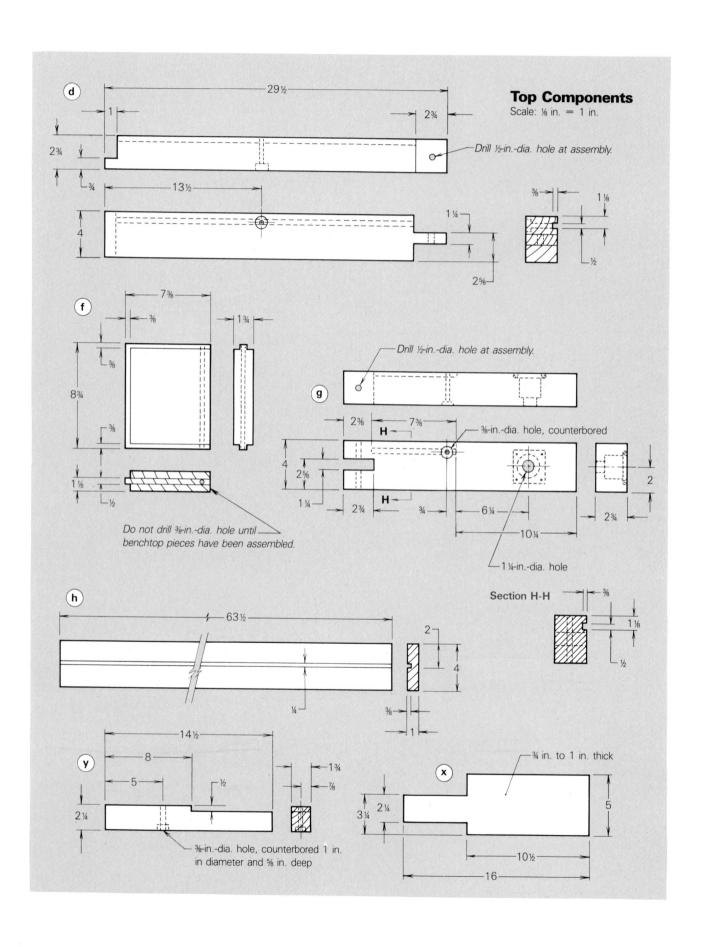

Top Components
Scale: ⅛ in. = 1 in.

Drill ½-in.-dia. hole at assembly.

Drill ½-in.-dia. hole at assembly.

⅜-in.-dia. hole, counterbored

1 ¼-in.-dia. hole

Do not drill ⅜-in.-dia. hole until benchtop pieces have been assembled.

Section H-H

¾ in. to 1 in. thick

⅜-in.-dia. hole, counterbored 1 in.
in diameter and ⅝ in. deep

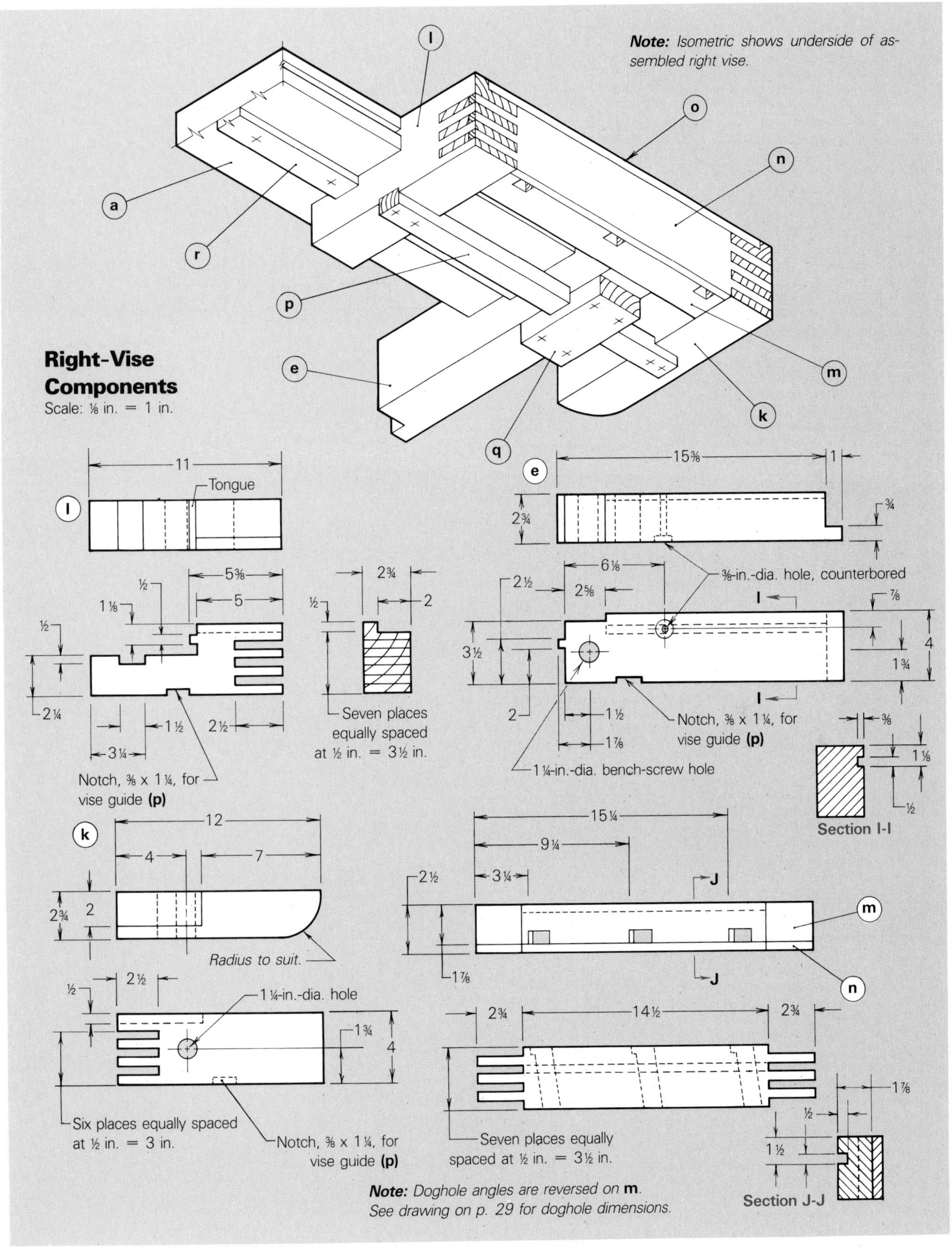
Note: Isometric shows underside of assembled right vise.
l
o
n
a
r
p
e
m
k
q
Right-Vise Components
Scale: ⅛ in. = 1 in.
11
Tongue
5⅜
5
½
1⅛
½
2¼
1½
2½
3¼
Notch, ⅜ x 1¼, for vise guide (p)
2¾
2
½
Seven places equally spaced at ½ in. = 3½ in.
15⅜
1
2¾
¾
6⅛
2½
2⅝
⅜-in.-dia. hole, counterbored
I
⅞
3½
4
1¾
2
1½
1⅞
Notch, ⅜ x 1¼, for vise guide (p)
1¼-in.-dia. bench-screw hole
⅜
1⅛
½
Section I-I
12
4
7
2¾
2
Radius to suit.
2½
1¼-in.-dia. hole
1¾
4
Six places equally spaced at ½ in. = 3 in.
Notch, ⅜ x 1¼, for vise guide (p)
15¼
9¼
3¼
J
1⅞
14½
Seven places equally spaced at ½ in. = 3½ in.
1⅞
1½
Section J-J
Note: Doghole angles are reversed on m.
See drawing on p. 29 for doghole dimensions.

Base Components
Scale: ⅛ in. = 1 in.

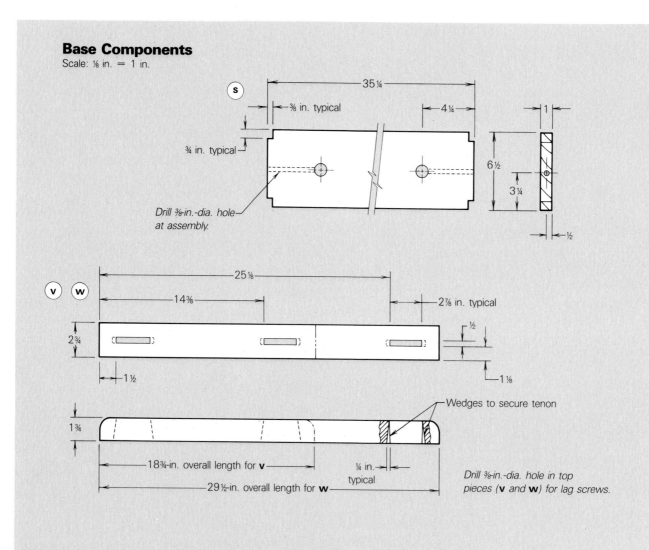

ⓢ

35¼

⅜ in. typical

4¼

1

¾ in. typical

6½

3¼

½

Drill ⅜-in.-dia. hole
at assembly.

ⓥ ⓦ

25⅛

14⅜

2⅞ in. typical

½

2¾

1½

1⅛

Wedges to secure tenon

1¾

18¾-in. overall length for **v**

¼ in.
typical

29½-in. overall length for **w**

Drill ⅜-in.-dia. hole in top
pieces (**v** and **w**) for lag screws.

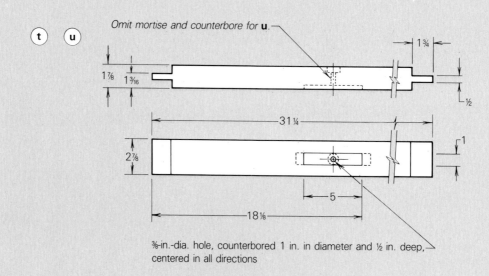

ⓣ ⓤ

Omit mortise and counterbore for **u**.

1¾

1⅞ 1³⁄₁₆

½

31¼

2⅞

1

5

18⅛

⅜-in.-dia. hole, counterbored 1 in. in diameter and ½ in. deep,
centered in all directions

Tables
Chapter 4

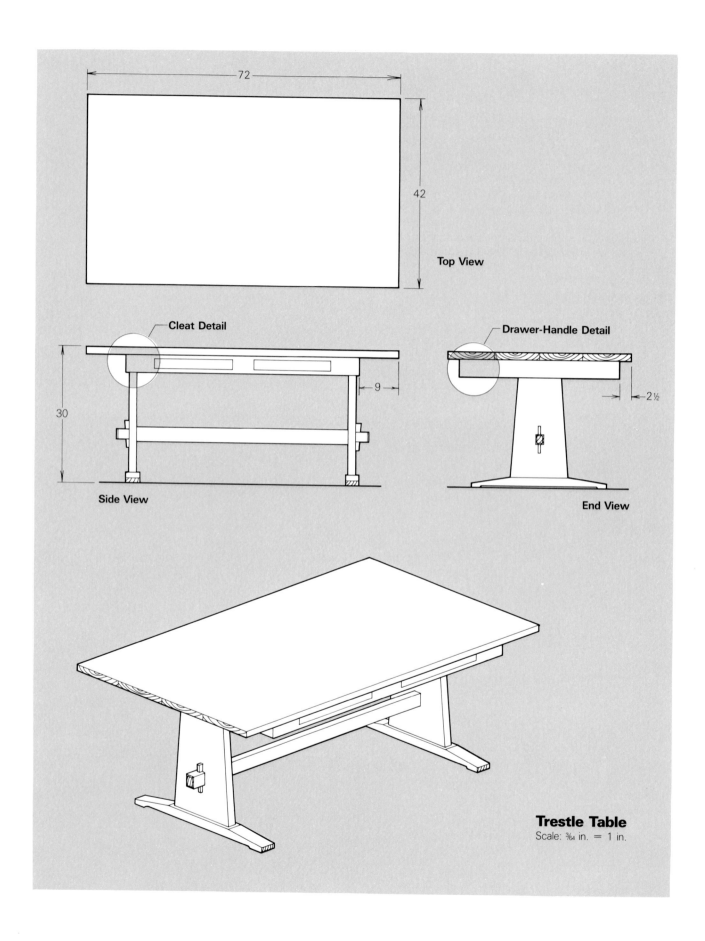

72

42

Top View

Cleat Detail

Drawer-Handle Detail

9

30

2½

Side View

End View

Trestle Table
Scale: ³⁄₆₄ in. = 1 in.

Trestle

Some people eat to live and some live to eat. I don't do either, but I enjoy good food. For the last 17 years I have belonged to a gourmet club of seven men who cook for each other once a month. I feel that half the success of a meal is the result of how it is presented and how comfortable each person is. Of course, the furniture plays an important role.

There are several important dimensions to consider when designing a dining table. Since the seat height of a dining chair is usually about 18 in., for the average person the height of a table should be about 30 in. Because people differ in height more from the hip down than from the seat up, I'd make the distance from the floor to the bottom of the table apron at least 24 in., so that someone's long legs aren't holding up the table (see p. 4). In determining the size of the tabletop, you should allow 24 in. per person for elbow room, so no one feels squeezed in (although you can get by with 20 in.). Place settings are about 14 in. deep, so the minimum width of a dining table should be 30 in. to keep you from drinking the wine of the person across from you. Whenever possible, I make dining tables 42 in. wide to leave enough space in the center for serving dishes, wine, condiments and flowers.

Try to position the table legs so that no one ends up having to straddle one of them. This usually means that the legs have to be very close to the corners, which makes the table more stable but the legs easier to kick and trip over. The best way to solve this problem is to make a pedestal or trestle table.

If the design is not restricted by the room, the most logical shape for a table is round or oval so that everyone can see each other. There is nothing worse than being seated near one end of a long, rectangular table and trying to talk with someone on the same side at the other end. If you want to see that person, you have to lean in so far that you might get gravy on your ear.

We needed a dining table in our house, which is over 200 years old. The house had several small rooms when we bought it and was built in the post-and-beam style. The beams are exposed and there are oak floors. There's a big central chimney with three fireplaces. The interior partitions were not bearing walls, so we knocked down a couple of them and combined three rooms into a good-size L-shaped living and dining room. The dining area is only 10 ft. by 11 ft., so I decided that a simple, rectangular table would be best. A delicate dining table would not look right in this house, so I made a trestle table with heavier members, which fit in much better with the architecture. A table 42 in. wide by 72 in. long is about the largest that would look good in the space, and it's also a very practical size because it seats six people comfortably and eight can easily squeeze in, which has happened many times over the years. I left details like the edges of the top square, rather than chamfered or rounded, to emphasize the heaviness of the members.

The top overhangs the base by 9 in. on each end, which is the minimum distance you need to avoid banging your knees on the trestles.

There are two drawers underneath the top **(1)**, which hold silverware and serving utensils. They go the full width of the table and open from one side, but they could be made half as deep to allow for two drawers on each side. Full-length drawers that open from one side create more space on the other side of the table, though.

1

The apron   The apron with the drawers is the only unusual part of this table's construction, so here are a few tips on how to make it. Make the grain of the drawer fronts match the apron by cutting them out of the same piece. Select the stock for the apron and rough-mill it oversize, allowing 2 in. extra in the length and ½ in. extra in the width. Then joint and thickness-plane the apron to 1½ in. by 4¾ in. Now mark the fronts of the boards so that after they have been cut up, they can be put back together in the same order. Joint the top edge and then rip off ¾ in., allowing a bit extra for planing off the sawmarks (¾ in. is the final dimension).

Rejoint the new edge of the wider piece and rip off another piece 2½ in. wide (again allowing for planing off the sawmarks). Now crosscut this piece into the drawer fronts and the center and end sections. Cut them to their exact final lengths. Joint off all the sawmarks and glue the whole thing back together, except for the drawer fronts. Include the drawer fronts in the assembly, but don't put any glue on them. Remove them as soon as the apron is clamped up so they won't be permanently glued in. Then use a damp rag to clean up the excess glue. Don't forget to get in the corners. When the glue has dried, cut, joint and thickness-plane everything to final dimension. Remember to thickness-plane all four sides of the apron at the same time to ensure uniformity.

Before gluing the apron unit together, cut grooves in the apron for the six stretchers that will carry the drawers. Then make a ¼-in. groove on the inside of the ends of the apron, about ¹³⁄₁₆ in. below the top edge. The top is made out of solid wood, so it will move considerably in its width. Tongued cleats will be used to hold the top down firmly; they can slide in the groove as the top expands and contracts. After the grooves have been cut, glue the whole unit together. Make sure it's square.

The apron unit is joined at the corners with full-blind dovetails [*Book 1*, pp. 75-77]. Since this table was made, I've been using full-blind multiple splines [*Book 1*, pp. 110-113] in similar situations. They are stronger and easier to make (see p. 55).

Apron Assembly (drawer-front side)

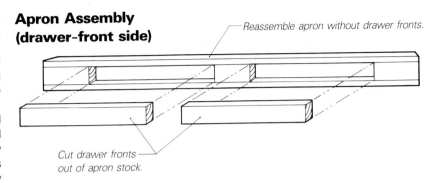

Reassemble apron without drawer fronts.

Cut drawer fronts out of apron stock.

Cleat Detail
Scale: ½ in. = 1 in.

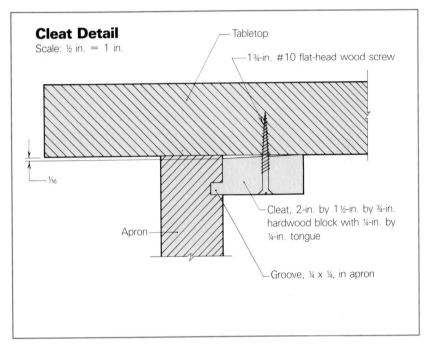

Tabletop

1¾-in. #10 flat-head wood screw

¹⁄₁₆

Apron

Cleat, 2-in. by 1½-in. by ¾-in. hardwood block with ¼-in. by ¼-in. tongue

Groove, ¼ x ¼, in apron

Drawer-Handle Detail

Scale: ¼ in. = 1 in.

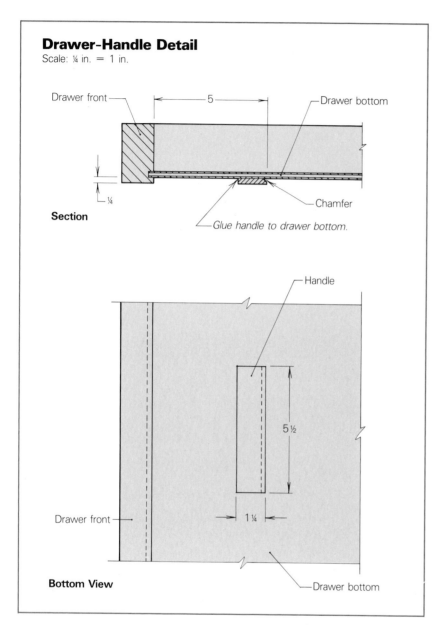

Drawer front

5

Drawer bottom

¼

Section

Chamfer

Glue handle to drawer bottom.

Handle

5½

1¼

Drawer front

Bottom View

Drawer bottom

The drawers   Once the apron section is together, the drawers can be made. First cut the drawer backs to the exact same length as the fronts in the apron. Rip the drawer-side pieces so that they fit very tightly into the opening, then cut them to length. Dovetail and glue the drawers together. When the glue is dry, do the final fitting by sanding lightly. (See pp. 12-15 for more about drawers.)

Next attach the drawer guides. Put in one drawer at a time, and with a piece of paper between the drawer side and the guide, glue down the guides. The paper will prevent the guide from being glued to the drawer side and will give just the right amount of play in the fit. It also helps if you cut a little bevel or chamfer on the inside bottom edge of the guide. Use hot hide glue on the guides and you won't need clamps—just put a little on the bottoms and rub the guides back and forth until they stick. Hot hide glue will stick as soon as it cools.

After about 15 minutes, carefully pull out the drawer and the paper, and let the glue cure. Attach the stop block in the back the same way. While you are waiting for these to dry, put the handles on the drawers. I did not want to advertise the fact that there are drawers in the apron, so the handles are attached to the drawer bottoms instead of to the fronts. To open one of the drawers, you have to reach under the apron and pull the drawer out a little and then grab onto the drawer front. To make the drawers slide easier, rub paraffin on the surfaces that slide against the runners.

The base The base of this trestle table is of simple, wedged, through-mortise-and-tenon construction. The very bottoms of the base pieces (the feet) are relieved by about ⅛ in. in their centers so that the whole table rests on four points, for stability.

The lower stretcher is 1¾ in. thick and 3½ in. wide, and it stabilizes the base by holding the two trestle ends together. It is joined to the uprights with a loose-wedged through-tenon **(2)**, which keeps the joint tight but can be easily knocked apart for disassembly (see p. 52). Because the mortise for the loose wedge extends ⅛ in. inside the upright, the shoulders of the stretcher are pulled tight against the upright as the wedge is pushed down. This feature makes it easy to keep the joint tight when the wood shrinks, but it works only with vertical wedges; a horizontal wedge will eventually work itself loose. This table is heavy and hard to move, so it made a lot of sense to design it to be easy to take apart.

The apron unit rests on the top shoulder of the trestles and is bolted to them with three ⅛-in. bolts with T-nuts (see p. 55). The center bolt should fit its hole tightly, but I've drilled slots in the upright of the trestle for the two outside bolts to allow for wood movement. Screws could also be used here, but T-nuts will survive being taken apart and put back together many more times.

Because the tabletop is meant to overhang the apron by the same amount on both sides, it should be fastened permanently in the center of each end so it will move equally in both directions. I use a piece of angle iron, screwed to both the trestle and the top, for this.

Wedged Tenon

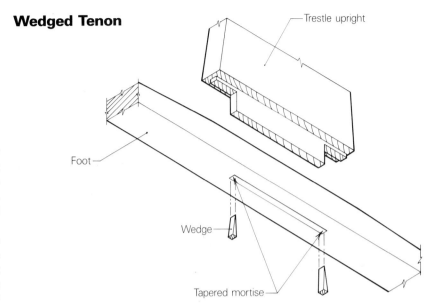

Trestle upright

Foot

Wedge

Tapered mortise

2

3

Finishing up This table has an oil finish, as do most of the dining tables I make. I think that an oil finish is the most sensible for a dining table because oil and grease spills won't hurt it, and might even improve it. It is water- and heat-resistant, and when it gets damaged, it is easy to repair. Here **(3)** I used a three-coat linseed-oil finish [*Book 2*, pp. 186-187], which I like even though the Food and Drug Administration does not agree with me.

The dining chairs for this table (see pp. 124-133) are simple but solidly constructed. They were originally designed for the boardroom in the old building of the Museum of Contemporary Crafts in New York. But they fit right in with my table, so I made a few extras for myself.

We also needed a sideboard that would blend in with the table and chairs. While I didn't want it to look too delicate, it couldn't be so heavy that the room would look smaller than it already is. To avoid having the piece appear to take up too much floor space, I designed the pedestal sideboard described on pp. 178-186. The doors in the room are of frame-and-raised-panel construction and that's where I got the idea to make the sideboard look like a raised panel without its frame. I used black walnut, which looks solid and heavy, and looks good against the white walls, too. A smaller version of the same design is now in the permanent collection of the Boston Museum of Fine Arts. □

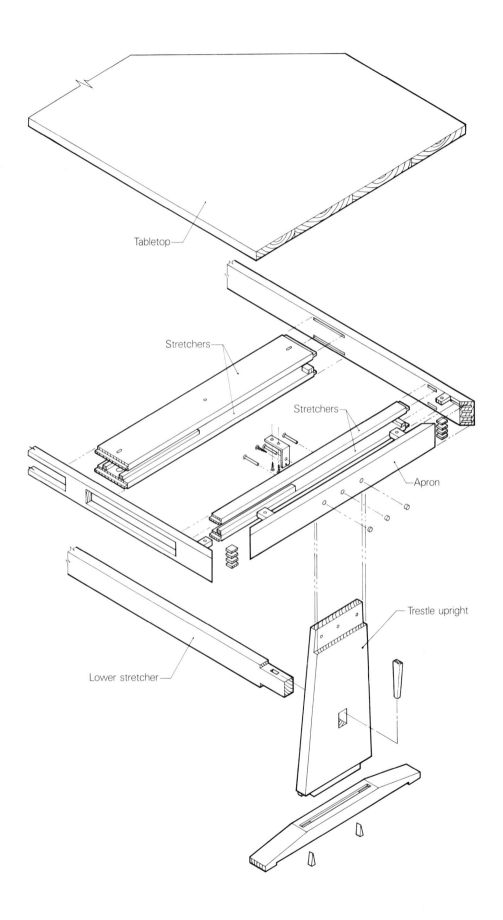

Tabletop

Stretchers

Stretchers

Apron

Trestle upright

Lower stretcher

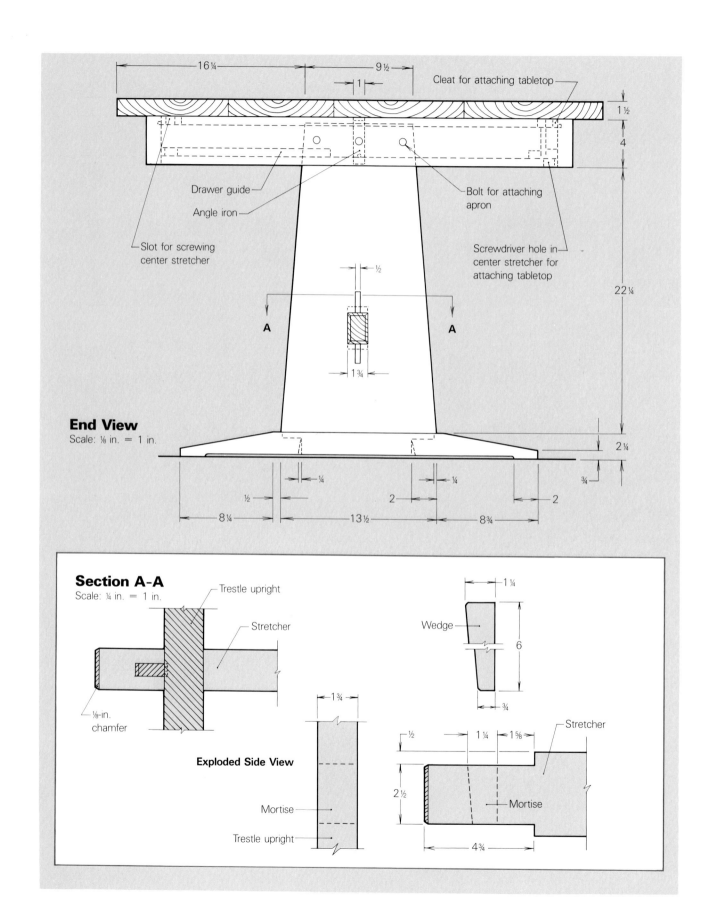

End View
Scale: ⅛ in. = 1 in.

Section A-A
Scale: ¼ in. = 1 in.

Trestle upright

Stretcher

⅛-in.
chamfer

Exploded Side View

Wedge

Mortise

Trestle upright

Mortise

Stretcher

Cleat for attaching tabletop

Bolt for attaching
apron

Screwdriver hole in
center stretcher for
attaching tabletop

Drawer guide

Angle iron

Slot for screwing
center stretcher

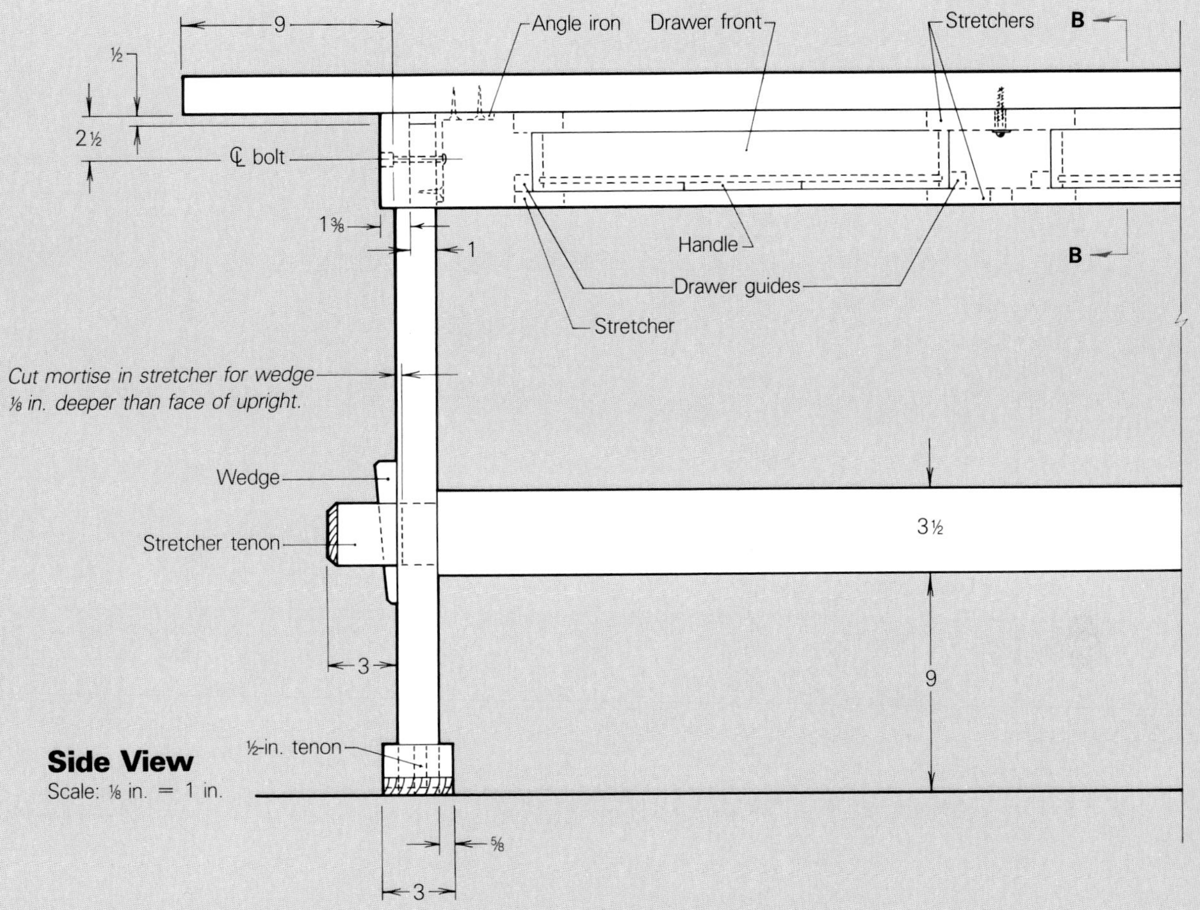
9
½
2½
℄ bolt
Angle iron
Drawer front
Stretchers
B
B
1⅜
1
Handle
Drawer guides
Stretcher
Cut mortise in stretcher for wedge
⅛ in. deeper than face of upright.
Wedge
Stretcher tenon
3½
3
9
½-in. tenon
⅝
3

Side View
Scale: ⅛ in. = 1 in.

Section B-B
Scale: ¼ in. = 1 in.

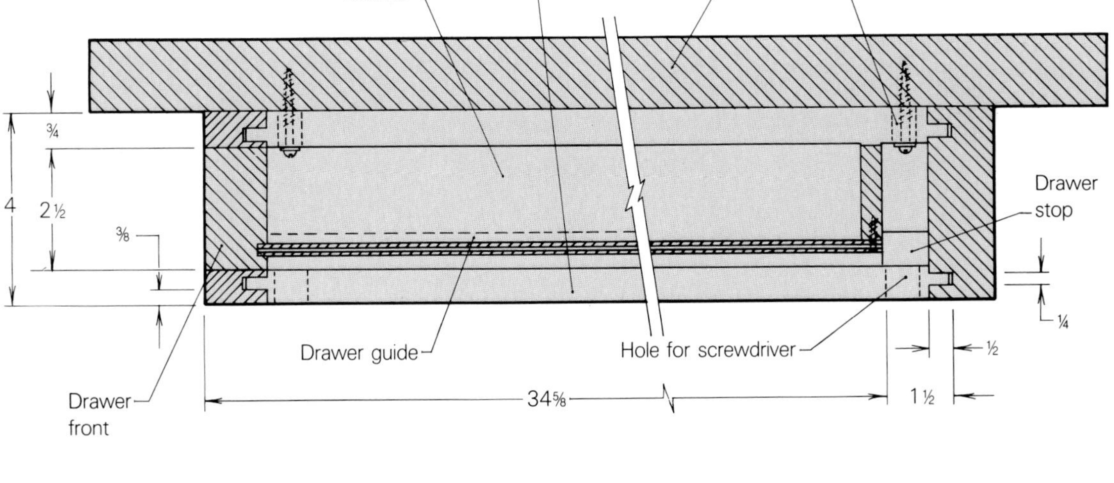
Stretchers
Tabletop
Drawer
Slot for screw
¾
4
2½
⅜
Drawer
stop
¼
Drawer guide
Hole for screwdriver
½
34⅝
1½
Drawer
front

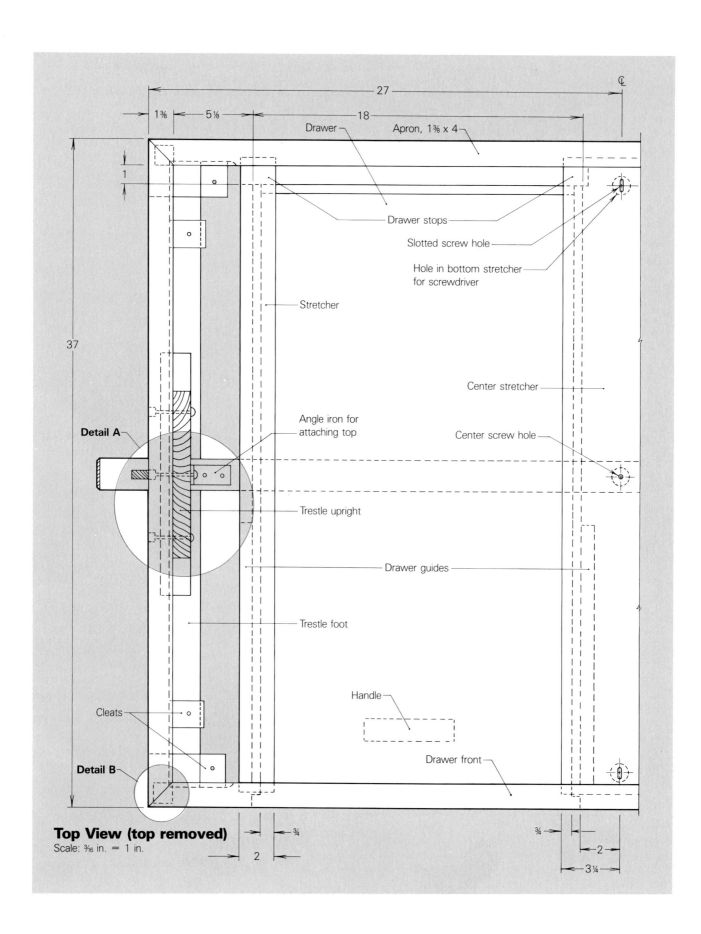

27

1⅜ 5⅛ 18

Drawer

Apron, 1⅜ x 4

1

Drawer stops

Slotted screw hole

Hole in bottom stretcher
for screwdriver

Stretcher

Center stretcher

37

Angle iron for
attaching top

Center screw hole

Detail A

Trestle upright

Drawer guides

Trestle foot

Handle

Cleats

Drawer front

Detail B

Top View (top removed)
Scale: ³⁄₁₆ in. = 1 in.

¾

2

¾

2

3¼

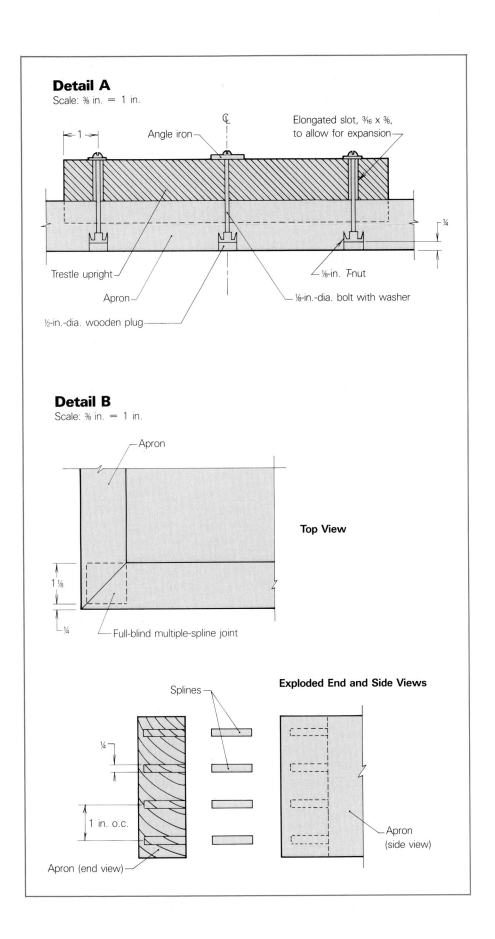

Detail A

Scale: ⅜ in. = 1 in.

1

Angle iron

Elongated slot, ³⁄₁₆ x ⅜, to allow for expansion

Trestle upright

Apron

½-in.-dia. wooden plug

⅛-in. T-nut

⅛-in.-dia. bolt with washer

¼

Detail B

Scale: ⅜ in. = 1 in.

Apron

Top View

1 ⅛

¼

Full-blind multiple-spline joint

Exploded End and Side Views

Splines

¼

1 in. o.c.

Apron (end view)

Apron (side view)

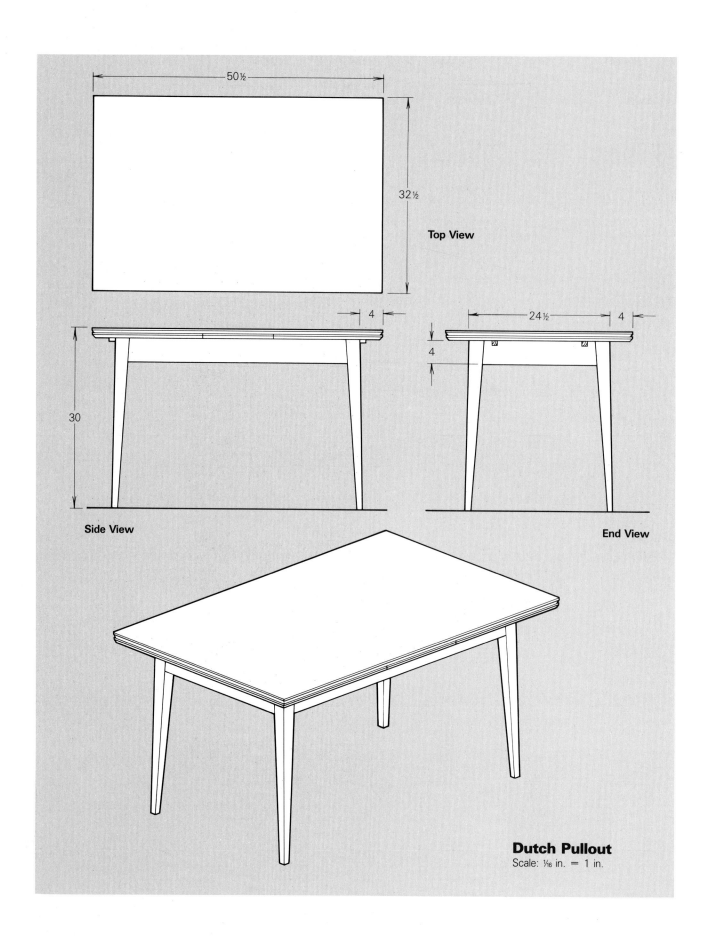

50½

32½

Top View

4

Side View

30

24½   4

4

End View

Dutch Pullout
Scale: ¹⁄₁₆ in. = 1 in.

Dutch Pullout

Few houses have a formal dining room anymore, so there is a great demand for extension tables. Such a table can be kept small to be used as a breakfast table, and opened up for company as needed. There are many different systems to choose from when making an extension table, but my favorite is the Dutch pullout. It is good-looking, simple and fast to make.

In addition, the extension leaves store right inside the table so they can't get lost, and they are easy to pull out, even with the table already set. With most extension systems, if unexpected guests show up just when you are putting the food on the table, you have to clear everything off the table before you can enlarge it. But with the Dutch pullout, you can pull out the leaves without disturbing the setting at all, and invite your guests to join you.

The tabletop consists of two pieces of plywood, both the same size, one mounted right above the other on the base. The lower piece is cut into three sections—the outer two are the leaves and the third is a fixed center piece. The top piece rests on these, held in place by two vertical dowels that sit loosely in guide holes in the center piece. The top is thus free to move up and down but not from side to side. The leaves are mounted on long, tapered slides that allow them to be pulled out from the ends. The slides travel in grooves in the end aprons and in a supporting stretcher across the center of the base. As each leaf is extended, the taper makes it rise slowly to the level of the top. As the leaf rises, so does the top, until the leaf is fully extended and clear of the top. Then the top drops down again, flush with the leaf. To close the table, the top has to be lifted high enough for the edge of the leaf to slip underneath. The top settles back down as the leaf travels back to its original position.

Pullout System

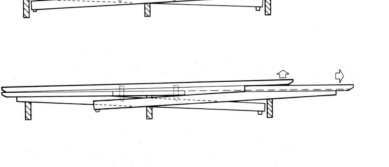

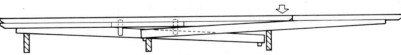

Top rises as extension leaves are pulled out.

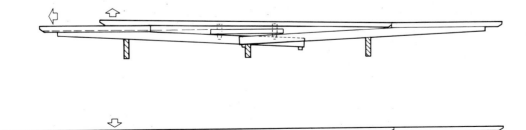

1

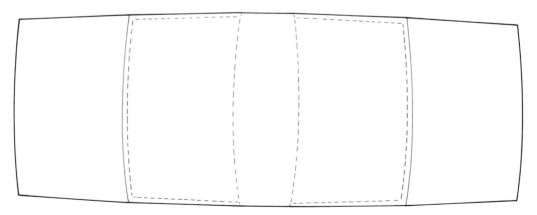

2

I made the table illustrated here **(1,2)** about thirty years ago. It was designed for a very small room and is only 32½ in. wide—about the smallest I'd use. It took four or five days to make, including veneering and edging the plywood top.

A simple Dutch pullout cannot be used on a round table, although more complex systems using the same principle have been tried. A Dutch-pullout system can be used for a table with curved sides, although the overhang between the top and the leaves will not be the same all the way around. But sometimes a curved top is preferable—it may fit in better with the design of the room.

In designing a Dutch pullout, remember that the less overhang there is between the top and the base, the bigger the leaves can be. This is because each leaf must travel its full length outward before it can clear the top. The tail ends of the slides to which the leaf is attached travel the exact same distance. But the slides can't go any farther than the distance between the inside of the apron and the center stretcher, less about an inch for the stop. Therefore, when you have chosen the length of the closed table, you can decide how much the top will overhang the base and calculate the length of the leaves. Or, you can decide the length of the leaves first, and then figure out the overhang. In either case, one determines the other.

Curved Dutch Pullout

*Dutch-pullout system
works with curved sides,
although overhang is uneven.*

The measurements used in the drawings were taken from the table in the photos and I'll use them to explain the system. Use your own dimensions to make the table to suit your own dining area.

When the table is closed, it is 50½ in. long and will seat four to six people comfortably. The top overhangs the apron by 4 in. all around and the apron is ⅞ in. thick. The overhang plus the thickness of the apron totals 9¾ in. Deduct that from 50½ in. and you get 40¾ in., which is the inside length of the base. Half of that is 20⅜ in., and when you subtract 1⅜ in. for the stop and half the thickness of the center stretcher, you get 19 in. for each leaf, because that's how far the slides can travel. Thus the length of the table can be extended by 38 in. to 88½ in. The width of the center piece will be the difference between the leaves and the top, or 12½ in.

If you start with both the open and closed dimensions, you can follow the same calculations in reverse to determine the overhang. Since my table measures 50½ in. closed and 88½ in. open, simple subtraction gives 38 in. for the combined length of the leaves. Add the thickness of the two aprons (1¾ in.) to the thickness of the two stops (1⅞ in.) and the center stretcher (⅞ in.) and you get 42½ in. Deducting this from the length of the top gives 8 in., so the top should be allowed to overhang the base by 4 in. at each end.

Once you understand the mechanical system, the work is easy and should go very quickly. The table consists of four tapered legs joined to an apron that is 4 in. wide. The center stretcher is also 4 in. wide, and will guide the four slides and serve as a place to run the stops against so the leaves won't fall out. Other than the solid wood used for the base, slides and stops, you'll need hardwood veneer-core plywood, two ¾-in. dowels and hardwood edging for the top.

Use standard mortise-and-tenon construction for the base [*Book 1*, p. 160]. Taper or shape the legs according to your own design after all the joints have been cut.

Because the tabletop is loose and the slides are glued and screwed to the bottoms of the leaves, the top and leaves should be made out of plywood. If you want to use solid-wood stock, then you must use frame-and-panel construction to prevent warpage. But I suggest plywood, and I recommend that you get a top grade. You can use plywood with the face veneer already on if you don't mind having the edging exposed, or you can veneer the top yourself after attaching the edging [*Book 2*, pp. 118-145]. If you want to veneer it yourself, Philippine mahogany, lauan or shina (a commercial name for limewood) makes the best veneer blanks. When the table is completed, you can paint the top, stencil it or finish it however you like.

On this table, I applied solid-wood edging to the plywood and then I veneered the top and leaves at the same time so the grain would match when the table is open. I also beveled the edging all the way around. There are two reasons for doing this. First, if the table gets used a lot, there might be a little play in the dowels and the beveled edge will help to hide any misalignment. Second, when the leaves are pulled out all the way, the top will slide down on the bevel, instead of dropping suddenly off a square edge.

Tapering Jig, Top View

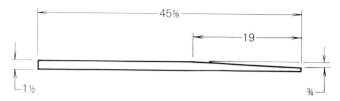

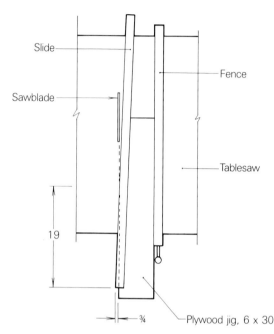

Lay out slide, then transfer marks to plywood to make tapering jig.

The slides   The success of your table will depend on your accuracy in cutting and positioning the four slides. Be sure that the wood you use is straight, and machine it carefully. I usually cut the slides slightly oversize and leave them for a few days to give them a chance to warp. Then I joint and thickness-plane them to size, which in this case was ⅞ in. thick by 1 ½ in. wide. Their length is the inside measurement of the base (40¾ in.) plus the ⅞-in. thickness of the apron and the 4-in. overhang, or 45⅝ in. The slides will be trimmed shorter later for appearances, but leave them full-length now for measuring.

The part of each slide that attaches to the leaf must be tapered so that it will wedge the leaf up to the level of the tabletop as the leaf is extended. On this table, the top and the leaves are ¾ in. thick, so each leaf must rise ¾ in. when it has traveled its full extension of 19 in. Measure 19 in. from one end of one of the slides, and square off the line. Then make a mark ¾ in. from one corner of the same end. A line connecting this point with the edge at the 19-in. mark will give the angle for the taper on the slides. In this case, that also leaves ¾ in. of wood at the end of the slides. If you make the slides wider, there will be more wood left at the ends when the ¾-in. taper is removed, and you will have to deepen the openings in the aprons and center stretcher.

To be sure that all the slides will have the same angle, you should make a tapering jig, as shown in the drawing at left. Cut a piece of plywood about 6 in. wide and 30 in. long. Place the marked slide over the plywood so that both marks (the ends of the lines you have drawn) just touch the bottom edge of the plywood. Then trace the end and the other side of the slide onto the plywood, and bandsaw out the wedge-shaped piece.

With the tablesaw fence still at the identical setting you used to cut the plywood jig to width, insert the slide into the jig and make the cut. Use the same setup for all four slides to ensure that they will all turn out exactly the same. Be careful to hold each slide securely against the jig when making these cuts, and watch your fingers.

The slides run in slots in the end aprons and the center stretcher **(3)**. One pair of slides travels inside the other pair and the two run side-by-side in the slots in the center stretcher. To lay out these slots, mark centerlines on top of both ends of the apron 1¼ in. from the inside edge of all four legs. With a long straightedge, transfer these lines to the center stretcher. Mark the thickness of the slide outside the lines on one apron and inside the lines on the other. On the center stretcher, mark the thickness of the slide to both sides of the centerline.

3

The grooves in the end aprons must be the same depth as the slides at that point so the leaf will clear the apron properly as it is extended. Cut the grooves to the exact depth of the slides, as measured at a point 4 in. from the tapered end, or ⅞ in. deep in this case.

To find the depth of the grooves in the center stretcher, first mark the location of the stretcher on the slides, which in this case is 25¼ in. from the tapered end, or half the length of the closed table. Then push the tapered side of a slide down on a flat surface and measure the depth at the marked point, in this case 1⅞ in. **(4)**. This is the minimum depth that will allow the leaf to rise ¾ in. in its travel. The grooves may be cut out a little deeper if you wish.

4

By the way, it's better to make all these grooves after the base of the table has been glued together. If anything has shifted out of square in the gluing-up, you can still make the leaves work properly by correcting the position of the grooves.

Now that all the measurements and cuts have been made, the tapered ends of the slides can be trimmed. I wanted the slides to extend 1 in. beyond the apron when the table was closed, so I cut off 3 in. and chamfered the ends.

5

6

7

8

9

Assembling the tabletop To assemble the tabletop, place the slides in the grooves with their tapered sides up **(5)**. Put the leaves in position (don't forget that you just trimmed 3 in. off the end of each slide), and glue and screw the slides to the leaves.

The center piece of plywood is screwed to the apron above the center stretcher. It prevents the leaves from tilting down when they are extended and it locates the tabletop. Drill two ¾-in. holes near opposite edges of the center piece, between the slides and the apron **(6)**; these are the guide holes for the dowels in the top.

Now push the leaves in and locate the top in its correct position. Clamp it down to the leaves and, from underneath, mark the location of the guide holes on the underside of the top **(7)**. Then drill two ½-in.-deep holes in the underside of the top using a Forstner bit, and glue two ¾-in. dowels into them. The dowels should be about 2¾ in. long, since the top has to move up a full ¾ in. while the leaves are being extended. Taper the bottom 1½ in. of the dowels so that you will be able to lift the top easily.

To locate the stops, extend the leaves to their open position and mark where the slides pass through the center stretcher. Then screw the stops to the ends of the slides at this point **(8)**.

When the leaves are pushed back in to close the table, the tabletop must be lifted. To prevent scratches that would result from the leaves sliding underneath the tabletop, glue two strips of felt to the bottom of the top **(9)**. Use hot hide glue or rubber cement.   □

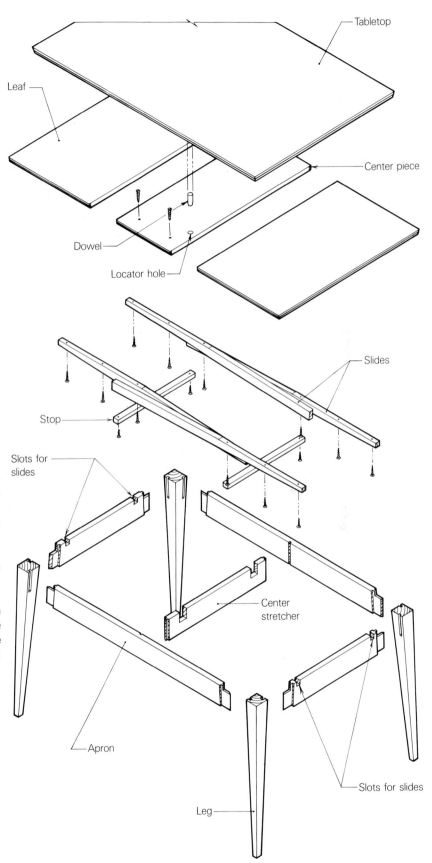

Tabletop

Leaf

Center piece

Dowel

Locator hole

Slides

Stop

Slots for slides

Center stretcher

Apron

Leg

Slots for slides

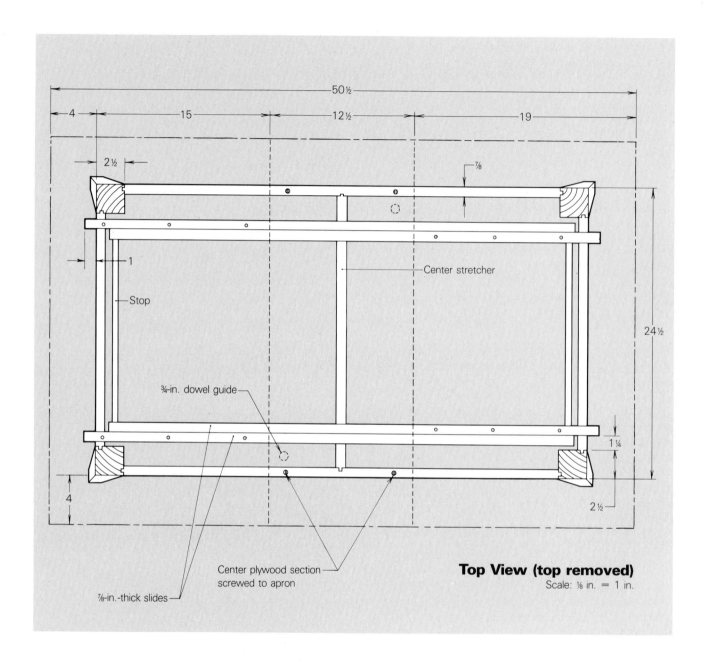

50½

4   15   12½   19

2½

⅞

1

Stop

Center stretcher

24½

¾-in. dowel guide

1¼

4

2½

Center plywood section—
screwed to apron

⅞-in.-thick slides—

Top View (top removed)
Scale: ⅛ in. = 1 in.

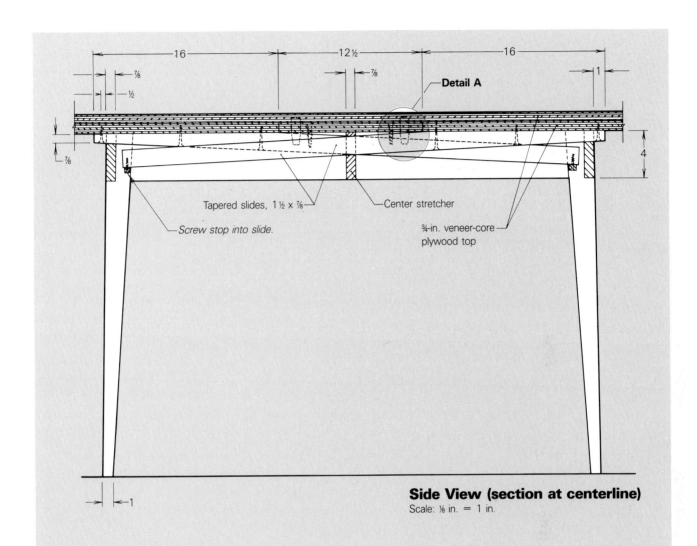

16 12½ 16
⅞ ⅞ 1
½
Detail A
⅞
4

Tapered slides, 1 ½ x ⅞
Center stretcher
Screw stop into slide.
¾-in. veneer-core
plywood top

1

Side View (section at centerline)
Scale: ⅛ in. = 1 in.

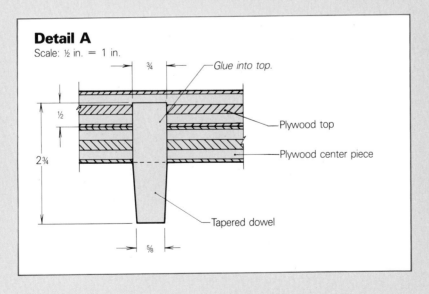

Detail A
Scale: ½ in. = 1 in.

¾
Glue into top.
½
Plywood top
2¾
Plywood center piece
Tapered dowel
⅝

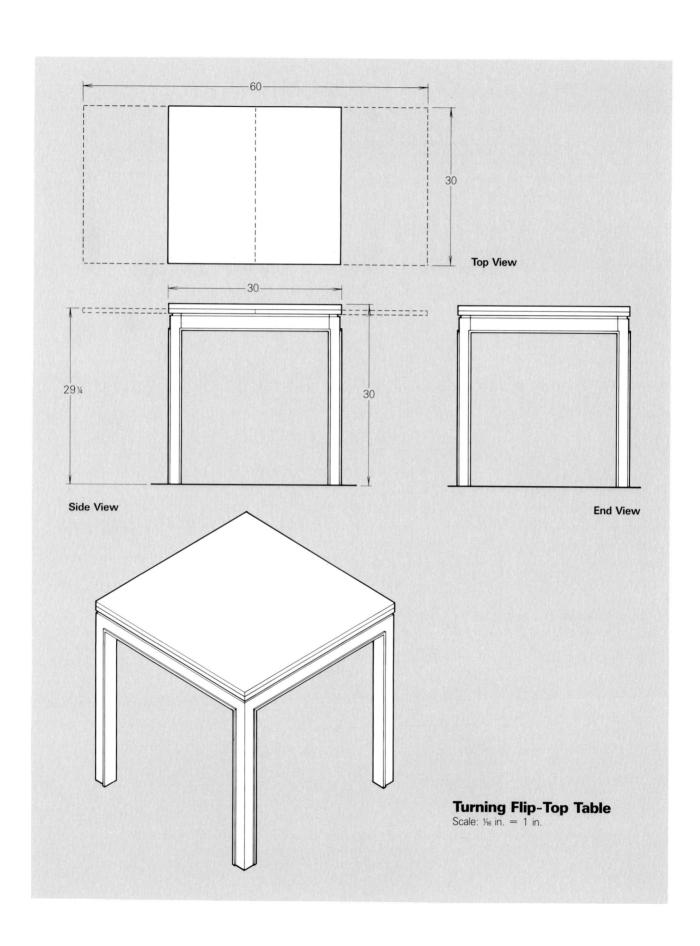

60

30

Top View

30

29¼

30

Side View

End View

Turning Flip-Top Table
Scale: ¹⁄₁₆ in. = 1 in.

Turning Flip-Top

A flip-top table is ideal for a small apartment, a summer cottage or a breakfast nook. It is small when closed but doubles its size when opened. It can be made as either a turning flip-top or a sliding flip-top (see p. 74).

The turning flip-top table shown here **(1)** is 30 in. by 30 in. when closed, which is good for two people and just big enough for four to enjoy breakfast or a light lunch. When open, it's 30 in. by 60 in., which is plenty of room for four people; six could be squeezed in.

As with all furniture, you should begin by making a good working drawing. The drawing is especially important here because the pivot point has to be exact. On this table, the top and the base are the same size, and any discrepancies in their alignment will be really obvious. It is difficult to get the top and the apron to line up perfectly over a long period of time because there will be some play in the hinges and the pivot plug. If you make some decorative detail on the edges of the top, the base or both, this will hide such minor misalignment. Rounding over the edges will do the job, but I thought the legs and apron would look too plain. A heavy apron and legs are needed for a stable base, but I didn't want the base to look too heavy. I decided on some simple details, which give the base the appearance of being lighter than it is **(2)**. They also create a better proportional relationship between the base and the top. A table of this type should always have as little overhang as possible so that when the top is folded open, it will be well supported on a broad base **(3,4,5)**.

1

2

3

4

5

The top of the table is made from ¾-in. lauan veneer-core plywood. The plywood is edged on four sides with ½-in.-thick facing, mitered at the corners. It is veneered with fiddleback mahogany on both sides [*Book 2*, p. 115]. The same veneer has to go on both sides of both pieces so that they match when the top is open and so the top won't warp. It is especially important that the top be flat because it is attached to the base only at the pivot point.

When the top pieces have been edged and veneered and are dry, they are ready to be hinged together. Lay out the brass hinges with a square and mark them with an awl. Then remove the wood with a router to the thickness of the hinges and clean up with a sharp knife. After you attach the hinges, file and sand them perfectly flush with the surface of the veneer. The hinges will be visible from one side of the table when it is closed.

The base of the table is made from solid Honduras mahogany. It is put together with haunched mortise-and-tenon joints [*Book 1*, p. 161].

After I made all the joints, I clamped the base together without glue and made the leg and apron surfaces flush with a hand plane. Then I disassembled the base and cut the ¼-in. half-round bead on the shaper. (I had to grind my own cutter to get the shape I wanted.) You can do the same with a router mounted in a router table. I ran the half-round detail on the apron pieces right through the ends, but the cut on the legs had to be stopped where it would meet the bottom of the apron. I finished the corner between them by hand after the base was glued together. First, I glued up the two opposite leg and apron sections to be sure they were square. Then, when the glue was dry, I glued the whole base together. When this was dry, I rough-sanded the base with 80-grit paper and touched up the top edges with a hand plane to make sure that the top would have a level surface to sit on.

I wanted another decorative detail on the top of the base to visually narrow the width of the apron and give it a more consistent proportional relationship to the

legs. To achieve this, I cut a rabbet around the top of the base with a hand router, using a fence, after the base was glued together and sanded. I rounded over the bottom edges of the cut with a rabbet plane and chamfered the top edges with a smoothing plane and sandpaper. To be consistent, I also rounded the edges of the tabletop slightly with a smoothing plane and sanded them.

Leg and Apron

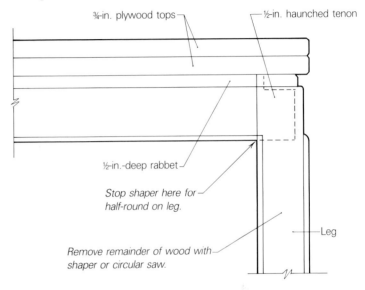

¾-in. plywood tops

½-in. haunched tenon

½-in.-deep rabbet

Stop shaper here for half-round on leg.

Remove remainder of wood with shaper or circular saw.

Leg

Leg Cross Section

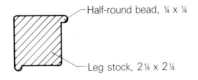

Half-round bead, ¼ x ¼

Leg stock, 2 ¼ x 2 ¼

6

The swivel A turning flip-top table is not difficult to make, but the swivel mechanism and the stretcher it sits in have to be accurately located **(6)** for the table to work properly. Here's how to do it.

To get the pivot point right, lay it out on the top and transfer it to the base. Finding the pivot point when the top is square is easy. Divide the top into four equal squares, and on one of them draw diagonal lines from corner to corner, as shown below. Where the lines cross is the center of the pivot point.

Remember that the top is not the same size as the base. Because ¼ in. was removed from the legs to make the half-round bead and another ¼ in. from the apron for the decorative rabbet, the top overhangs the base by ½ in. on all sides. The pivot point on the top measures 7½ in. from the edges, so subtract the extra ½ in. and then measure in 7 in. from the edges of the base to locate the pivot point on the 4½-in.-wide swivel stretcher.

Inlay the swivel stretcher flush with the top of the apron so the pivot point is centered in its width, then screw it down. Don't glue it—you may have to replace it if you mark and drill wrong, which is what

Locating the Pivot Point

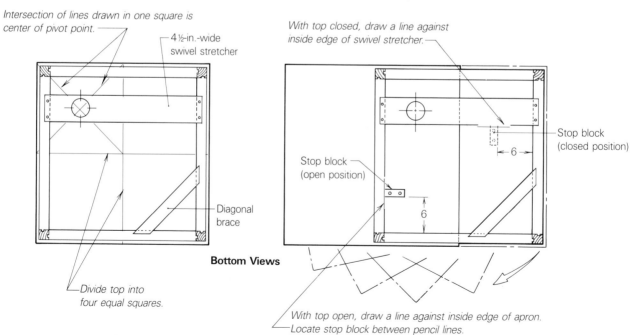

Intersection of lines drawn in one square is center of pivot point.

4½-in.-wide swivel stretcher

Diagonal brace

Divide top into four equal squares.

Bottom Views

Locating the Stop Block

With top closed, draw a line against inside edge of swivel stretcher.

Stop block (closed position)

6

Stop block (open position)

6

With top open, draw a line against inside edge of apron.
Locate stop block between pencil lines.

I did the first time. Inlay the diagonal brace, too, for the top to slide on when it's being opened and closed. Be sure the brace is flush with the top of the base and glue it in permanently. The swivel stretcher and the diagonal brace also help to keep the base square and rigid.

With both pieces in place, locate the center of the pivot point for the swivel mechanism, which fits in a 3-in.-dia. hole in the swivel stretcher. Now remove the stretcher and drill the hole in it using a wing cutter. Do this carefully on a drill press because accuracy is very important in this step.

On the lathe, turn a wooden plug to fit snugly in the 3-in.-dia. hole in the swivel stretcher [*Book 2,* pp. 80-83]. Allow an extra ⅛ in. in the thickness of the plug for the felt pieces that will be added later.

With the top closed and in the proper position, clamp it to the base and then screw the wooden plug onto the bottom of the top.

Now turn the tabletop and open it. The corner of the top slides on the diagonal brace. Make sure the mechanism works smoothly. With the top open, measure to determine if the overhang is the same on both sides and the ends, which it should be if the hole in the swivel stretcher has been drilled correctly. Then run a pencil along the inside of the apron to mark the bottom of the top for the stop block. Close the top, position it correctly and make a pencil mark against the inside edge of the swivel stretcher, as shown in the drawing on the facing page. Cut a stop block to fit between the two pencil lines, with the grain running lengthwise so it won't shrink in the critical direction that would change the stopping position of the top. Screw on the stop block, fitting it exactly between the two pencil lines. Be sure the block clears the diagonal brace.

When you are satisfied that everything is working as it should, remove the top, then finish-sand and apply finish to the whole table. I used an oil finish on mine. I left the two top pieces together for finishing because I didn't want to remove the hinges.

Now glue strips of heavy felt onto the top edges of the base to prevent the top from being scratched when it is opened and to make it slide smoothly and quickly. Attach the felt with hot hide glue, but be careful to let the glue cool a little before putting down the felt so the felt will not absorb the glue. If the glue gets soaked up, the felt will become hard and useless for its job. You can also use contact cement to attach the felt, but it is not as good as hot hide glue.

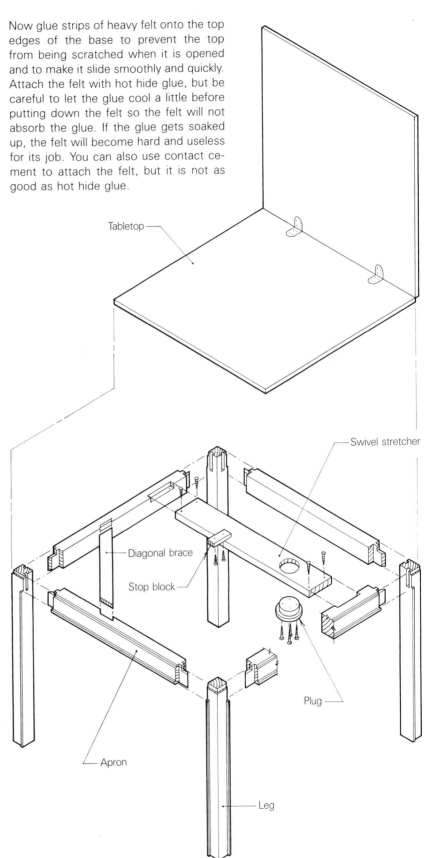

Tabletop

Swivel stretcher

Diagonal brace

Stop block

Plug

Apron

Leg

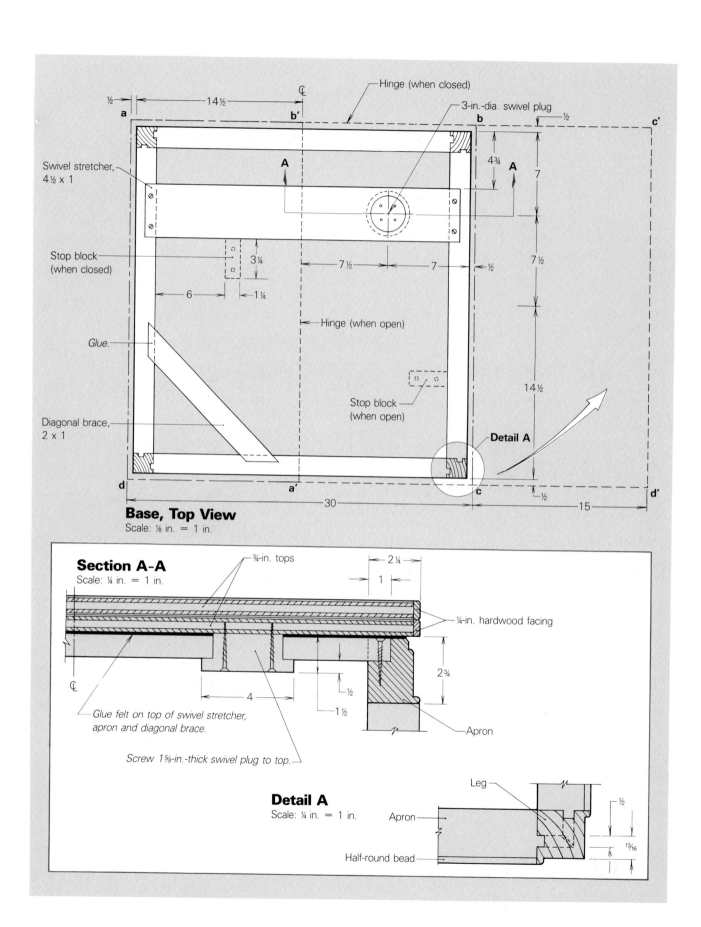

Hinge (when closed)

3-in.-dia. swivel plug

Swivel stretcher, 4 ½ x 1

Stop block (when closed)

Glue.

Diagonal brace, 2 x 1

Hinge (when open)

Stop block (when open)

Detail A

Base, Top View
Scale: ⅛ in. = 1 in.

Section A-A
Scale: ¼ in. = 1 in.

¾-in. tops

¼-in. hardwood facing

Apron

Glue felt on top of swivel stretcher, apron and diagonal brace.

Screw 1⅝-in.-thick swivel plug to top.

Detail A
Scale: ¼ in. = 1 in.

Leg

Apron

Half-round bead

A rectangular turning flip-top To make this table with a rectangular top, the system for finding the center of the pivot point is similar to that used on the square table. The top in this example is 24 in. by 42 in. when closed. Divide it into four equal sections, each being 12 in. by 21 in. This top overhangs 2 in. on all four sides, which makes the base 20 in. by 38 in. The center of the base in length is 19 in. from the outside of the apron. In width, it is 10 in. from the outside edge. The hinged side has to be right on the 19-in. centerline after the tabletop is turned 90°. Because each section of the top is 12 in. by 21 in., the pivot point must be located 6 in. from both the centerline and the outside edge of the table.

As noted, the overhang of the tabletop is 2 in., so measure in 4 in. from the outside edge of the base. Where these lines intersect is the center of the pivot point.

A piece like the diagonal brace in the square table is not needed here because the corner will slide on the top of the base. Remember to put felt on the top of the base to prevent the top from being scratched when it is opened.   □

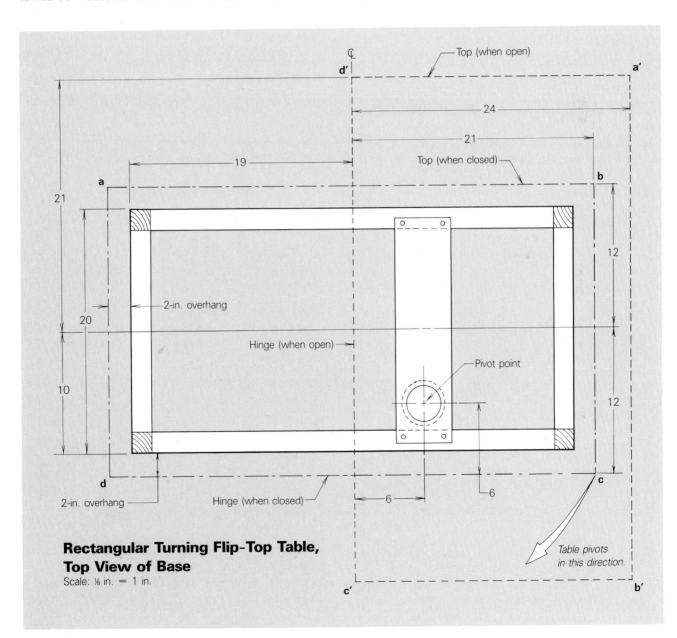

Rectangular Turning Flip-Top Table, Top View of Base
Scale: ⅛ in. = 1 in.

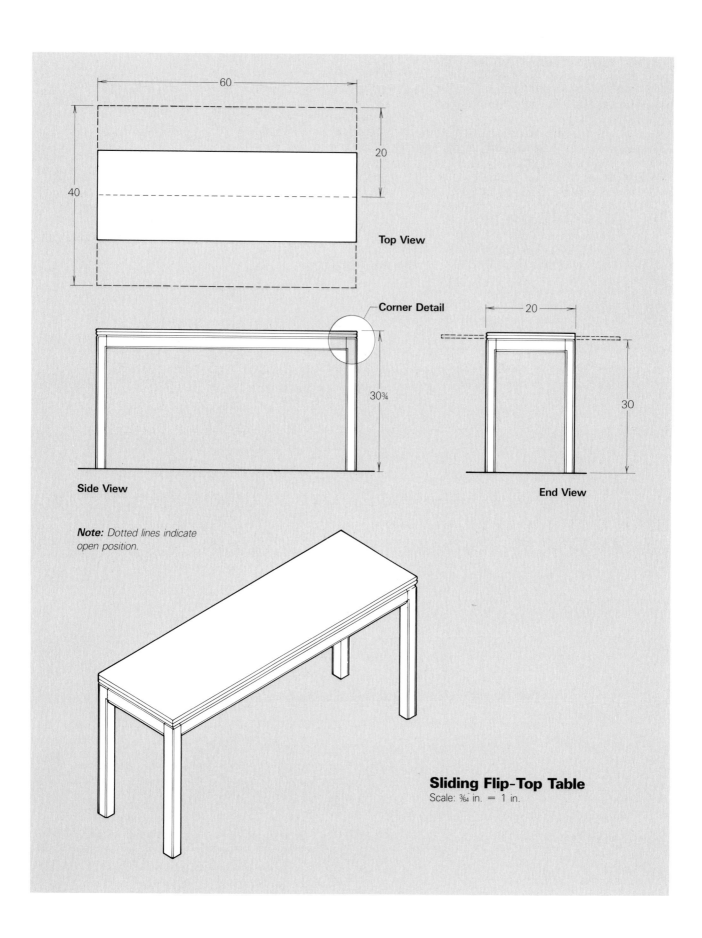

60

20

40

Top View

Corner Detail

20

Side View

30¾

30

End View

Note: Dotted lines indicate open position.

Sliding Flip-Top Table
Scale: ¾₄ in. = 1 in.

Sliding Flip-Top

Another way to make a flip-top table is with a sliding mechanism instead of a piv-ot. Like the turning flip-top (see p. 66), this table also has a plywood top and felt on top of the apron. The main advantage of the sliding system is that the dimen-sions of the top are more flexible than with the turning flip-top. The sliding mechanism is easy to make, but it is greatly affected by changes in humidity. It will usually be loose in the winter as the wood contracts, and tight in the summer as the wood expands. To help prevent this problem, and to make the top slide more easily, cover the slides with the paraffin and turpentine mixture described on p. 35.

Some years ago, I designed and made the furniture for the trustees' meeting room in the old building of the Museum of Contemporary Craft in New York City. I built chairs, a conference table, and a sliding flip-top table about the same size as the one explained here, but with a dif-ferent base. The meeting room at the museum was also sometimes used for lunches and dinners, when the flip-top table would double as a sideboard. For large gatherings, the flip-top could be added to the conference table as an ex-tension because it was the same height and width when opened.

The table shown here is 20 in. by 60 in. when closed and 40 in. by 60 in. when open. Like the turning flip-top table, the sliding flip-top has as large a base as possible to provide stability when the ta-bletop is open.

The solid-wood base is put together with haunched mortise-and-tenon joints. No-tice that the end aprons are the same thickness as the legs, so they are flush on the inside for the slides to work against. The two side aprons, however, are only 1½ in. thick. This creates more room in-side the table and allows the slides to be as long as possible. The distance be-tween the two side aprons is 17 in. Be-cause the top has to slide 10 in. for the hinged edge to be in the center when the table is opened, the slides are 7 in. long. The slides also serve as stops for the top in both the open and closed positions.

Just like on the turning flip-top table, I wanted some simple edge details to make the base look lighter in relation to the top, and to hide any future misalign-ment. The cove detail can be cut with a hand router after the base has been put together, flushed up and sanded. You won't be able to cut all the way into the corners with the router; you will have to carve the cove with a gouge where the legs meet the aprons.

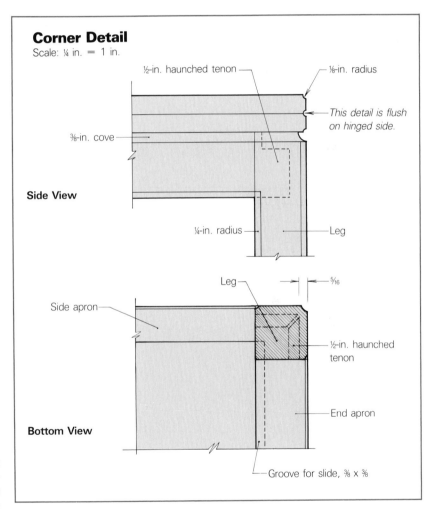

Corner Detail
Scale: ¼ in. = 1 in.

At each end of the table, a ⅜-in. by ⅜-in. groove is cut on the insides of the end aprons and part of the legs for the slides to travel in. First glue the two end sections together. Plane them flush on the inside and top, then cut the groove using a hand router with a fence. Using the same setting, rout both grooves in the center stretcher.

Because of the length of the table, a center stretcher is necessary. A piece 2 in. wide by 2¾ in. thick, with the ⅜-in. by ⅜-in. grooves cut into it, is mortised into the apron in the center. I used a double-tenon joint here for extra strength [*Book 1*, p. 162]. The double tenon provides additional gluing surface and prevents twisting. All the slides are 1½ in. thick by 2⅜ in. wide by 7 in. long, with ⅜-in. by ⅜-in. tongues.

It is especially important that the base of this table be glued up perfectly square, or else the table won't work. After the base is finished, glue down the felt strips on top of the apron and center stretcher. Then put the top in place and hold it securely with clamps. Attach the slides by putting them in place in the grooves and screwing them to the bottom side of the top. Remember to coat them with paraffin first. □

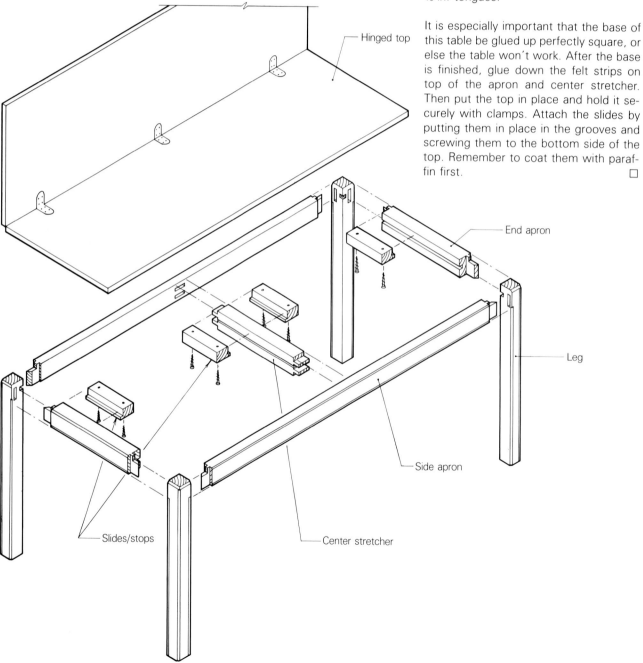

Hinged top

End apron

Leg

Side apron

Slides/stops

Center stretcher

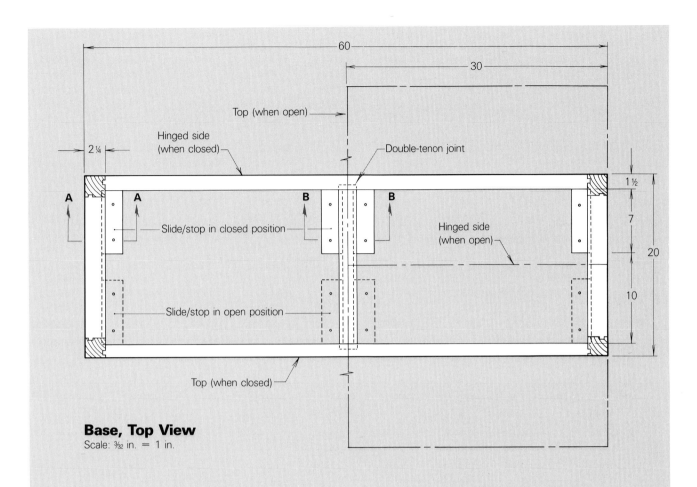

Base, Top View
Scale: ³⁄₃₂ in. = 1 in.

60

30

Top (when open)

Hinged side
(when closed)

Double-tenon joint

2¼

Slide/stop in closed position

Hinged side
(when open)

1½

7

20

10

Slide/stop in open position

Top (when closed)

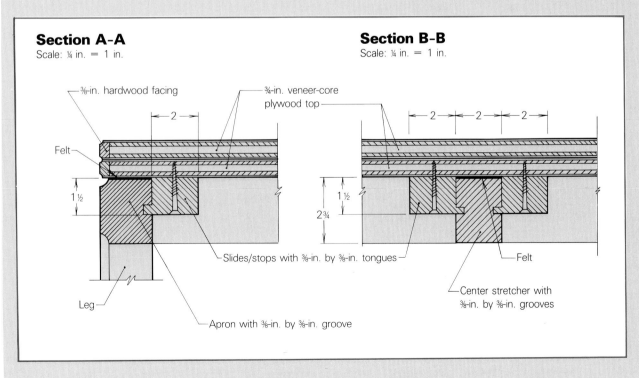

Section A-A
Scale: ¼ in. = 1 in.

Section B-B
Scale: ¼ in. = 1 in.

³⁄₈-in. hardwood facing

¾-in. veneer-core
plywood top

Felt

2

2   2   2

1½

1½

2¾

Slides/stops with ³⁄₈-in. by ³⁄₈-in. tongues

Felt

Leg

Center stretcher with
³⁄₈-in. by ³⁄₈-in. grooves

Apron with ³⁄₈-in. by ³⁄₈-in. groove

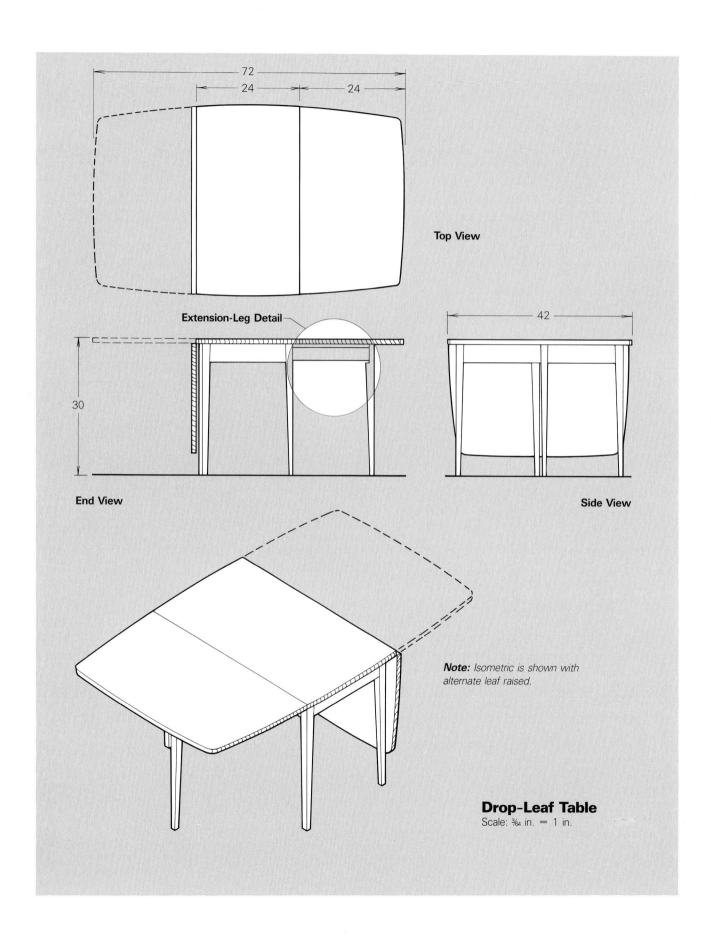

Top View

Extension-Leg Detail

End View

30

72

24

24

42

Side View

Note: Isometric is shown with alternate leaf raised.

Drop–Leaf Table
Scale: ³⁄₆₄ in. = 1 in.

Drop-Leaf

Because drop-leaf tables don't require much space, they are good extension tables for small apartments. There are several types of drop-leafs, but since they've been described so many times in other books and magazines, I will not cover them all again here. I would like to show you one of my favorites.

About 28 years ago, we bought our first house in a subdivision in Rochester, New York. It was comfortable but small, and it had 19 ft. of picture windows—without curtains, which we couldn't afford. (Of course, this helped to make the house feel bigger than it was.) We had two children and we needed a dining table, but there wasn't enough room in this house for a regular one. I did not want a gate-leg table because such tables look too heavy and complicated, so I came up with this drop-leaf design, which I had never seen before.

What is different about this table is that the stretchers for the two extension legs slide through the apron to support the leaves. Before starting, make a full-scale drawing of the mechanics of these pull-out stretchers (like the drawings on the following page).

The table is simple to use and simple to make. It is stable when open and doesn't take up much space when closed, considering its size when open. Closed, the top is 24 in. by 42 in., a comfortable size for two people to eat at when seated at the ends. With one leaf open, the top is 42 in. by 48 in.; with both open, it is 42 in. by 72 in. When the table is closed, most of the base is covered up and only the bottom 5 in. of the center extension legs is visible. The extension legs are off-set on opposite sides of the center, although this is not noticeable.

The base of the table is put together with haunched mortise-and-tenon joints. The construction and assembly are standard, but there are a couple of unusual things about making this table.

Apron Assembly

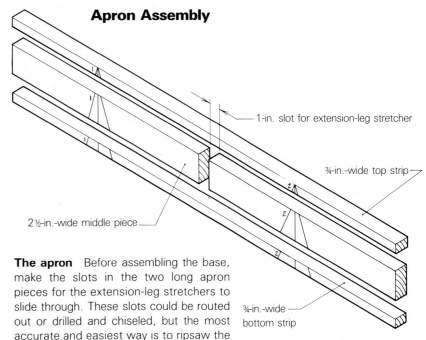

1-in. slot for extension-leg stretcher

¾-in.-wide top strip

2½-in.-wide middle piece

¾-in.-wide bottom strip

The apron Before assembling the base, make the slots in the two long apron pieces for the extension-leg stretchers to slide through. These slots could be routed out or drilled and chiseled, but the most accurate and easiest way is to ripsaw the pieces and reglue them after removing the slot section. (The process is the same as for preparing the drawer fronts in the apron of the trestle table on p. 47.)

First joint and plane the boards to about 1⅛ in. thick by 4¾ in. wide and about 2 in. longer than needed. Be sure to mark them before ripping so you can put the pieces back together in the same order with the grain matching. Joint the top edge of each piece and then rip off a ¾-in.-wide strip. Actually, cut the strip a little wider than ¾ in. so that after the sawcuts have been planed off for the gluing surface, the remaining strip will be ¾ in. wide. Now joint the edge of the boards again and rip off a 2½-in.-wide piece (again, allowing extra for planing the sawmarks). Then joint the edges of the remaining pieces. Remove the 1-in. section in each apron for the extension-leg stretchers by crosscutting on the tablesaw. Remember, the slots are not in the center, so check the drawing. Now glue the four pieces for each apron back together. Don't forget to insert a small block the same dimension as the extension-leg stretcher in the slot when you glue up the apron. When the glue is dry, joint one side of each stretcher and thickness-plane the aprons down to 1 in. Cut the aprons to their final width and length. Finally, cut the tenons on the ends to fit the mortises in the legs.

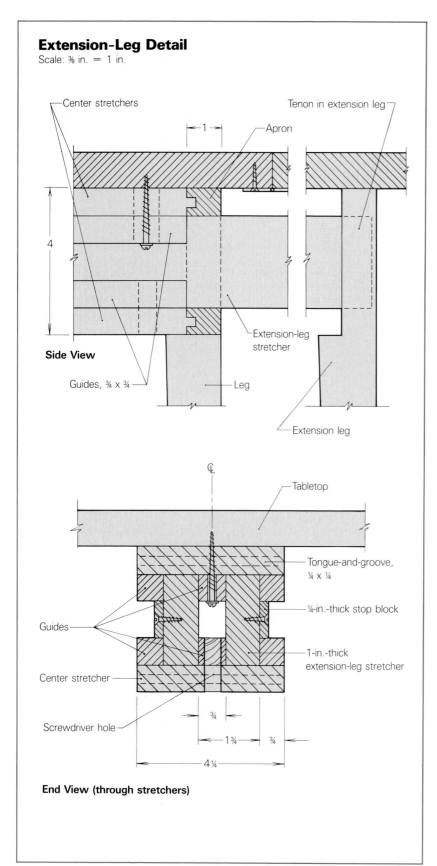

Extension-Leg Detail
Scale: ⅜ in. = 1 in.

Center stretchers

Tenon in extension leg

1

Apron

4

Side View

Guides, ¾ x ¾

Extension-leg stretcher

Leg

Extension leg

℄

Tabletop

Tongue-and-groove, ¼ x ¼

¼-in.-thick stop block

Guides

1-in.-thick extension-leg stretcher

Center stretcher

Screwdriver hole

¾

1¾   ¾

4¼

End View (through stretchers)

Extension-leg assembly   Before gluing the base together, tongue-and-groove two ¾-in. by 4¼-in. center stretchers into the top and bottom of the two long aprons, as shown in the drawings. The extension-leg stretchers slide between these center stretchers, which also help to make the table more rigid.

Glue in the center guides after the table is together. It's important that these guides go in straight. Then fit the extension-leg stretchers and glue on the four outside guides. The stops are screwed on the stretchers so they can be removed if anything goes wrong. Rub all moving parts with paraffin.

Finishing up   In the closed position the top overhangs the extension legs by ½ in. This allows the top to shrink without interference from the legs. I made the top of this table out of solid wood, so it is fastened permanently only in the center with three screws. The two outside screw holes in the center stretcher are slotted to allow the top to move. The rest of the top is held down with cleats that run in slots cut on the insides of the short aprons. The cleats allow the top to expand and contract with changes in humidity. Of course, if you make the top out of plywood, this is unnecessary.

When finishing the table, especially the leaves, be sure to put the same amount of finish on both sides to prevent warpage. If you make the top out of solid wood, try to use stable, quartersawn stock. This table has an oil finish [*Book 2*, pp. 186-187]. Also, as a last step, it's a good idea to put a little rubber bumper on the bottom of each leaf where it hits the center leg.   □

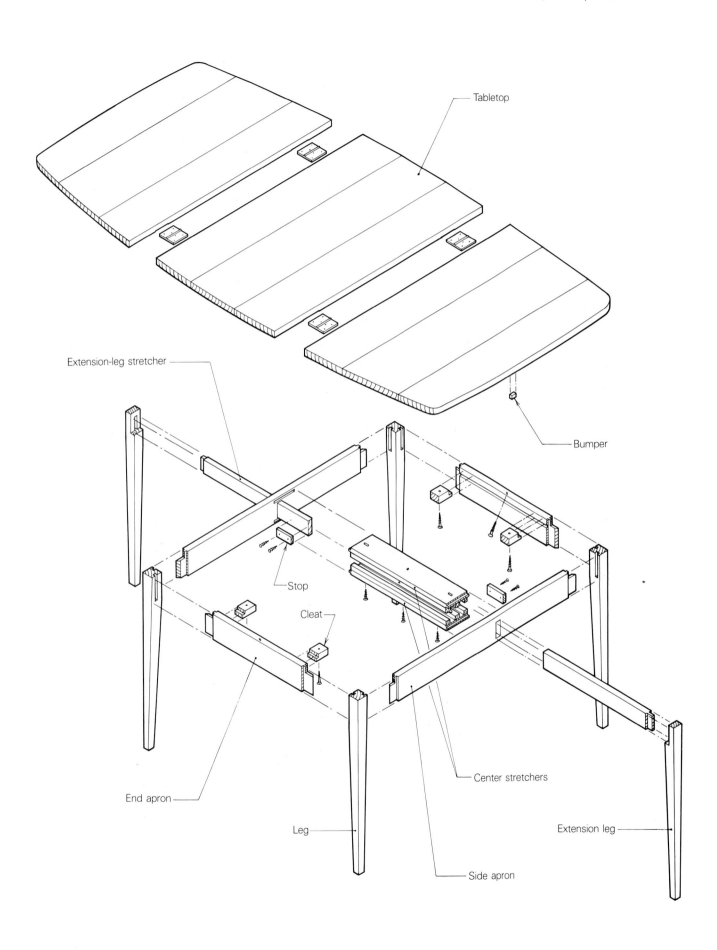

Tabletop

Extension-leg stretcher

Bumper

Stop

Cleat

Center stretchers

End apron

Leg

Side apron

Extension leg

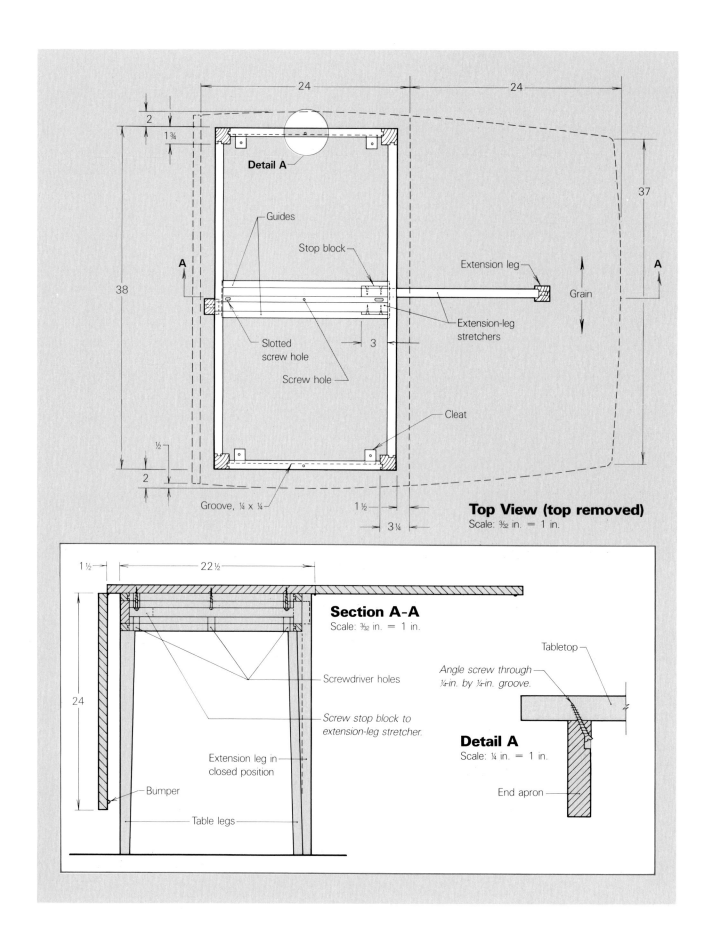

24

24

2

1¾

Detail A

37

Guides

Stop block

Extension leg

A

A

Grain

38

Slotted
screw hole

Extension-leg
stretchers

3

Screw hole

Cleat

½

2

Groove, ¼ x ¼

1½

Top View (top removed)
Scale: ³⁄₃₂ in. = 1 in.

3¼

1½

22½

Section A-A
Scale: ³⁄₃₂ in. = 1 in.

Tabletop

*Angle screw through
¼-in. by ¼-in. groove.*

24

Screwdriver holes

*Screw stop block to
extension-leg stretcher.*

Detail A
Scale: ¼ in. = 1 in.

Extension leg in
closed position

Bumper

End apron

Table legs

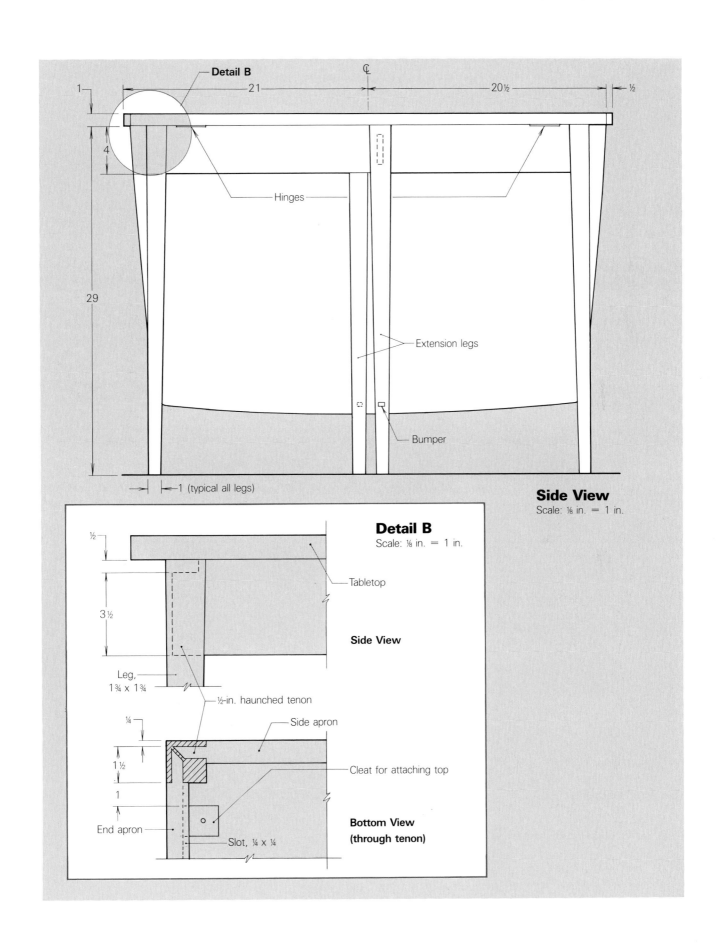

Detail B

Detail B

1 ← 21 → Ⓒ ← 20½ → ½

4

29

Hinges

Extension legs

Bumper

1 (typical all legs)

Side View
Scale: ⅛ in. = 1 in.

Detail B
Scale: ⅛ in. = 1 in.

½

Tabletop

3 ½

Side View

Leg,
1¾ x 1¾

½-in. haunched tenon

¼

Side apron

1 ½

Cleat for attaching top

1

End apron

Slot, ¼ x ¼

**Bottom View
(through tenon)**

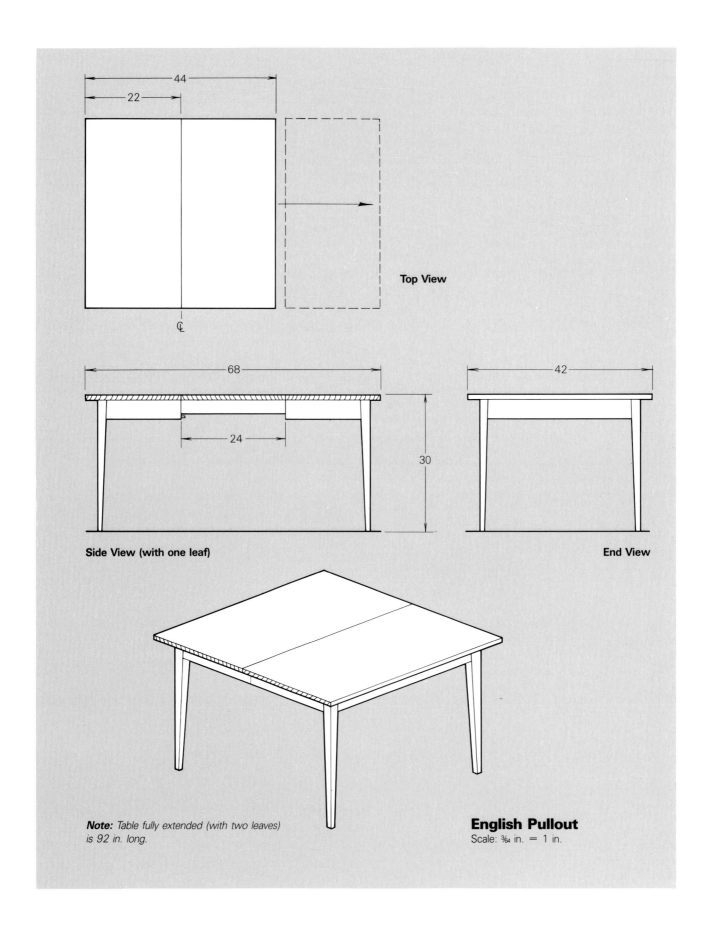

Top View

Side View (with one leaf)

End View

Note: *Table fully extended (with two leaves) is 92 in. long.*

English Pullout
Scale: ¾₄ in. = 1 in.

English Pullout

For large extension tables, the English pullout is usually the best system to use because the legs move out to support the ends and the table remains stable. The two halves of the base follow the two halves of the top, which are attached to extension slides, and for very long extensions an extra leg can be added in the center of the table.

The only real disadvantage with the English pullout is that the leaves can't be stored inside the table when they aren't being used.

Laying out the slides There are some commercial extension slides available in both metal and wood that are good, but I prefer to make my own so that I can make them as long and strong as possible. Here is how to lay out the slides. At first glance, this may all look confusing, but it's actually pretty straightforward. You will find that a full-scale drawing is very helpful in figuring out this type of extension system.

First determine how large you want to make your table. Let's assume that you want a table that is 44 in. long when closed and 92 in. long when opened, which is the size I chose for the table illustrated in these drawings. This is about the minimum size for a small table that could seat four people comfortably when closed and eight when open. Make the leaves 24 in. wide to allow for the comfortable addition of two place settings, one on each side of the table, when each leaf is inserted. Or, if you prefer, four 12-in.-wide leaves could be used, which might be easier to handle and store. This table would have to open up 49 in. in the center to accommodate the two 24-in. or four 12-in. leaves (including an extra inch for the locator splines or dowels between the leaves).

Next determine the amount of overlap of the slides. I wanted the slides to overlap each other by at least 12 in. when the table is open. You would not want less than that to be sure of sufficient strength in a table this size. Here is the method I used to figure out the size and number of slides.

Assuming the top overhangs by 2½ in. and the apron is 1 in. thick, subtract 7 in. (the sum of the aprons and overhang on both ends) from 44 in. This leaves you with 37 in. between the aprons. Leaving ¼ in. of space at each end to compensate for any misalignment of the aprons gives you a maximum length of 36½ in. for the slides.

Now figure out how many 36½-in. slides to use. Half of the inside slide and half of the outside slide are screwed to opposite sides of the tabletop. The two halves added together equal 36½ in. Add that to 49 in. (the desired leaf opening) for 85½ in. If you use two slides, their total length when placed end-to-end is 73 in. Subtracting 12 in. for the single overlap gives you 61 in. This is well short of the required extension. Four slides have a total length of 146 in. If you subtract 36 in. from this for the three 12-in. overlaps, you get 110 in., or 24½ in. more extension than is necessary. Three slides will work just right. Their total length is 109½ in. Subtract 24 in. for the total of the overlaps (three slides will overlap twice) to get 85½ in.

Extension-Slide Diagram

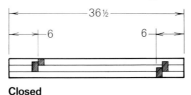

Closed

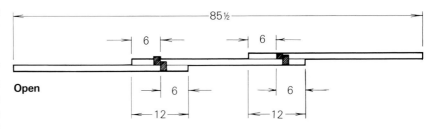

Partially Open

Open

Perhaps you want a slightly larger table, say, 48 in. when closed and 96 in. when open, but the apron thickness and the overhang are to remain the same. In this case, you'll find that if you use three longer slides (40½ in.) and a 12-in. overlap, you will have an extra 8 in. This gives you several options. You could make the slides shorter, you could increase the overlap, or you could extend the width of the leaves. If I were making a much larger table that was going to have three 24-in. extension leaves, I would use five slides on each side instead of three, and I would have them overlap by at least 18 in. I would also add a fifth leg in the center of the table for extra support, as described on p. 95.

If you happen to have a set of slides already, or have decided to buy them, you can always figure out the size of the table by working these measurements in reverse.

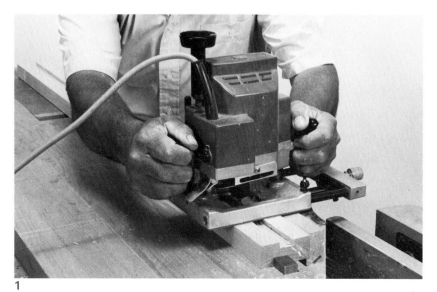

1

Making the slides Now that you know how to lay out the slides, here's how to make them.

Use a hardwood like maple or oak with a straight grain and be sure that it is dry. Rough-cut it two or three weeks ahead of when you'll need it and let the pieces stand free so they get a chance to warp if they're going to. (Discard them if they move a lot.) Then joint and plane them to their final dimensions.

Now make a straight-sided groove in the center of each slide. You can use a hand router, a shaper, or a tablesaw with a dado head. I used a router with a fence, and to stabilize the router at both ends of the cut, I screwed a long piece of wood to the fence.

Then, using a ½-in. dovetail bit, make the first cut on one side of the groove for the dovetailed spline to ride in **(1)**.

For the next cut, move the fence so the bit cuts the slot to the desired width of the dovetail. Keep the fence running against the same side of the slide, but start from the opposite end, so the bit will push the work tight against the fence. If you mark one edge of the slide and always keep the fence referenced to that edge, the grooves will be exactly the same width along their entire length.

The splines that fit into the grooves in the slides should be ³⁄₃₂ in. thicker than the grooves are deep. It is a good idea to have extra pieces for testing, and in case any are ruined.

Keep the same dovetail bit in the router to cut the dovetailed splines, but mount the router in a router table. A fence is necessary and a featherboard clamped to the fence will help hold the splines down.

Here you can see the router-table setup (without the featherboard). The edge of plywood piece 1 that holds the uncut spline against the fence is square, but the edge on plywood piece 2 that holds the routed spline against the fence is cut at the same angle as the dovetail bit. This is so that the spline will be held tight after it has been cut. It is important that the plywood hold the spline tight against the fence to ensure that it will be uniform in width.

First do one edge and then reset the fence and do the other edge **(2)**. It is best to make the splines a little bigger on the first pass so that you can try them in the grooves and then recut them to fit perfectly.

When the splines have been fitted, drill and countersink holes for 1-in.-long #10 flathead wood screws about every 6 in.

The screws aren't put in until after the splines have been glued to the slides. Put the splines back in the grooves and then run a bead of glue down the center, being careful not to overdo it.

Router-Table Setup

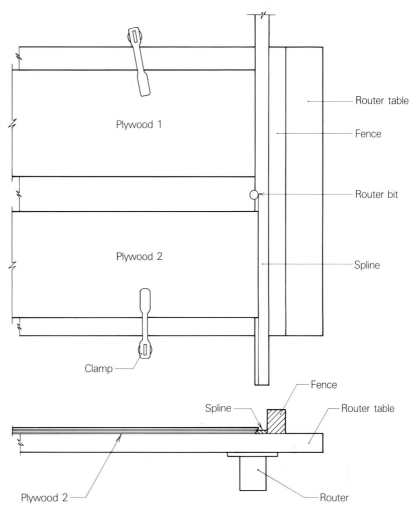

2

3

4

5

Assemble the slides. Be sure to have them in the right order, with the edges that were against the router fence all down on the bench. As you put the clamps on, make sure that both sides are square **(3)**. The clamps should apply pressure only in the middle where the splines are.

Notice that the space between the slides is the same **(4)**, which means that the unit is square. One of the advantages of having this space is that, even if you put on too much glue and it squeezed out, the slides will not stick together too badly. And if they cup slightly, they will still be able to slide.

As soon as the glue is set but not dry, separate the slides to be sure they don't stick together. The length of time actually depends on the glue used and the temperature in the shop. In this case, I used Titebond yellow glue and removed the clamps after about 45 minutes.

After the glue is completely dry, do the final fitting. Because the splines are tapered and are ³⁄₃₂ in. thicker than the grooves are deep, you will have to plane and sand the tops of the splines a little where necessary until they work easily **(5)**. Don't take off too much. When everything is working smoothly, put in the screws. You will have to drill a pilot hole for the part of the screw that runs into the slide. It is a good idea to rub paraffin on the threads before you put the screws in.

Reassemble the slides and send them through the thickness planer as a unit, being careful to have them together correctly. Make sure that for the first pass through the planer, the edges that were against the router fence are placed down on the table, or bed, of the planer. When you've taken off the smallest amount possible to get the opposite side even, flip the unit over and take a fine cut off the other side, just in case it wasn't perfect already.

Locating the stops You will have to make and fit stops on the slides. The same stops should work when opening and closing the table. Because the slides will overlap each other by 12 in., measure in 6 in. from each end of the assembly **(6)**. Next draw out the width of the stops. Locate stops **1** and **2** outside of the line, as shown in the drawing below. Place stops **3** and **4** on both sides of the line. (I made my stops 1¼ in. wide.) If your slides have a greater overlap than 12 in., you can position the stops using the same method—simply divide the overlap in half and measure in by that amount from each end of the slide assembly. Then lay out the stops as described above.

Glue and screw the stops onto the slides in the positions shown in the drawing below. Be sure to leave a slight space between the overlap on the stops and the slides **(7)**. This allows the stops to move without rubbing when the table is extended. Notice that stop **4** is square **(8)**, but the others are all rectangular in order to overlap the adjacent slides.

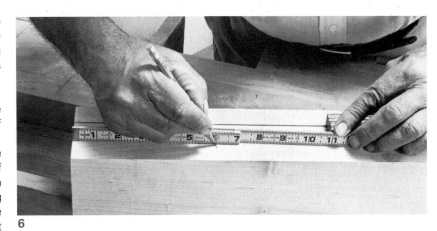

6

7

8

Extension Slides

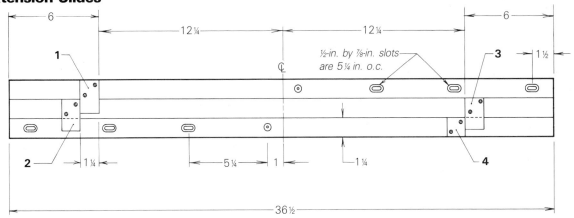

Note: Allow ³⁄₃₂-in. clearance between slides.

9

10

Making the top   Once the slides are made, make the top and leaves. If you are making a solid-wood top, be sure that the grain of the top runs at right angles to that of the slides. This is important because if you orient the grain of the slides in the same direction as that of the top, they will probably not work if the top warps or cups or moves more at one end than the other.

Now install the locator splines for lining up the top and the leaves. (I used splines instead of dowels because I like the way they look.) I cut the slots for the splines with this simple jig **(9)**. The short dowel on the right acts as a stop to locate the jig. The other two dowels are used to clamp the jig in position **(10)**. Use a plunge router with a template guide and a ¼-in. bit to make the slots. Cut the slots in one edge and then flip the jig over to make the matching slots in the edge of the adjacent board.

Installing the slides   When the top has been made and the splines glued in place, drill and countersink holes in the slides for the screws that will attach them to the top. Attach one end of the inside slide on each unit to one half of the top, and the opposite end of the outside slide to the other half of the top. Put a strip of ⅛-in.-thick veneer between the top and the slides when you attach them to leave a little space so the slides can't rub against the top. If you don't leave a space, the slides won't be able to move if the top warps slightly.

When screwing the slides to a solid-wood top, fasten them permanently in the center of the table and slot all the other holes so the top can expand and contract. The top is attached to the aprons with cleats that slide in routed grooves (see p. 47).

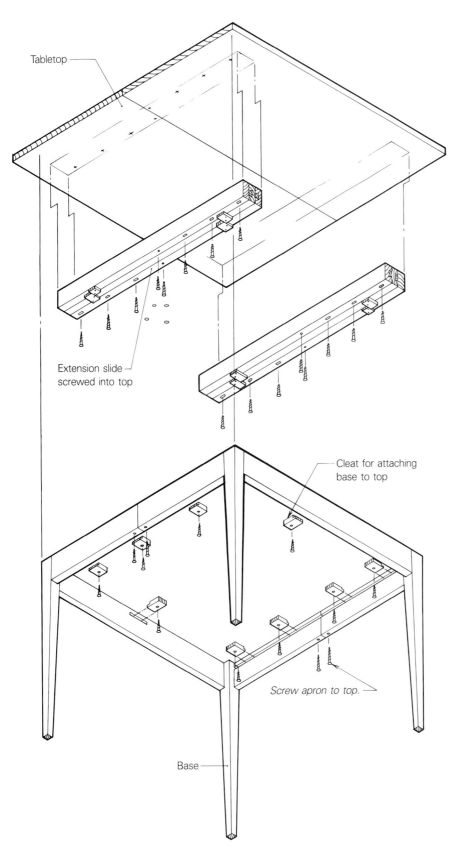

Tabletop

Extension slide
screwed into top

Cleat for attaching
base to top

Screw apron to top.

Base

Note: *View is from underside of table.*

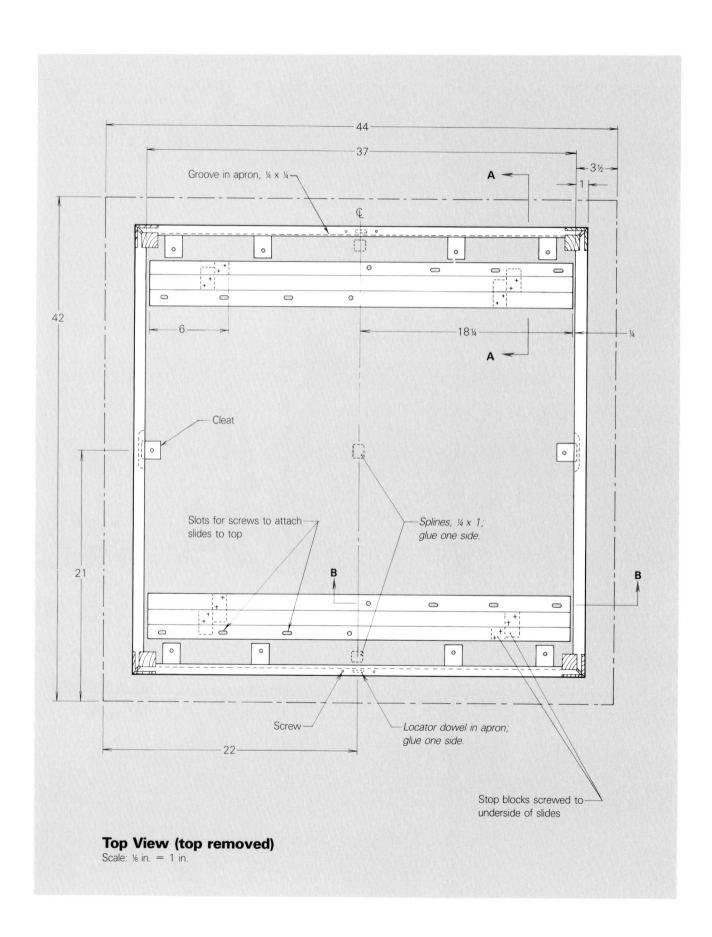

Groove in apron, ¼ x ¼

Cleat

Slots for screws to attach slides to top

*Splines, ¼ x 1;
glue one side.*

Screw

*Locator dowel in apron;
glue one side.*

Stop blocks screwed to
underside of slides

Top View (top removed)
Scale: ⅛ in. = 1 in.

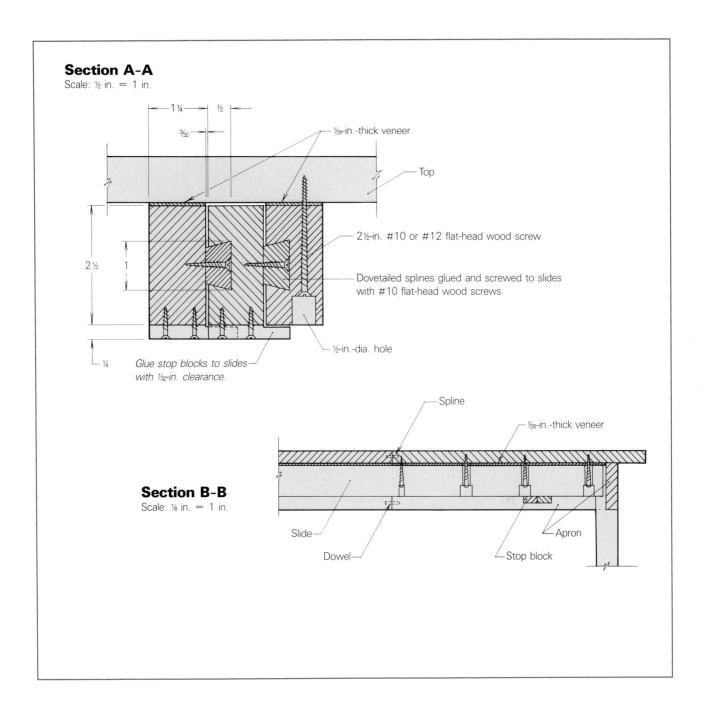

Section A-A
Scale: ½ in. = 1 in.

1 ¼

½

3⁄32

2 ½

1

¼

½8-in.-thick veneer

Top

2 ½-in. #10 or #12 flat-head wood screw

Dovetailed splines glued and screwed to slides
with #10 flat-head wood screws

½-in.-dia. hole

*Glue stop blocks to slides
with ½32-in. clearance.*

Section B-B
Scale: ⅛ in. = 1 in.

Spline

½8-in.-thick veneer

Slide

Dowel

Stop block

Apron

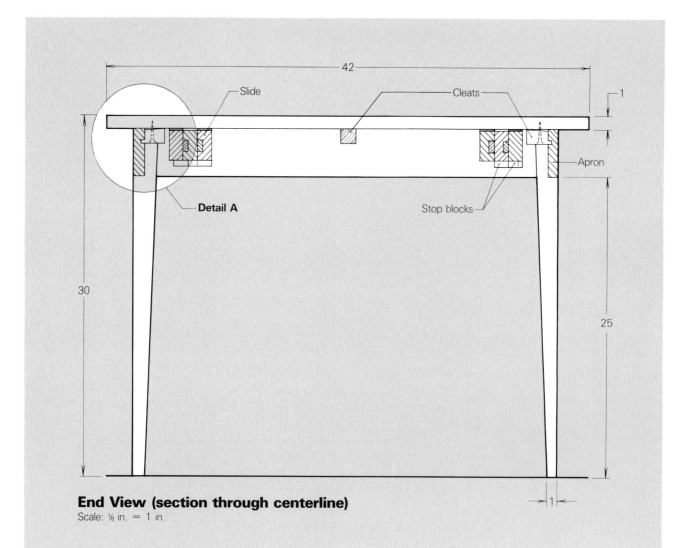

End View (section through centerline)
Scale: ⅛ in. = 1 in.

Slide

Cleats

Detail A

Stop blocks

Apron

42

1

30

25

1

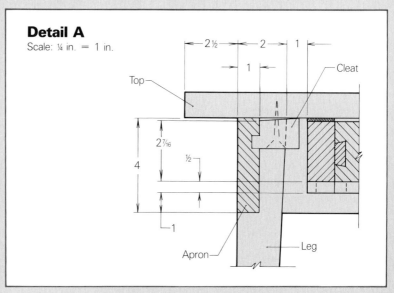

Detail A
Scale: ¼ in. = 1 in.

2½

2

1

1

Cleat

Top

2⁷⁄₁₆

4

½

1

Apron

Leg

The fifth leg Any table that extends more than 4 ft. should have an extra support leg in the center. The special hardware usually available to stabilize this type of leg is sometimes not too reliable, so I do it differently. I prefer to have a fifth leg that is bolted to a piece of wood glued and screwed to the bottom of the inside slides. The leg is attached using a bolt with a wing-nut head and a T-nut. It is then bolted in place when the full extensions are used and removed and stored away when not needed.   ☐

Note: *A table with three 24-in. leaves would require five slides and an extra center leg.*

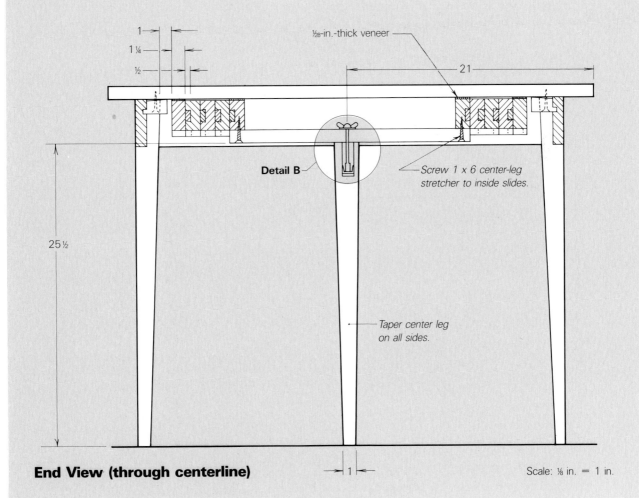

Detail B
Scale: ¼ in. = 1 in.

- Recess dowel ⅟₁₆ in.
- Stretcher
- 1-in.-dia. dowel glued in leg
- ¼-in.-dia. bolt with wing-nut head
- Space below T-nut
- T-nut
- Center leg

2   1   2½

½₈-in.-thick veneer

21

Screw 1 x 6 center-leg stretcher to inside slides.

Detail B

1   1¼   ½

25½

Taper center leg on all sides.

End View (through centerline)   1   Scale: ⅛ in. = 1 in.

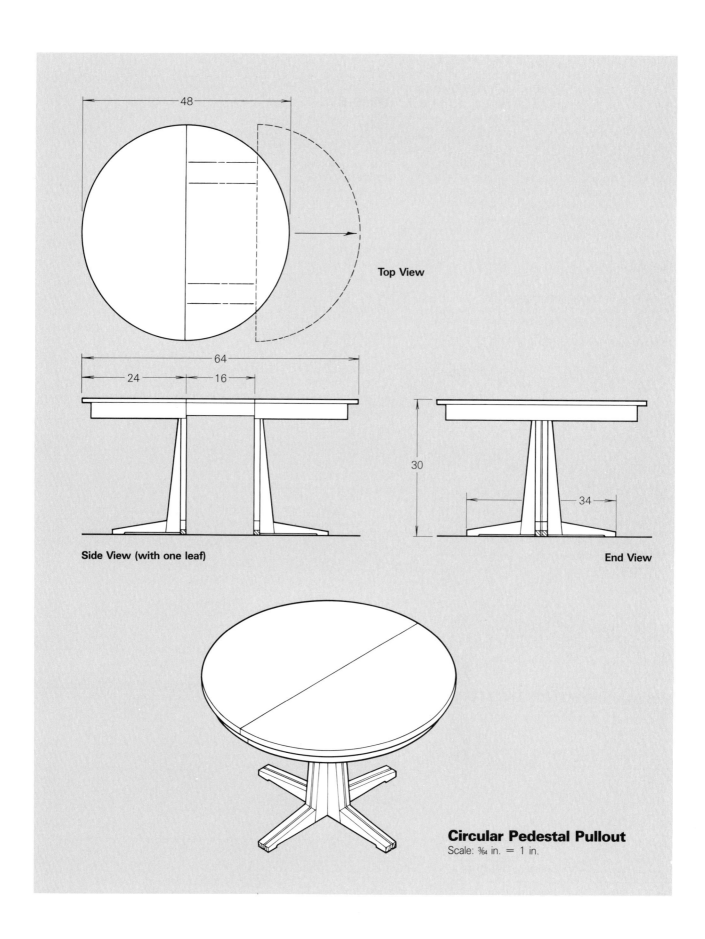

Top View

Side View (with one leaf)

End View

48

64

24

16

30

34

Circular Pedestal Pullout
Scale: ¾₄ in. = 1 in.

Circular Pedestal Pullout

While it is helpful to have drawings of the rectangular English pullout, it is absolutely essential to draw the round version because the slides are more difficult to figure out mathematically. The process is similar to the one used for the rectangular table, but the round top means that each slide will be a different length. To figure out the length of each slide and the position of the stops, a full-scale drawing of half of the top view is most useful.

Laying out the slides First determine how large you want your table to be. For this table, I decided on a 48-in.-dia. top that will expand to 96 in. in length when three 16-in. leaves are inserted. Again, this means my slides have to extend at least 49 in. (including an extra inch for the locator splines). I also wanted the slides to overlap at least 12 in.

Now locate the centerline of the two slide assemblies. This is somewhat arbitrary, although the farther apart you place them, the more stable the leaves will be when the table is open. At the same time, the farther apart the assemblies are, the shorter the slides will be and the more of them you will need to make up the span. In this case, I positioned the slide assemblies at a point where the centerline would be 30½ in. long—allowing about ¹⁄₁₆ in. between the ends of the slides and the inside of the apron.

As before, half of each outside slide will be screwed to opposite sides of the tabletop, so add the average slide length (30½ in.) to the desired opening (49 in.) for 79½ in. This is the total minimum distance the slides must extend. If you use four slides in each assembly, they will have a total length of 122 in. Subtract 36 in. for the total of the overlaps (12 in. times 3) to get 86 in. Because this is 6½ in. more than what you need, you can overlap the slides by an extra 2 in. for greater strength. Three slides would have given only 67½ in. of extension.

Next lay out all four slides on your drawing with the 30½-in. length as the centerline. Notice that the ends of the slides follow the curve of the inside of the apron. I made the slides 1¼ in. thick, so that makes them 28 in. long, 30½ in. long, 32¾ in. long and 34½ in. long, as shown in the drawing below.

I used maple for the slides. The process for making them is the same as the one used for the rectangular English pullout table (see pp. 86-88).

Extension-Slide Diagram

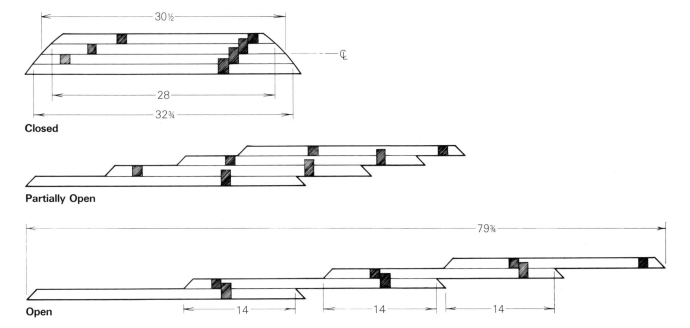

Closed

Partially Open

Open

Locating the stops   Because of the difference in the lengths of the slides, the stops have to be placed differently than on the rectangular English pullout. You can see from the drawing that stop **4** at the end of the short slide is square, while stops **1**, **2** and **3** are rectangular and overlap the adjacent slides. Stops **5**, **6** and **7** on the other end are all square.

Lay out the stops right on the slides. Begin again at the centerline of the assembly. Subtract the 14-in. overlap from 30½ in. to get an extension length of 16½ in. Divide that in half and lay out stop **1** so that its outside edge is 8¼ in. from the midpoint of slide **a**. Next draw in stops **2**, **3** and **4** in the stepped fashion shown below. Then measure in 14 in. from the left end of slides **b**, **c** and **d** and make marks at those positions. Move slide **a** so that its right end is on the 14-in. mark on slide **b**. Stop **1** overlaps slide **b** at the location for stop **5**. Do the same thing with slides **b** and **c** to locate stops **6** and **7**.

The apron   As with most tables, an apron helps to stabilize the top and in this case it also hides the slides. The easiest and strongest way to make a round apron

is to bricklay it [*Book 2*, pp. 98-104]. For this table, I glued four layers of basswood on top of each other. Basswood is soft and glues easily. When the glue was dry, I cut the outside to a perfect circle on a jig made for the bandsaw.

The jig **(1)** is a piece of ¾-in. plywood, clamped to the bandsaw table. Draw a line on the jig between the front of the blade and the edge of the plywood. Measuring out from the blade along the line, mark the radius of the circle to be cut and drill a hole at that point. (My jig has been used before, so there are lots of holes.)

Now fit and screw a board to the bottom of the bricklaid piece and drill a hole in the center of it that will match the hole in the plywood jig **(2)**. It's important that the hole be perfectly centered.

Turn the piece over and move the bricklaid ring up to the blade until the center hole in the board and the hole in the plywood line up. Then insert a tight-fitting dowel in the holes for a pivot point and start the saw. It is easy to pivot the ring on the dowel to cut the outside of the apron to a perfect circle **(3)**.

Extension Slides

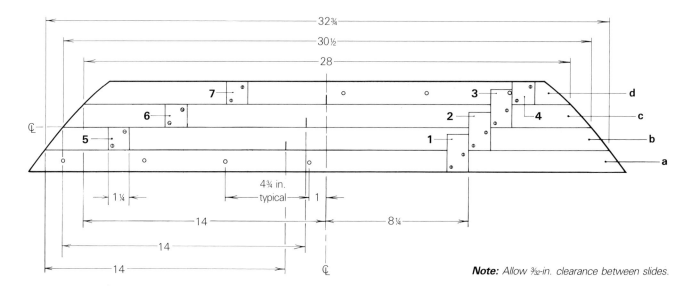

Note: Allow ³⁄₃₂-in. clearance between slides.

1

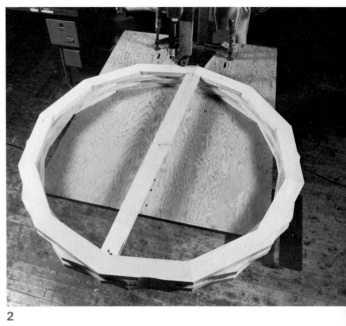

2

3

4

This apron has to be cut in half because it is for an extension table, so it is simple to cut the inside curve. If you ever have to cut the inside of a circular apron for a solid table, however, here's a quick way to do it (without having to break and reweld the bandsaw blade).

Mark the inside circle before removing the centerboard so you don't lose the center. Then cut a long scarf from the outside edge to the inside circle marked on the apron **(4)**.

After you have cut the inside freehand, glue a piece of wood the same thickness as the sawkerf between the two scarfs to make a joint **(5)**. I used a different-color wood in these photos so it would be more visible.

I glued a ¼-in.-thick facing on the outside of the apron **(6)**. Even if you are going to veneer the apron, a facing should still be glued on (but it could be thinner) to prevent the bricklaying from telegraphing through the veneer.

5

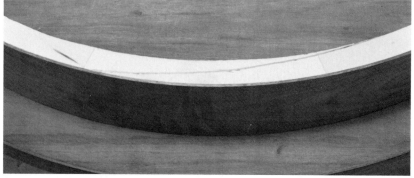

6

The top To make the top perfectly round, you can use the same jig as for the apron. First, drill a pivot hole ½ in. deep (don't drill all the way through) at what will be the center of the underside of the tabletop. Then bandsaw out the top.

To smooth the edge, I used a shaper with the same jig I used on the bandsaw **(1)**, but I bolted the jig to the shaper table instead of clamping it. The two bolt holes in the jig are slotted so you can move the jig to adjust its position. Draw a line on the jig from the center of the cutter to the edge of the plywood, then drill a hole in it to locate the center hole on the underside of the top. Fit a dowel tightly in the center hole of the top and set the top on the jig. For security, glue the dowel in and cut it off later. With the two bolts loosely in place, move the edge of the top up to the cutter but not touching it.

Now tighten the bolt in the slot on the jig's right side. Start the machine and pivot the jig until the cutter reaches a pencil line marking the top's outside diameter **(7)**. Then tighten the bolt in the left slot.

Rotating the top on the center dowel, cut all the way around until it is a perfectly smooth circle. This operation takes two people **(8)**. The shaper's safety guard has been removed just for these pictures.

A router mounted in a router table could be used for this job instead, but it must have at least 1½ HP and should accept a ½-in.-shank bit. A small router won't work.

Another way to do it, which can be managed by one person, is to use a router with a fence. Drill a hole in the top of a router fence and thread it for a ³⁄₁₆-in. stove bolt. The bolt should stick out a little less than the depth of the hole drilled in the underside of the tabletop. A nut on the inside of the fence will keep the bolt from unscrewing. (When used, the fence is attached upside down, as shown in **9**.) Extend the fence with two steel rods and set it up with the bolt in the pivot hole. With this particular router, the rods can be extended to cut a large circle. Carefully move the router into the pencil line as you did on the shaper. Then stop the router and secure the two steel rods. Now run the router in a circle to smooth the top.

7

8

9

10

11

The top and the leaves of the table in the photos are made out of 1-in. plywood. Since this is an extension table, you have to cut the top in half on the tablesaw. To do this, clamp a straightedge to the underside to act like a fence riding against the edge of the saw table.

After cutting the top, glue hardwood facings on all exposed edges to cover the plywood. First glue a very thin facing, about 1/16 in. thick, to the inside straight edges and to both straight edges of the leaves as well. Then glue a 1/8-in.-thick facing to the outside perimeter of the top: Set up the two halves with blocks between them and glue the facing to one half at a time using a strap clamp **(10)**. To be sure that the ends are glued well enough, hammer in a couple of wedges to force them tight **(11)**. When one half is dry, glue the facing to the other half in the same manner. Then glue the 1/8-in. facing to the outside edges of the leaves.

Now cut the slots for the locator splines in both halves of the top and in the leaves, as described on p. 90. Then install the splines. The splines are offset slightly to make it easier to line up the leaves and put them in right side up.

If you make a circular tabletop that does not expand, you can glue on the facing the whole way around except for the last 10 in. or so on both ends, where they overlap. When the glue has dried, scarf the two ends together and clamp them down with a strap clamp.

Pedestal base This table has a pedestal base that has to separate in the center when the table is opened. So when I designed the base, I used a ¼-in. by ¼-in. rabbet as a detail to cover up the joint between the two halves and to make the base look lighter. I also ran the rabbet down the legs and feet that do not separate so the table would look the same from all directions. The base is assembled using standard mortise-and-tenon construction. Each half of the plywood top is screwed to a piece of ¾-in. plywood, which is bolted to the base with ⁵⁄₁₆-in. T-nuts. The top is secured to the apron with tongued hardwood cleats that run in a ¼-in. by ¼-in. continuous groove in the inside of the apron. If you make the top from solid wood instead of plywood, the screw holes in the plywood underneath and in the two cleats on the ends must be slotted to allow for expansion and contraction.

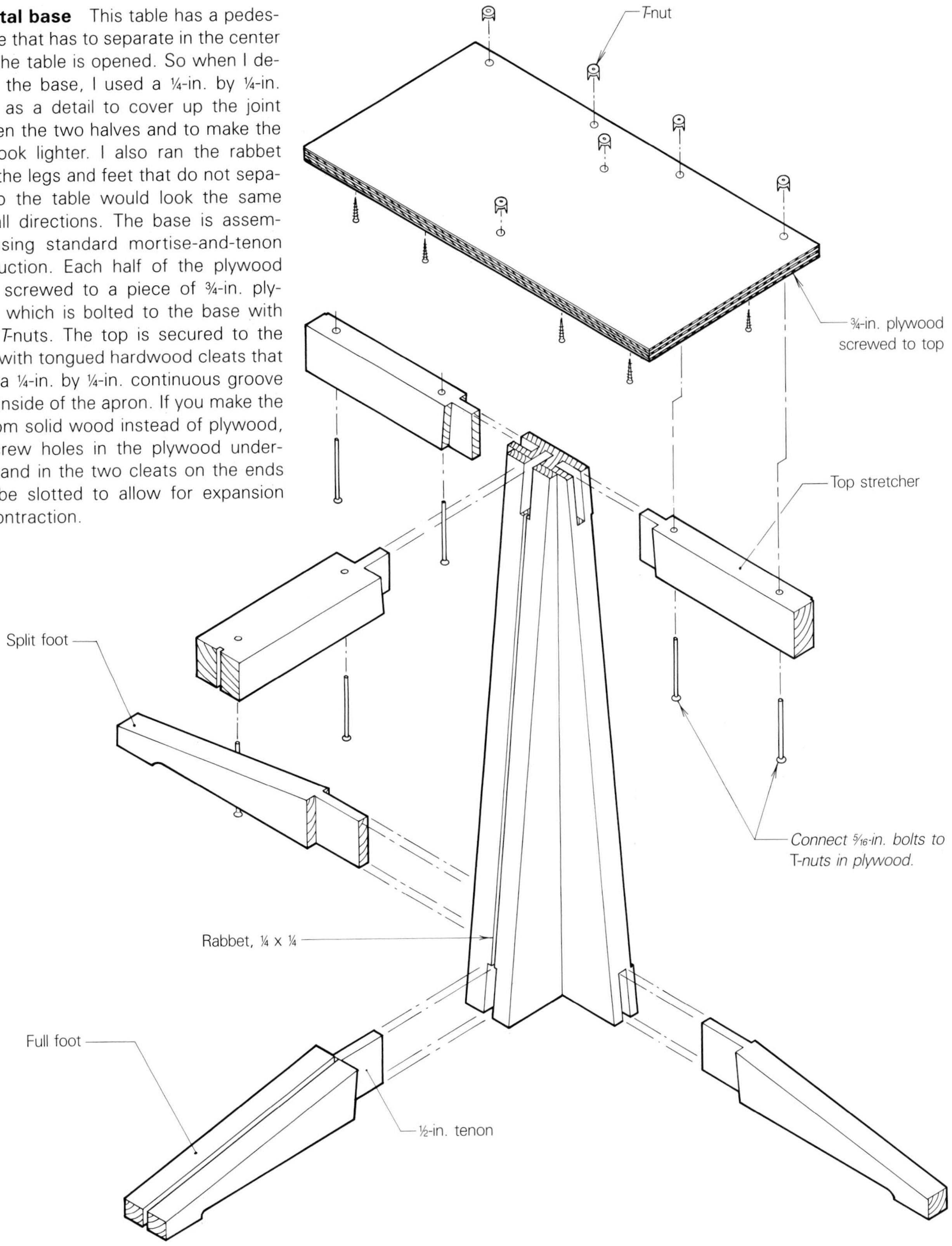

T-nut

¾-in. plywood screwed to top

Top stretcher

Connect ⁵⁄₁₆-in. bolts to T-nuts in plywood.

Split foot

Rabbet, ¼ x ¼

Full foot

½-in. tenon

Note: *Isometric is of base only and is taken from centerline.*

The finished piece Here is the table closed **(12)**, with one 16-in.-wide leaf inserted **(13)**, and open without the leaves **(14)**. I later added apron pieces to the undersides of the leaves to hide the slides. □

12

13

14

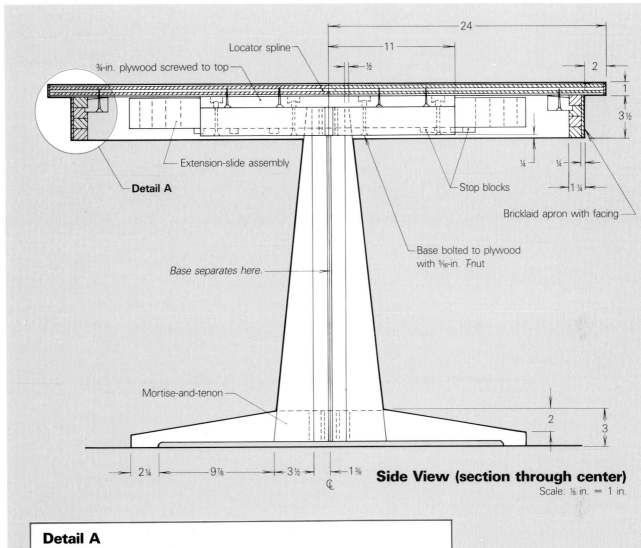

24

11

½

2

¾-in. plywood screwed to top

Locator spline

1

3½

Detail A

Extension-slide assembly

Stop blocks

¼   ¼

1¼

Bricklaid apron with facing

Base bolted to plywood
with ⁵⁄₁₆-in. T-nut

Base separates here.

Mortise-and-tenon

2

3

2¼   9⅞   3½   1⅜

C̸

Side View (section through center)
Scale: ⅛ in. = 1 in.

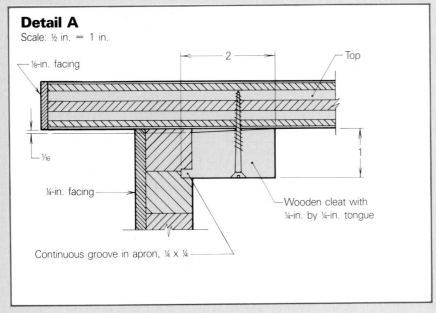

Detail A
Scale: ½ in. = 1 in.

⅛-in. facing

2

Top

1

1⁄16

¼-in. facing

Wooden cleat with
¼-in. by ¼-in. tongue

Continuous groove in apron, ¼ x ¼

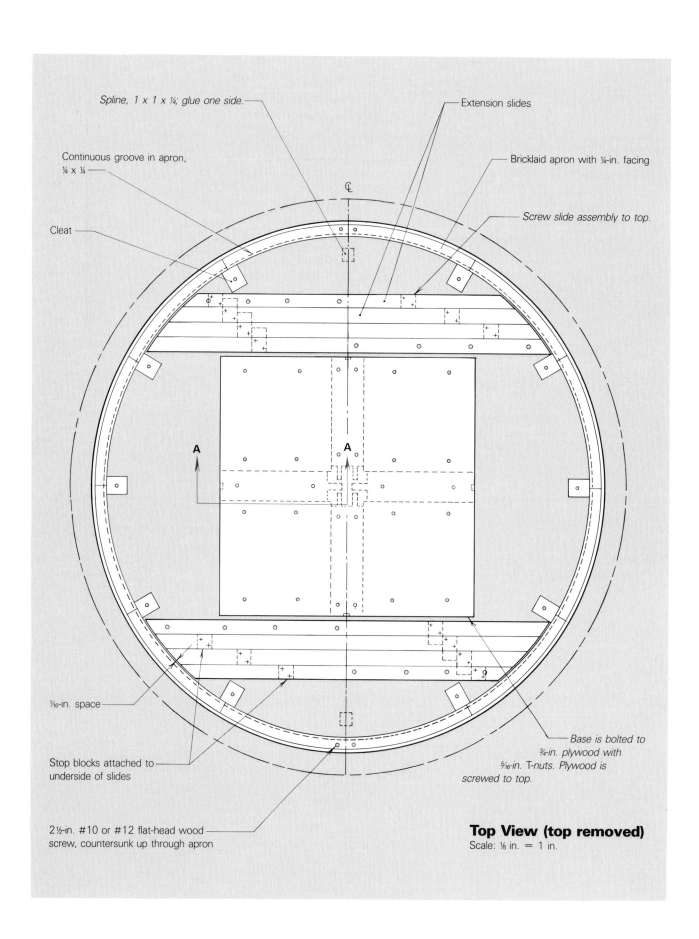

Spline, 1 x 1 x ¼; glue one side.

Extension slides

Continuous groove in apron, ¼ x ¼

Bricklaid apron with ¼-in. facing

Screw slide assembly to top.

Cleat

℄

A

A

¹⁄₁₆-in. space

Base is bolted to ¾-in. plywood with ⁵⁄₁₆-in. T-nuts. Plywood is screwed to top.

Stop blocks attached to underside of slides

2½-in. #10 or #12 flat-head wood screw, countersunk up through apron

Top View (top removed)
Scale: ⅛ in. = 1 in.

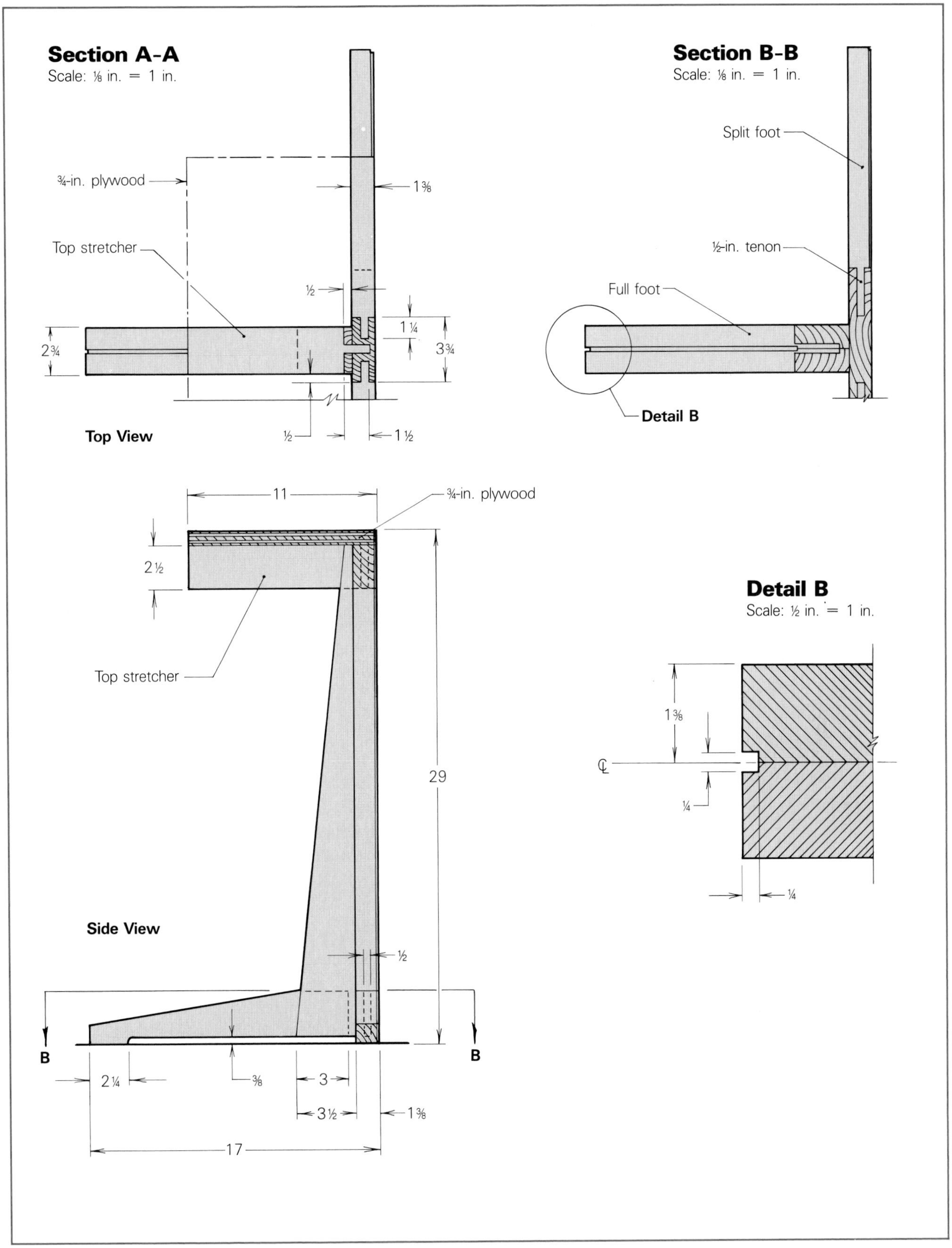
Section A-A
Scale: ⅛ in. = 1 in.
¾-in. plywood
Top stretcher
1⅜
½
1¼
3¾
2¾
½
1½
Top View
Section B-B
Scale: ⅛ in. = 1 in.
Split foot
½-in. tenon
Full foot
Detail B
11
¾-in. plywood
2½
Top stretcher
29
Side View
½
B
B
2¼
⅜
3
3½
1⅜
17
Detail B
Scale: ½ in. = 1 in.
1⅜
℄
¼
¼

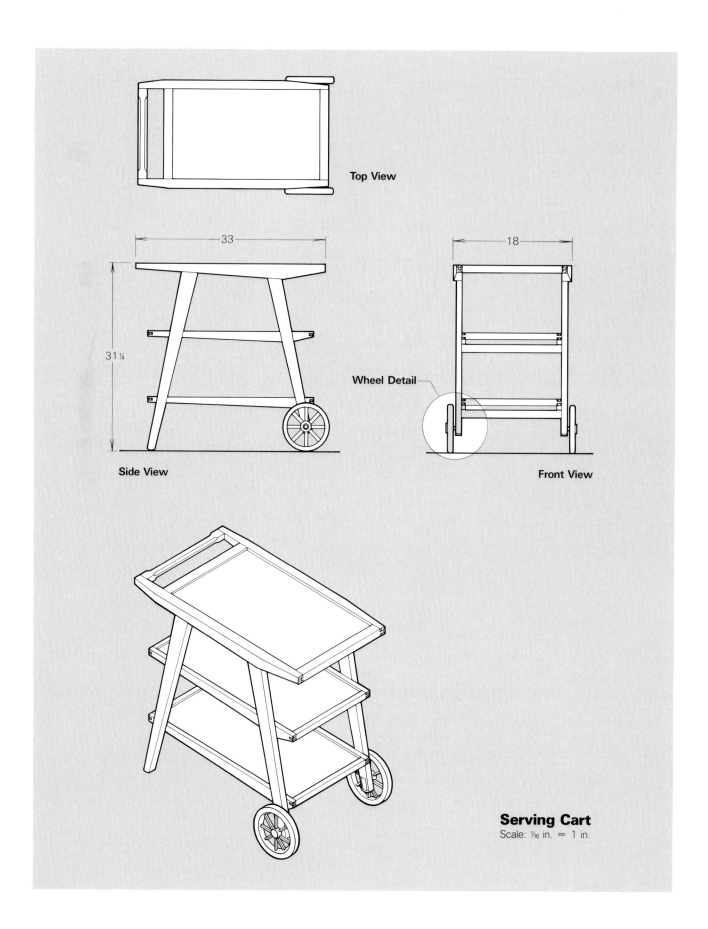

Top View

Side View

Front View

Wheel Detail

Serving Cart
Scale: ⅟₁₆ in. = 1 in.

Serving Cart

A serving cart is a handy thing to have. It saves a lot of steps in serving a meal. Unfortunately, serving carts are usually made very light and have small casters on them, so they cannot carry much weight. I wanted to make a cart that could bear a heavy load but would still look light **(1)**. It had to be stable enough for me to carve meat on the top on a removable cutting board, and I wanted two shelves below to hold plates and utensils. I wanted wheels only in the front, but they had to be large enough for the cart to roll smoothly under weight. The placement of the handle would allow it to be used for hanging a towel.

This cart is easy to make using standard mortise-and-tenon construction. For strength, I used slip joints on the corners of the two bottom trays. But I used full-width tenons, which are not exposed on the sides, for the top tray. The drawings show the construction details well. The only unusual thing about building this piece is making the wheels.

Wheel construction might seem difficult because of all the jigs involved, but once the jigs are made, the process actually goes quickly, especially if more than one wheel is being made at the same time.

1

Making the rims I made the rims of the wheels out of three layers of bricklaid walnut [*Book 2*, pp. 98-103]. Each layer has eight pieces. To make the rims, begin by cutting 24 pieces for each wheel on the tablesaw to match the pattern in the drawing below. The angle for the mitered ends is based on eight pieces in each layer and a wheel with a 4⅛-in. radius. As in any bricklaying, the joints in one layer should be centered between the joints in the adjacent layers.

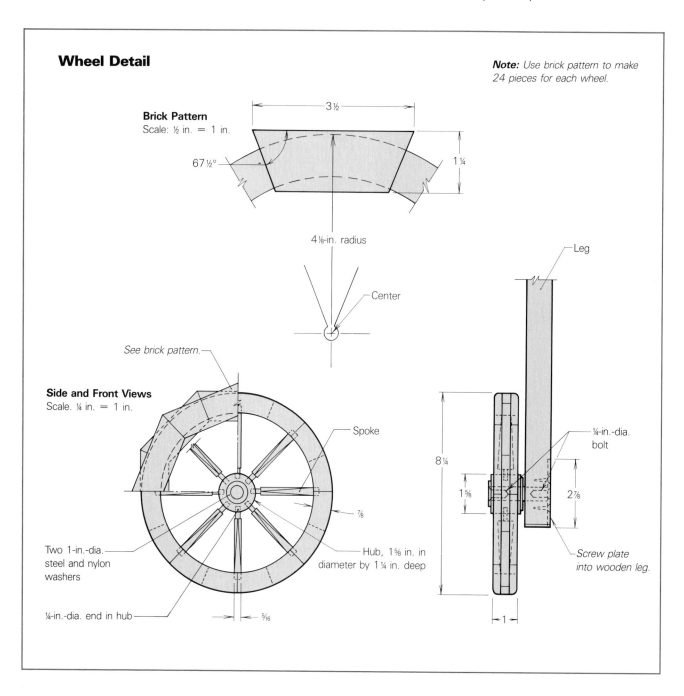

Wheel Detail

Note: Use brick pattern to make 24 pieces for each wheel.

Brick Pattern
Scale: ½ in. = 1 in.

3½

67½°

1¼

4⅛-in. radius

Center

Leg

See brick pattern.

Side and Front Views
Scale. ¼ in. = 1 in.

Spoke

Two 1-in.-dia. steel and nylon washers

Hub, 1⅝ in. in diameter by 1¼ in. deep

¼-in.-dia. end in hub

⅞

⅝

¼-in.-dia. bolt

Screw plate into wooden leg.

8¼

1⅝

2⅞

1

For each rim, first glue two layers together and then glue them to a piece of plywood. I used hot glue and placed a piece of brown paper between the plywood and the two rings so they could be easily separated later [*Book 2*, pp. 88-90]. (When the pieces are separated, the paper splits in half and you can remove it from the bricklaid section with a scraper or hot water.) Now screw this assembly to another, larger piece of plywood and drill a hole in the center for a steel pin (pivot point) in the jig. The top layer will be routed for the spokes before the wheel is assembled. The third layer will be glued up and shaped by itself, using the same jig, after the first two are completed.

Fit a wooden fence to the two rods on the router and drill a corresponding hole in it for the steel pin.

Set the wooden fence to the correct radius for cutting the inside of the rim and begin routing. To prevent the bit from chattering, remove only one-third of the thickness on each pass. On the third or fourth pass, cut below the ring into the plywood (**2**) so it will be easier to separate the jig from the wheel later. Cut the outside of the rim the same way (**3,4**).

2

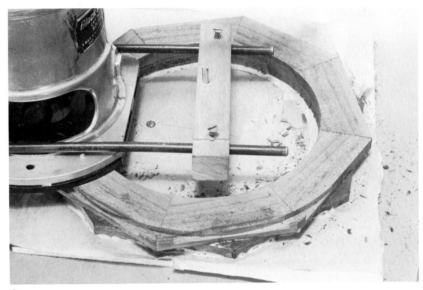

3

4

5

6

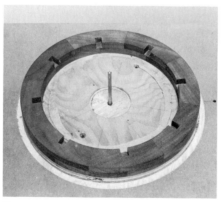

7

To cut the slots for the spokes to fit into, put another steel pin into the same jig outside the rings.

Now make another jig for the second steel pin to fit into. First drill a hole for the center pin, then drill eight outside holes at the right radius and distance apart. The radius is the same as the distance between the center pin and the outside pin on the first jig. The best way to drill the eight holes is to clamp another piece of plywood to the drill-press table. Drill a hole in the plywood, the same size as the steel pin, and measure out from it a distance equal to the distance between the two pins on the first jig. Drill another hole and insert a pin at that point. Then mount the center hole of the second plywood jig on that pin and turn the jig to drill the eight equally spaced holes.

When the eight holes have been drilled, cut a slot large enough to accept the router template guide at the correct spot on the jig **(5)**. I used a 5/16-in. bit and template guide to match the ends of the spokes I had in mind. This step has to be done precisely so the cuts in the ring below will be correct. It is not critical, but I suggest that you center the slot between joints in this layer of the rim. When the third layer is added, the outside joints will line up on the spokes.

Clamp the jig in place and make the first slot in the rim **(6)**. Then move the jig to the point where the outside pin in the bottom jig will fit into the next index hole in the top jig, and clamp the jig in place. Rout that slot and repeat the process until all the slots in the ring have been cut.

That done, chisel the ends square. Notice that I routed out the center of the jig to accept the hub **(7)**, which will be longer than the wheel rim is thick. Take the pin out and use a Forstner bit (or a router or chisel) to do this. This was not done before now because the center pin had to be as stable as possible for all that routing.

Making the spokes Next the spokes have to be made. In this case I did not want them turned; I wanted them to have crisp edges so they would fit in with the other design details of the cart.

Mill the wood for the spokes and cut it to length. Then on the tablesaw cut the square tenons that fit into the slots in the rim of the wheel. To remove waste, I drilled two relief holes at the other end of each spoke **(8)** on the drill press using a simple jig to align them.

To make the round tenon on the end of each spoke that fits into the hub, turn the drill-press table 90° and make another jig to hold the spokes **(9)**. Then cut the round tenons with a plug cutter **(10)**.

8

9

10

11

12

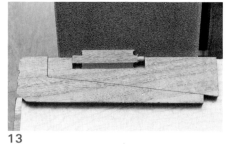

13

To bevel the four edges of each spoke, tilt the table on the stationary belt sander to the desired angle and make a wedge jig **(11)** that will sand the correct bevel when the wedge is pushed in **(12,13)**. The spoke has to be held down with a stick when it is being sanded to keep it from jumping out of the jig.

For tapering the spokes, reset the table on the sander at 90° to the face of the belt and make another jig. Glue and nail a piece of wood with a slot for the round tenon on the right side and fasten a stop on the left. Then place the spokes, one at a time, in the slot and push each side of the spoke against the sandpaper with a stick until it hits the stop **(14)**.

At this stage, the spokes are ready to be hand-sanded **(15)**. Use a file and sandpaper to trim the end.

14

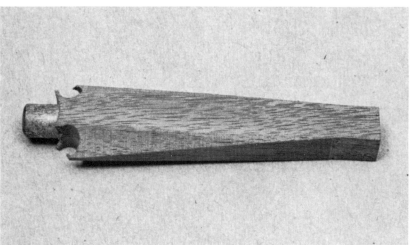

15

Making the hubs To make the hubs, use the tablesaw to cut the corners off a 1¾-in. by 1¾-in. piece of wood so that it is octagonal. Then cut it to length (1¼ in. for each hub). After that, drill the hole for the axle exactly in the center. Now position each block carefully and consistently on the drill-press table to drill the eight holes for the spokes, one in each face **(16)**.

To sand the hub round, set the table on the sander at 90° to the belt. Attach a board with a pin that fits the center hole in the hub so that it can slide in and out **(17)**. The distance between the pin and the edge of the board should be equal to the desired radius of the hub.

Place the hub on the pin, start the sander, and move the board in until it hits the sandpaper. Clamp the board in that position and turn the hub until it is round.

16

17

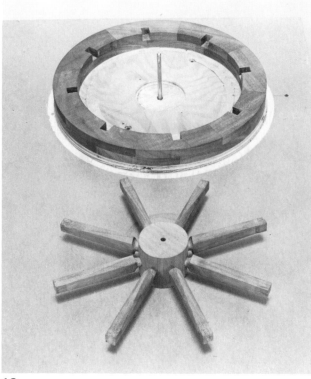

18

19

Assembling the wheel The spokes are now ready to be glued into the hub and rim **(18)**. Use a slow-drying glue, like plastic resin, because the hub, spokes and third ring are all glued at the same time, and it takes a long time to assemble everything.

Before gluing, cut away the plywood inside the third layer of the wheel using a saber saw. Just cut out the center of the plywood, leaving a ring attached to the rim **(19)**. Do not cut the inside surface of the rim. Now you can wash all the glue off and check to see if the rings line up on the inside.

When the glue is dry, sand the outside of the wheel round on the belt sander, the same way you sanded the hub. Drill the ⅝-in. hole for the oil-treated sleeve. Do this on the drill press and line up the bit using the small hole in the hub as a guide. Then remove the plywood from both sides and sand the wheel. The inside should be done by hand and the whole wheel finish-sanded by hand **(20)**.

20

Hardware The axle hardware I used was custom-made and designed to give a strong, smooth ride to the cart.   ☐

Wheel-Hardware Assembly

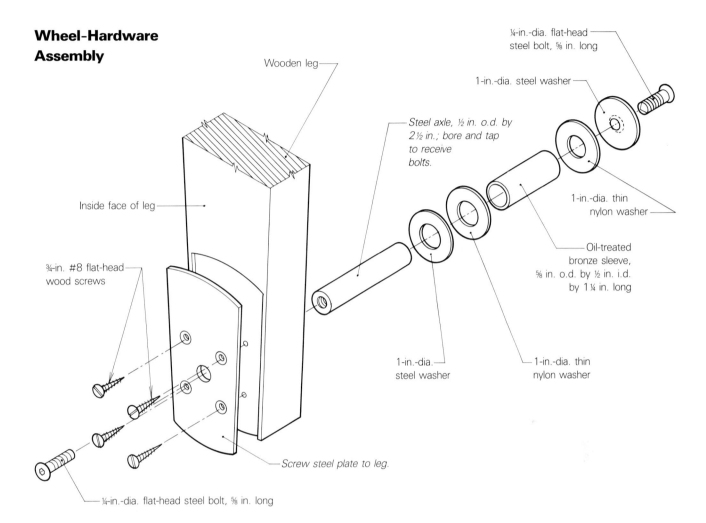

Wooden leg

Inside face of leg

¾-in. #8 flat-head wood screws

¼-in.-dia. flat-head steel bolt, ⅝ in. long

Screw steel plate to leg.

Steel axle, ½ in. o.d. by 2½ in.; bore and tap to receive bolts.

1-in.-dia. steel washer

1-in.-dia. thin nylon washer

¼-in.-dia. flat-head steel bolt, ⅝ in. long

1-in.-dia. steel washer

1-in.-dia. thin nylon washer

Oil-treated bronze sleeve, ⅝ in. o.d. by ½ in. i.d. by 1¼ in. long

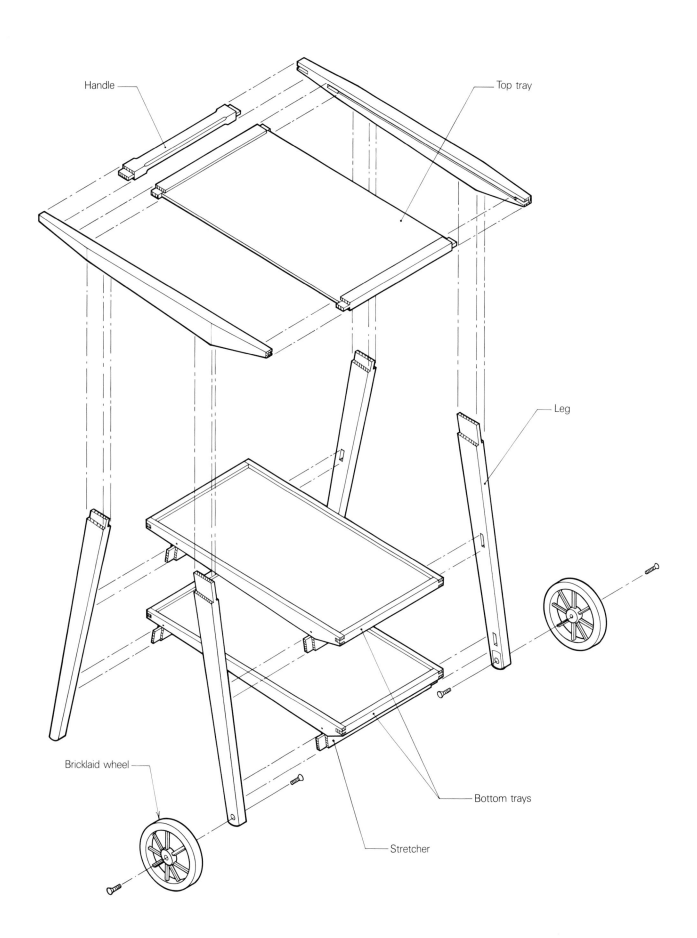

Handle

Top tray

Leg

Bricklaid wheel

Bottom trays

Stretcher

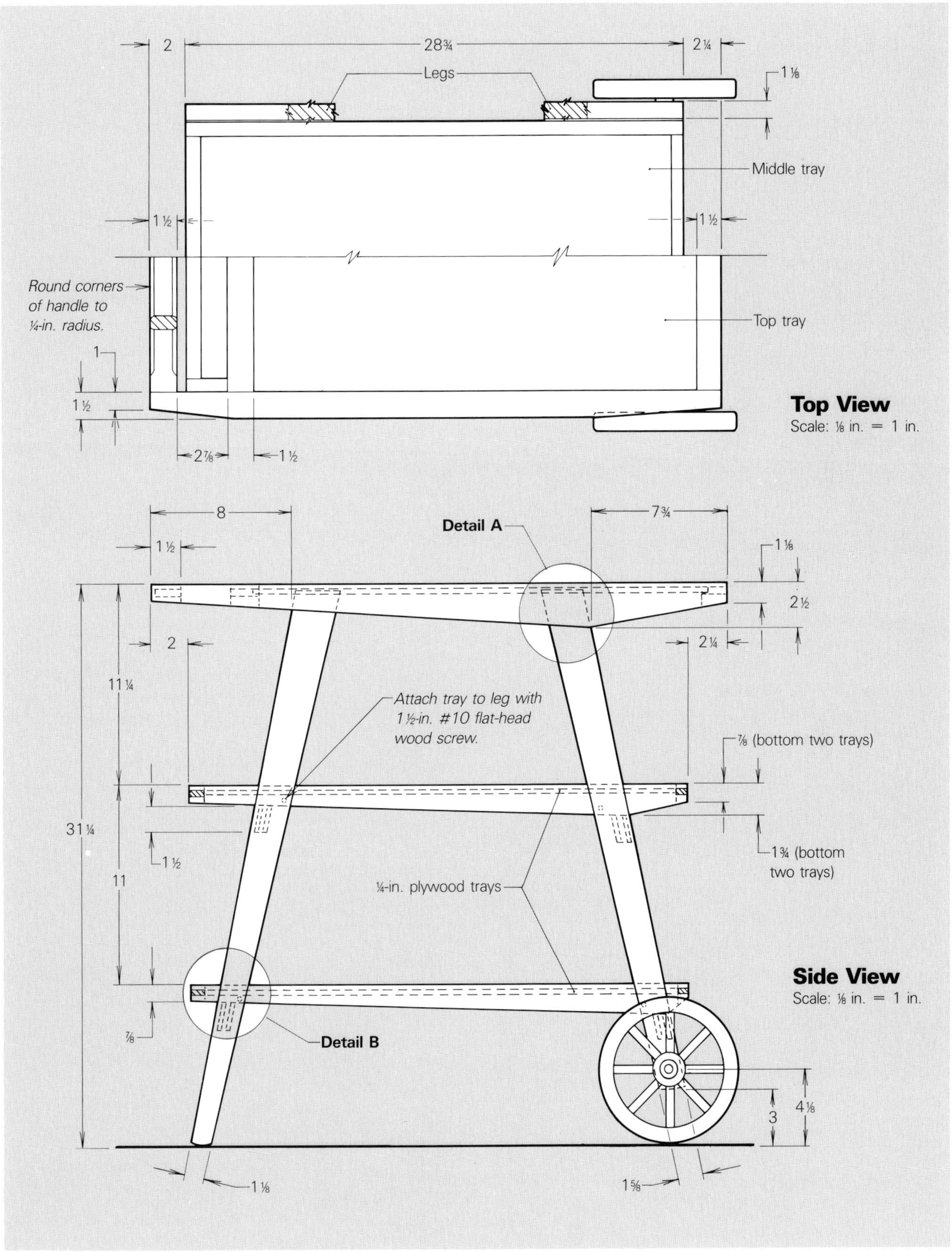

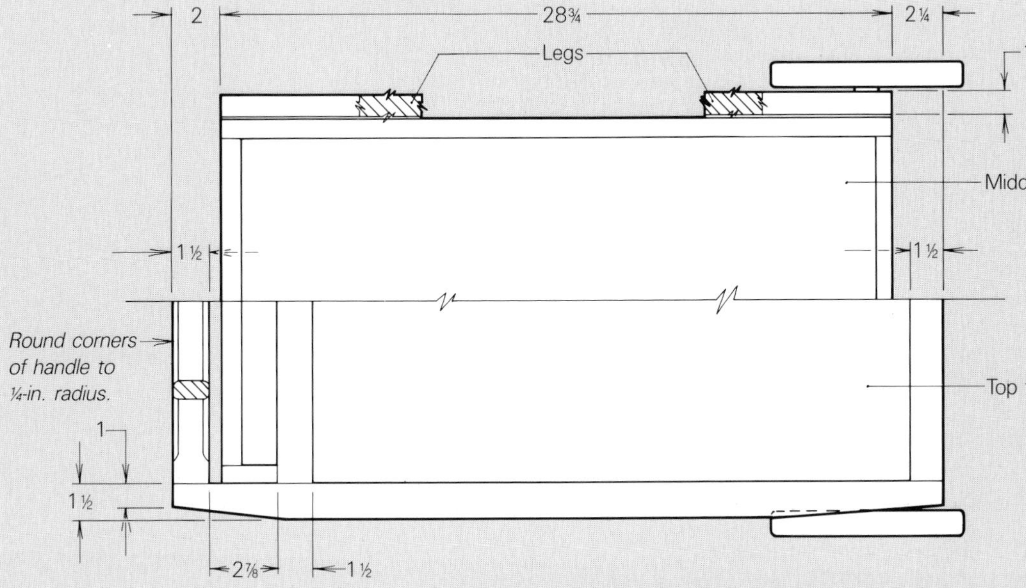
2
28¾
2¼
Legs
1⅛
Middle tray
1½
1½
Round corners of handle to ¼-in. radius.
Top tray
1
1½
2⅞
1½

Top View
Scale: ⅛ in. = 1 in.

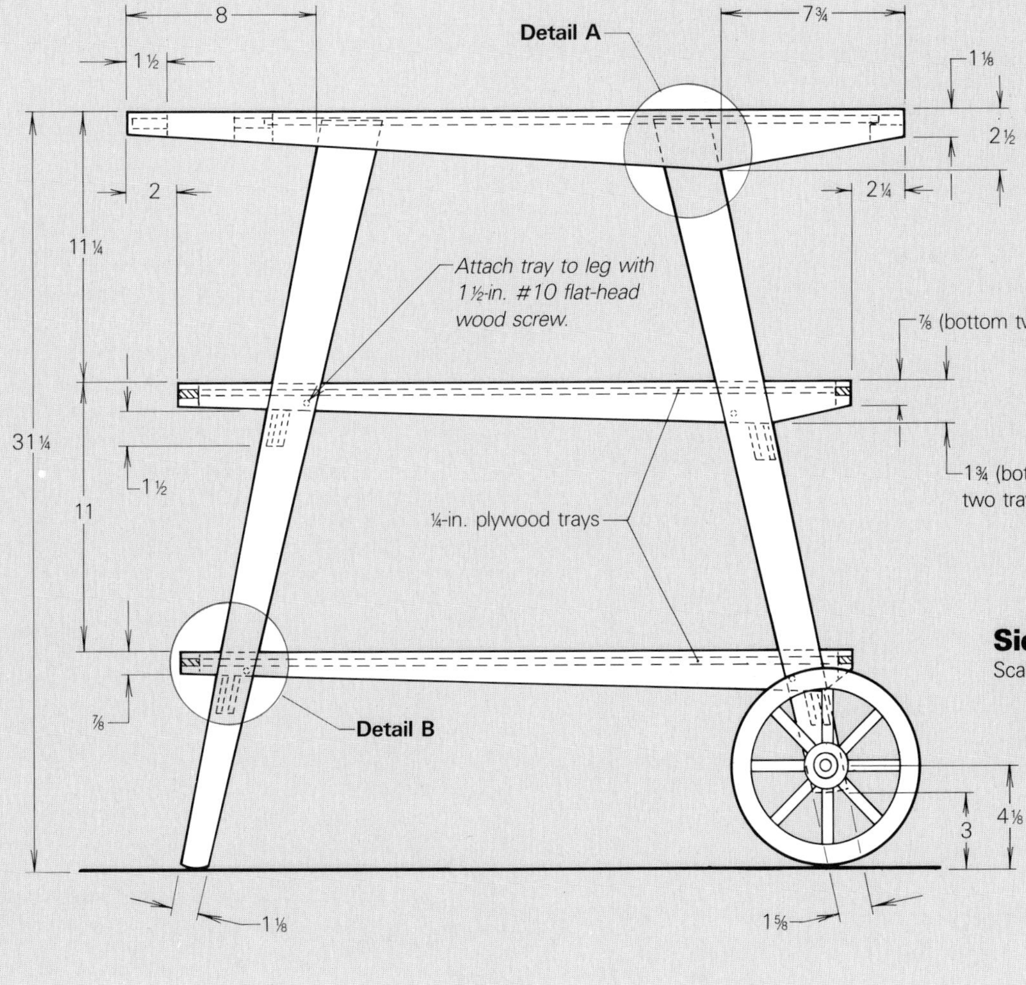
8
7¾
Detail A
1½
1⅛
2½
2
2¼
11¼
Attach tray to leg with 1½-in. #10 flat-head wood screw.
⅞ (bottom two trays)
31¼
1½
1¾ (bottom two trays)
11
¼-in. plywood trays
⅞
Detail B
3
4⅛
1⅛
1⅝

Side View
Scale: ⅛ in. = 1 in.

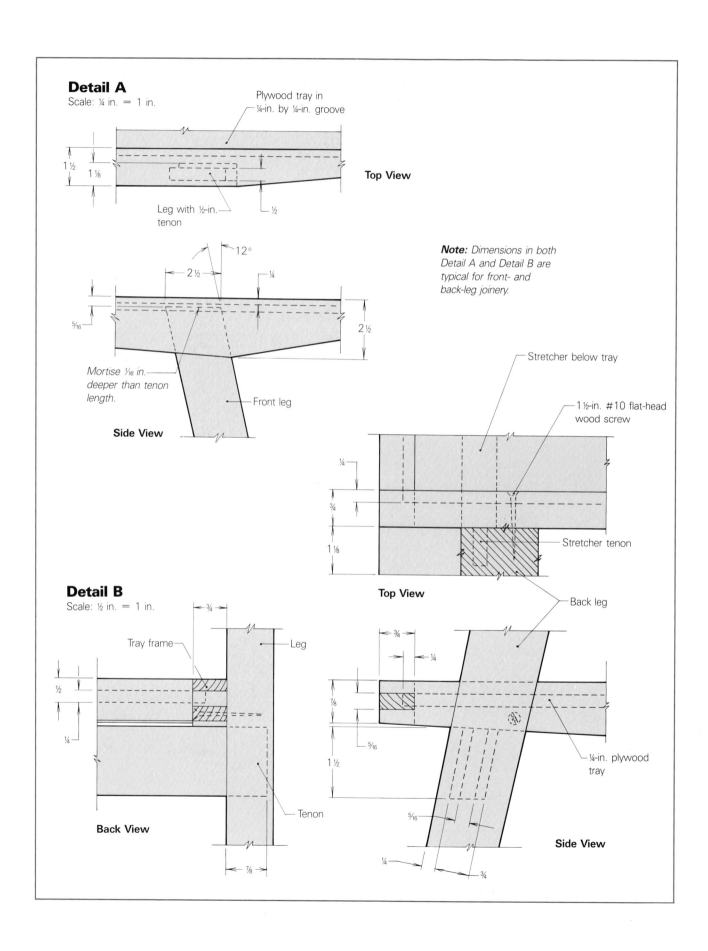

Detail A
Scale: ¼ in. = 1 in.

Plywood tray in ¼-in. by ¼-in. groove

Top View

1 ½

1 ⅛

Leg with ½-in. tenon

½

12°

2 ½

¼

5/16

2 ½

Mortise 1/16 in. deeper than tenon length.

Front leg

Side View

Note: Dimensions in both Detail A and Detail B are typical for front- and back-leg joinery.

Stretcher below tray

1 ½-in. #10 flat-head wood screw

¼

¾

1 ⅛

Stretcher tenon

Top View

Back leg

Detail B
Scale: ½ in. = 1 in.

¾

Tray frame

Leg

½

¼

Tenon

Back View

⅞

¾

¼

⅞

5/16

1 ½

¼-in. plywood tray

5/16

¼

¾

Side View

Chairs
Chapter 5

Design

Designing a chair is a great challenge because of the many requirements the design must satisfy.

A chair presents a person in a setting. It must be comfortable to sit on in a variety of positions, and it should look pleasing from all angles. Dining and occasional chairs are moved around a lot, so they should be made as light as possible yet strong enough to handle the sitter's weight. One of the ways to achieve this is to put the bulk of the wood at the joints and remove some of the wood where it is not needed, such as in the bottoms of the legs and the tops of the back legs. Of course, I don't mind occasionally adding some detail that isn't structurally necessary but that will improve the design.

As I've mentioned before, I always design around the construction instead of constructing around the design. This is especially important with chairs, because they tend to get a lot of use (or abuse) and must be built to withstand it. The part of the chair that takes the most stress is the joint between the side aprons and the back legs—people often throw themselves into a chair and hit the back hard, or they tip the chair back and lean it against the wall so that their whole weight is carried by the joints in the back legs. As for arms, if a chair is going to have them, either they should appear so delicate that no one will dare sit on them, or, if they look inviting to sit on, they should be strong enough to bear the weight.

Contoured chairs that are shaped to fit the body in one position are the most uncomfortable chairs to sit in for a long period of time. When you shift to a different position, the wrong thing gets in the wrong place.

I have been designing and making furniture for more than 55 years, and I've done a lot of experimenting with various techniques and designs. Along the way, I have developed a certain style of my own, but I still enjoy trying new approaches. Some examples of my chairs that illustrate this are shown here.

(1) Here's an armchair that I entered in a competition somewhere around 1952. In the early days, I liked to make chairs by designing the frame first and then placing the seat and back in it. I wish I had photos of my earlier chairs, but this one shows a later development of that idea. The wood is walnut and the seat and back are nylon cord. The chair is mortise-and-tenoned together and the back leg is bolted to the side frame, then plugged.

(2) This is a side chair that I designed for the trustees' meeting room at the old Museum of Contemporary Craft in New York City in 1957. I made 12 of them, also out of walnut, but with upholstered seats. Later I sold 240 of them, some with arms. This method of joining the front legs to the bottom of the side aprons, instead of at the front corners, was designed so that the user could avoid kicking the legs when sitting down. The bottom stretchers were added for extra strength. The design was an experiment that worked well and I have used it again since.

(3) Here's a more recent chair, from 1979. It is one of several I did for the permanent collection of the Museum of Fine Arts in Boston and is on display in their ancient Greek galleries. The construction is similar to the side chair in **(2)**, except that the back legs are laminated curves. The front legs are shaped out of solid wood. The klismos form of ancient classical furniture pictured on Grecian vases was the inspiration for this chair. While the piece is by no means an exact archaeological reproduction, I have tried to reflect the grace of the ancient furniture in my design. I also made a double chair-back settee based on this side chair for the museum.

(4) This chair was made in 1983 to go with the circular pedestal table on p. 96. You can see that a lot has changed over the years, but I've tried to hang on to the best aspects of the earlier chairs. This one is much more delicate than the earlier version, made in 1957. I removed the bottom stretchers because they would have looked too busy alongside the pedestal of the table. Instead, a stretcher is mortise-and-tenoned between the two front legs under the seat. □

1

2

3

4

Top View

15¾

18⅝

Seat Detail

17½

19¼

Front View

17¼

17¼

17¼

Side View

19

17¼

17

31¾

Back View

Upholstered seat

Dining Chair
Scale: ¹⁄₁₆ in. = 1 in.

Dining Chair

Dining chairs are usually made in groups of four or six, which amounts to a small production run. So it is helpful to consider your machinery before arriving at the final design. That doesn't mean that every part of every chair has to be machine-made, but as many parts and joints as possible should be machine-made for speed and consistency and then finished with handwork.

Drawing the chair Whatever the design, a chair is a complicated thing to make. This is one case where a full-scale drawing of the side, front and top views, and sometimes the back view, has to be made first. To get all the angles for the joints, it makes sense to figure them out on paper first. Each view can be drawn on a separate sheet of paper, but because measurements and angles have to be transferred from one sheet to another, it is easy to make mistakes.

A better way to draw a chair is to superimpose the three or four views on the same piece of paper. It is much harder to make mistakes because they become obvious right away when one view is drawn on top of the others. Even if you do make a mistake, the chair will still go together because the error will be transmitted to the other views.

First draw the side view. Then draw the front view, and place it far enough to the left so that the lines don't interfere with the side view. All the measurements from the front view are transferred to the top view, which is drawn near the middle of the side view. Usually I work on the front and top views at the same time.

This might seem a little confusing at first, but it is worth the effort once you get used to it. To help read the drawing, try using different colors for each view. By the way, in this type of drawing I don't always put in all the joints because too many lines would get confusing. If someone other than myself were going to make the chair, I would draw separate joint details. For most chairs I would make a mock-up (see p. 135), but because this one was similar to the earlier designs, that was not necessary.

With the drawing complete, make a cutting list and lay out the parts on the lumber. Then rough-cut all the parts, and joint and thickness-plane them. Rough-cut them 1 in. longer than their finished dimension to allow for the angles to be put on the ends later. All the simple tapers are cut on the tablesaw with a tapering jig (see p. 60) and left a little wide so they can be cleaned up on the jointer.

Superimposed Views

1

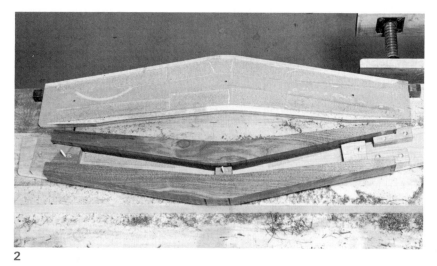

2

The legs   The back legs have compound angles and can't be cut on a tablesaw, so a jig has to be made to shape them. A shaper is most efficient for this, but not everyone has a shaper, so here's how to do it with a router; the principle is the same.

The jig is like a sandwich, with the legs in the middle **(1)**. The router has a template guide that runs along the top part of the jig and the wood is removed in several cuts. If you were using a shaper or a router table instead, the jig would be used upside down.

The template guide necessitates making the jig smaller than the actual finished dimension of the leg by half the difference between the diameter of the bit and the diameter of the template guide. Hold the jig together with three ¼-in. flat-head bolts with T-nuts in the bottom—one in the center and one at each end. Bolt stop blocks inside the jig for accurate positioning of the legs and countersink all bolt heads below the surface of the jig so they will not interfere with the router. Use a ½-in. router bit with a ½-in. shank—a smaller bit would produce vibration.

Bandsaw out the legs so that there is about ¹⁄₁₆ in. for the router to remove from each side. Place two legs in the jig and bolt it together. I glued sandpaper onto the jig **(2)** to prevent the legs from slipping.

The jig is made so that the front of each leg has to be shaped first. After the front has been cut, it is put into the back of the jig, which has been set up to fit it, and then the back edge can be cut. To begin, put the legs in the jig, but cut only the front of the first one **(3)**, then open the jig and reverse the legs. Now the back of the first leg and the front of the second one can be cut. Open the jig and reverse the legs again (or put a new leg in the front if more than one chair is to be made) to cut the back of the second one.

Remove the wood in two or three passes so there will not be too much pressure on the bit.

When the back legs have been routed in the jig, the inside faces get tapered top and bottom. It is easiest to saw out these tapers and then clean them up on the jointer.

It is okay to cut leg joints either before or after shaping, and the sequence is usually determined by the design. On this chair, I made most of the joints after I had shaped the legs and aprons. The construction is mortise-and-tenon, except for the joint between the backrest and the back legs, which is splined. It was easier to make the spline joint than to cut a compound tenon, and it is just as strong. After the joints were made, I cut a rabbet on the inside top edge of the aprons for the plywood seat bottom.

3

Back-Leg Pattern

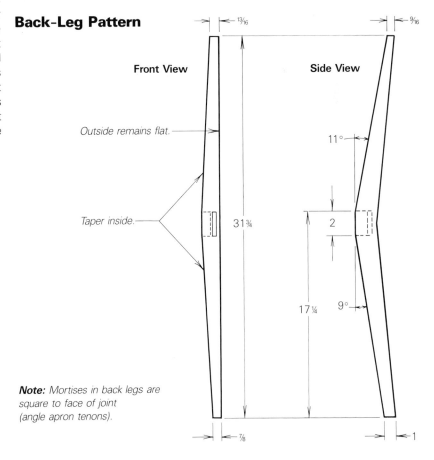

Front View

Side View

Outside remains flat.

Taper inside.

$13/16$

$9/16$

$11°$

2

$31¾$

$17¼$ $9°$

Note: Mortises in back legs are square to face of joint (angle apron tenons).

$7/8$ 1

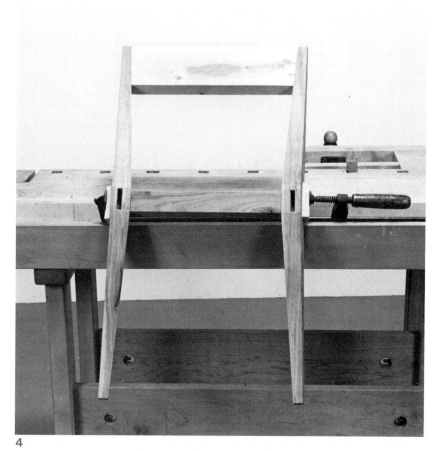

4

The backrest To fit the piece for the backrest, dry-clamp the two back legs and the back apron together. Check to be sure that the angle is the same on both back legs and that they correspond to the angle in the drawing. Take both angles for the backrest from the drawing and then set the miter gauge and tilt the tablesaw blade to match. Cut a piece of scrapwood the same dimension as the real backrest to test the setup **(4)**. With the miter gauge on the left side of the blade, make the first cut, then flip the piece upside down and end-for-end and make the second cut on the other end. Cut the backrest a little longer than what is shown on the drawing and check the angle. If the piece is a little off, reset the miter gauge or the blade, or both, until the fit is perfect. When you are sure of the angle, cut the real backrest for each chair.

To cut the grooves for the ¼-in. by 1-in. splines, use the plunge router with a long wooden fence attached for stability because of the narrow leg **(5)**. Mark the length of the groove on each leg. Running the fence along the front edge of the leg, cut the groove about ½ in. deep and chisel the corners square **(6)**.

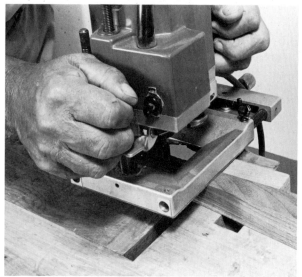

5

6

To rout the matching groove in the backrest, clamp the piece in the vise and mark the length of the groove **(7)**.

Without resetting the router fence, run it against the front face of the backrest **(8)**. Cut the grooves and chisel the corners square. Because the ends are cut at an angle to the face, be sure the base of the router rides flat on the ends so the splines will be square to them.

Fit the splines in the grooves so the grain runs in the same direction as that of the backrest and then dry-clamp the back together. Mark the front curve of the backrest **(9)** and then take the assembly apart and bandsaw out the backrest. Next mark the thickness from the front of the backrest and cut out the back curve. Now finish-shape and sand the back of the backrest, but don't do the front until after the chair back has been glued together. I cut the curves on the bandsaw and finished them off using a belt sander and a scraper.

7

8

9

10

11

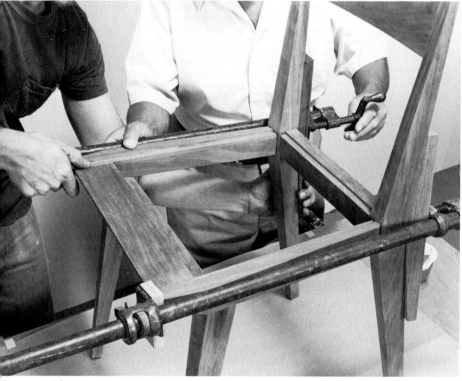

12

13

Assembling the chair Gluing chairs together can be complicated and it usually takes two people. Good planning helps, too.

It is a good idea to glue the back-leg assembly together first **(10)**. Check all the angles to make sure they agree with the drawing and with the other parts. When the glue is dry, plane and sand the front of the backrest flush with the upper legs.

Next glue the front legs to the side aprons. When the glue is dry, sand the joints flush. Always be sure to remove the excess glue with hot water right after gluing up. Wipe the joints dry with a rag.

Now the front stretcher and front apron are glued in. To make it easier to line up the parts, place the back tenons of the side aprons (without glue) partway into their mortises in the back legs **(11)**.

Set the sliding bevel to each angle in the drawing and check that all the chair's angles are correct. When this section is dry, plane the bottom of the front apron and sand it flush with the side aprons.

Finally, glue the front and back sections together **(12)**. This step has to be well thought out in advance and great care has to be taken. Don't forget to wash off the excess glue.

Check for squareness by measuring from corner to corner with a ruler. Also check the angles of the back legs.

(13) Here's Jamey Hutchinson washing the last two joints and smiling because everything went smoothly.

When the glue was dry, I applied my 4-F finish (Frid's Fast Fine Finish) [*Book 2*, pp. 188-89]. This oil and shellac combination dries quickly and looks nice. Then I installed the upholstered seat.   ☐

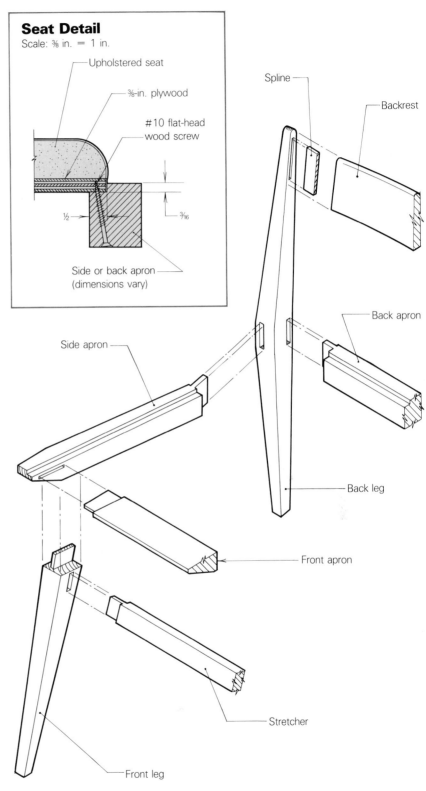

Seat Detail
Scale: ⅜ in. = 1 in.

Upholstered seat

⅜-in. plywood

#10 flat-head wood screw

½

³⁄₁₆

Side or back apron (dimensions vary)

Spline

Backrest

Back apron

Side apron

Back leg

Front apron

Stretcher

Front leg

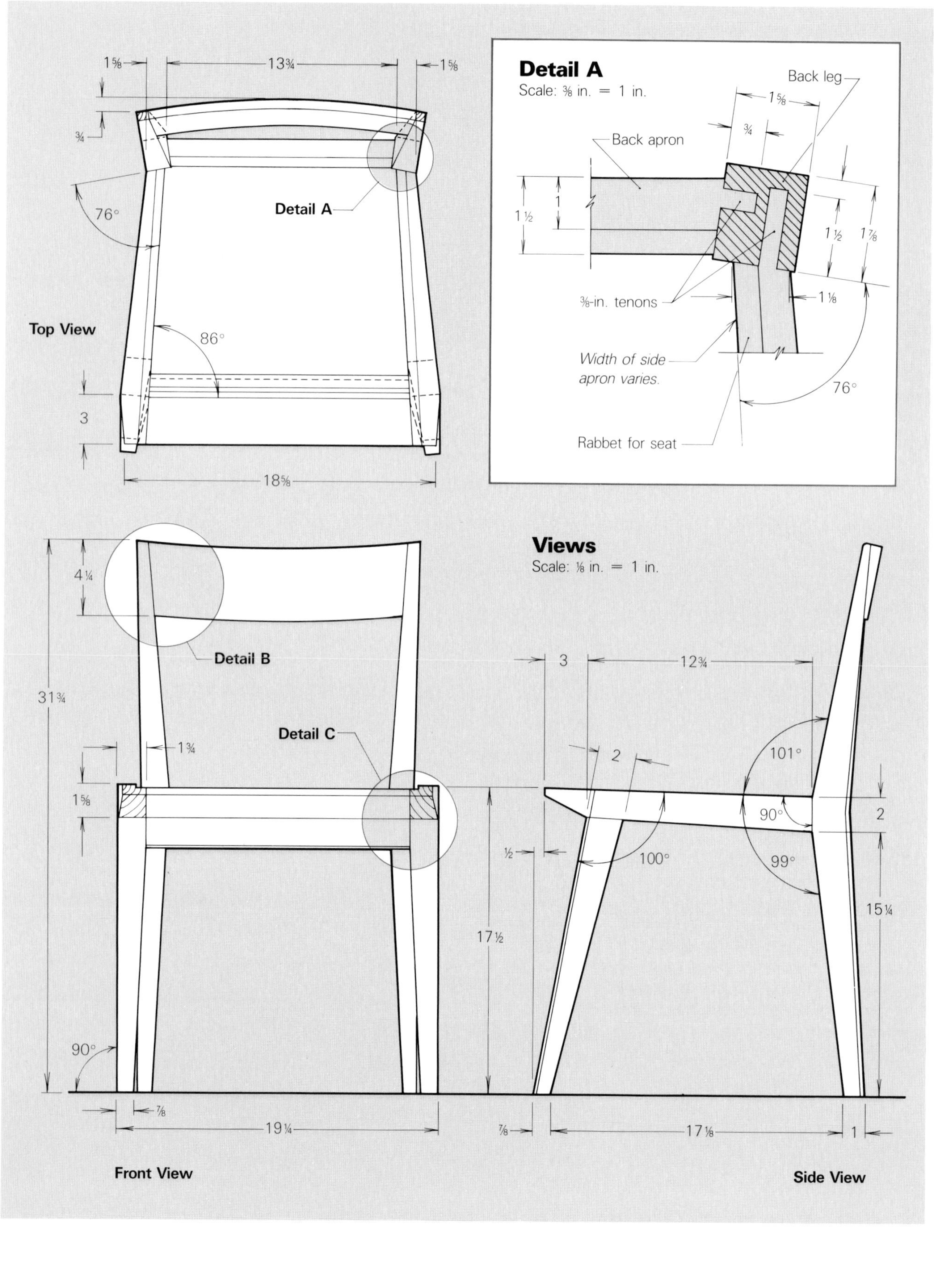
Top View
1⅝
13¾
1⅝
¾
76°
Detail A
86°
3
18⅝
Detail A
Scale: ⅜ in. = 1 in.
Back leg
1⅝
¾
Back apron
1½
1
1½
1⅞
⅜-in. tenons
1⅛
Width of side apron varies.
76°
Rabbet for seat
Views
Scale: ⅛ in. = 1 in.
4¼
Detail B
31¾
1¾
Detail C
1⅝
90°
⅞
19¼
Front View
3
12¾
2
101°
90°
2
100°
99°
½
17½
15¼
⅞
17⅛
1
Side View

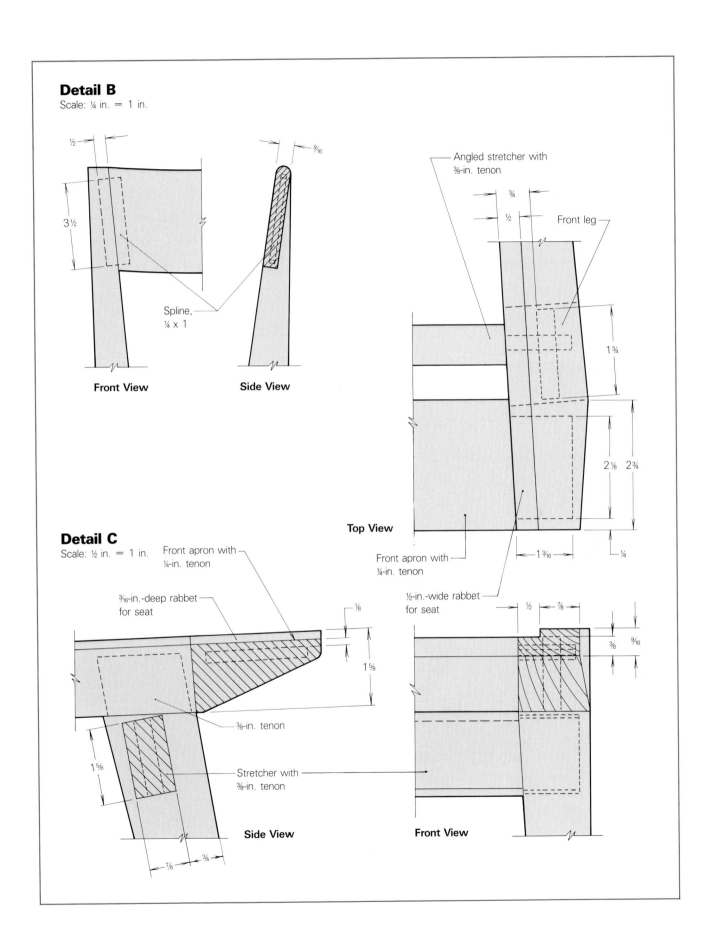

Detail B
Scale: ¼ in. = 1 in.

½   9/16

3½

Spline,
¼ × 1

Front View   **Side View**

Angled stretcher with
⅜-in. tenon

¾
½   Front leg

1¾

2⅛ 2¾

Top View

Front apron with
¼-in. tenon

½-in.-wide rabbet
for seat

1 3/16   ¼

Detail C
Scale: ½ in. = 1 in.   Front apron with
¼-in. tenon

3/16-in.-deep rabbet
for seat

⅛

1⅝

⅜-in. tenon

½   ⅞

⅜   9/16

1⅝

Stretcher with
⅜-in. tenon

⅞   ¾

Side View   **Front View**

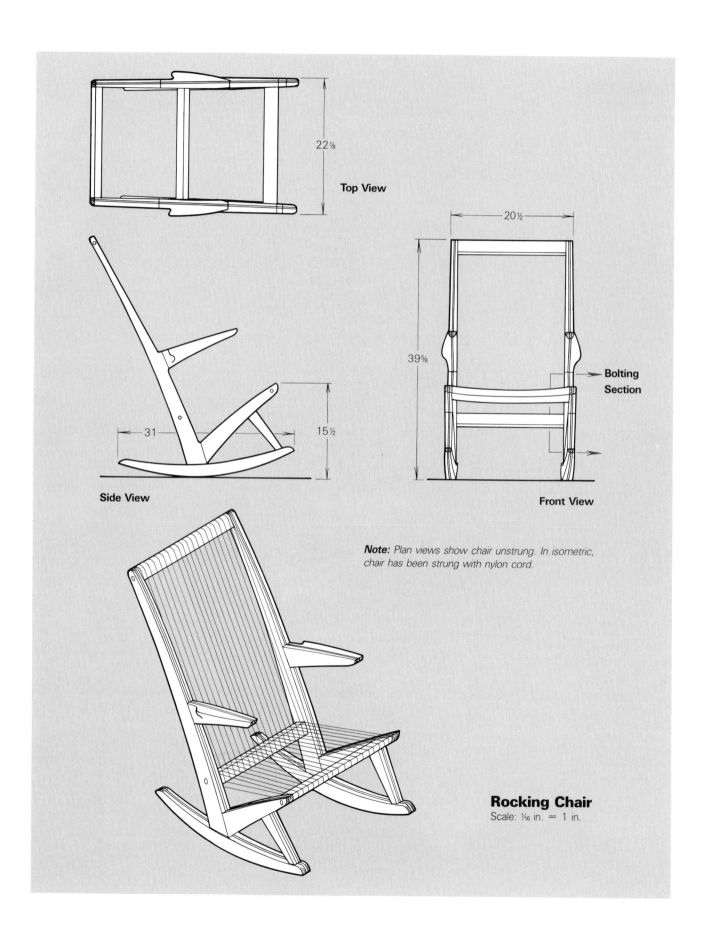

Top View

22⅛

20½

39⅝

Bolting
Section

Side View

31

15½

Front View

Note: *Plan views show chair unstrung. In isometric, chair has been strung with nylon cord.*

Rocking Chair
Scale: ¹⁄₁₆ in. = 1 in.

Rocking Chair

Recently I wanted to make a rocking chair that would be comfortable and well balanced and would rock easily. I wanted the seat to be low enough so that the user's feet would always touch the floor, even with the chair in motion. I didn't want a solid-wood or an upholstered seat and back, so I decided to use $\frac{3}{16}$-in. nylon cord instead, which I used a lot about 20 years ago. It's comfortable and it stands up well.

I don't know of any good formula for designing and making a rocking chair. I have an old Boston rocker (**1**), which is one of the best I've ever seen, and it met most of the requirements for the chair I was planning, so I studied it. The armrests on this rocker are high enough so your arms are spread slightly when you're sitting, letting your body breathe. Plus, your arms are well supported for reading. The angle and height of the seat are good, and the chair rocks well, too.

To find the point where the sitter's cheek bones would rest and to determine the correct height and curve of the back and armrests, I traced the profile of the Boston rocker on a piece of paper. (The rockers have a 37-in. radius.) Then, using this sketch as a rough guide, I designed my own rocking chair and made a mock-up out of scrapwood, screwing everything together so I could change the angles. I had several people try it out (**2**) before I made the final design.

1

2

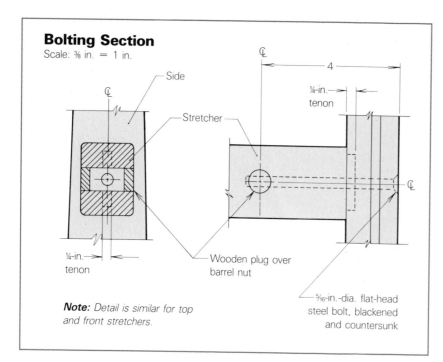

Bolting Section
Scale: ⅜ in. = 1 in.

Side

Stretcher

¼-in.
tenon

4

¼-in.
tenon

Wooden plug over
barrel nut

⁵⁄₁₆-in.-dia. flat-head
steel bolt, blackened
and countersunk

*Note: Detail is similar for top
and front stretchers.*

I wanted to make the sides out of ¼-in.-thick aluminum sandwiched between two pieces of wood. I had used that technique years before, too, and liked the way it looked. This method requires no wooden joints on the side pieces and yet it produces a strong construction.

I used contact cement (not the water-soluble kind) to glue the wood to the aluminum. I felt this would be safe because the glue is well sealed from the air due to the thickness of the pieces. I have contact-cemented aluminum and wood together for years and have a few 17-year-old scraps that are still hard to separate. I once tried epoxy glue, but it is not flexible like contact cement, so the pieces separated after about a year—the wood moved, but the aluminum and epoxy did not.

Because of the aluminum, I did not use regular mortise-and-tenon joints; instead, bolts and barrel nuts connect the side pieces and stretchers. I didn't want the barrel nuts exposed, so I drilled holes through the stretchers and plugged them.

To prevent the stretchers from swiveling on the bolts, I put small tenons on the ends. The drawing at left shows the tenon on the rear seat stretcher, but the idea is the same for all three stretchers.

Making templates With the construction planned and the mock-up done to satisfaction, I next made a full-scale working drawing of the side view. A pattern has to be made for each chair part and this should be taken directly off the drawing.

To transfer the lines from the full-scale side view to a piece of ¼-in. plywood, you can use the old shipbuilders' method of lofting. With an awl, prick little holes through the lines on the drawing into the plywood underneath **(3)**. Most lines need only three or four holes along their length, but the round ends and sharp curves need to be marked about every ⅛ in.

Remove the plywood from underneath the drawing and hammer small brads in the holes. Push a thin stick against the brads and draw the line. This operation usually takes two people **(4)**. Now band-saw out the pieces and carefully shape and sand their edges to the lines.

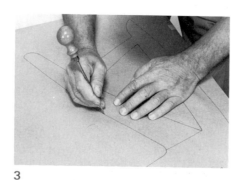

3

4

Cutting the aluminum   Using the plywood templates, scribe the shapes of the parts onto a ¼-in.-thick sheet of aluminum and then rough-cut the aluminum on the bandsaw. (I used a regular wood-cutting blade.) Glue the matching pieces together temporarily with rubber cement and make the final bandsaw cut with the pieces from opposite sides of the chair held together in pairs. Using the bandsaw saves a lot of time and makes for a more accurate job. I cleaned up the edges by filing them to the scribed lines.

When all the pieces have been shaped, it is time to put them together. Lay the ¼-in. plywood template pieces back on the drawing of the side view and glue and nail them together **(5)**. Fit all the aluminum pieces, which are still glued together, to this plywood template and then separate them. I sent the aluminum pieces and the plywood template off together to the welder. The welder used the plywood to position the aluminum.

I wanted to have the aluminum welded from small pieces, rather than cut out of a single piece. I figured this would give me greater flexibility—especially with some future designs I had in mind. But I hadn't considered the fact that metal warps when it is welded, as one side expands more than the other from the heat. I wasn't worried about the warping, because the stock is flattened later when it is glued between the wood pieces. The welder leveled off the joints and I used a belt sander **(6)** to clean off the grease and dirt before the sides could be glued up. I began with 80-grit sandpaper and then followed with a sanding block. As it turned out, it would have been cheaper and less time-consuming to cut the two complete sides out of a large sheet, and either sell or keep the scrap.

5

6

7

8

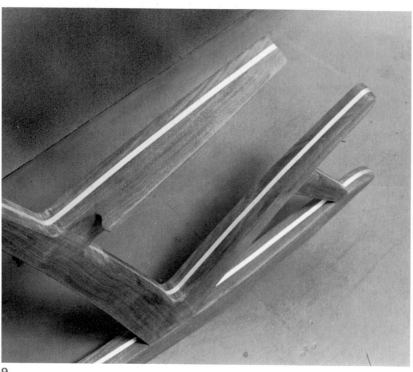

9

Attaching the wood   I used walnut for all the wood parts of this chair. I milled all the pieces that would be glued to the aluminum 1/16 in. oversize in width and length so they could be trimmed easily to the correct dimensions. It's a good idea to make the pieces out of thick stock so that you can get two sides out of each one. Fit the wood to the pattern and then resaw the pieces in half, thickness-plane them and they are ready to be glued to the aluminum. I allowed about 1/4 in. for waste in the cutting and planing. Because the arms are wider, they are made out of heavier stock and have to be fitted individually. Remember, if the pieces have to be tapered in thickness, do that before gluing them on.

Before actually gluing the wood pieces, clamp them in place on one side of the aluminum, on top of a piece of 3/4-in. plywood. (The plywood helps keep everything flat.)

First, remove the front leg and the back piece and put the contact cement on both surfaces **(7)**. Leave the rest of the pieces clamped in place to help in positioning the glue-covered pieces.

You have to wait about 30 minutes from the time you spread the contact cement until you can assemble the work. After that, you can clamp the pieces in place. The more pressure, the better the glue joint, but the clamps can be taken off right away. For convenience, I left the clamps on until the next piece was ready. This process continues until all the pieces have been glued to one side of the aluminum **(8)**. Then the whole thing is flipped over and the wood is glued to the other side.

Once all the wood has been glued to both sides, trim the edges so they are flush with the aluminum. I used a spokeshave, a wood file and a scraper blade for this, and then I finished up the job with sandpaper.

I didn't want sharp edges on the armrests and I didn't want them to look like they had been shaped with a router, so I did them by hand, using a spokeshave and a rasp. This gave me a chance to experiment and get the look I liked **(9)**.

When the sides are done, make the solid-wood stretchers and assemble the chair. Plug the holes for the barrel nuts and sand the whole assembly.

In the top and front stretchers, file shallow notches to keep the nylon cord spaced uniformly.

Finishing   I used a Watco oil finish on this chair, but in a slightly different way than usual. I applied the first coat but did not wipe it off. When it got tacky, I vigorously rubbed it with fine steel wool and then left it to dry. The next day I waxed the whole thing with bowling alley wax to keep the aluminum from oxidizing.

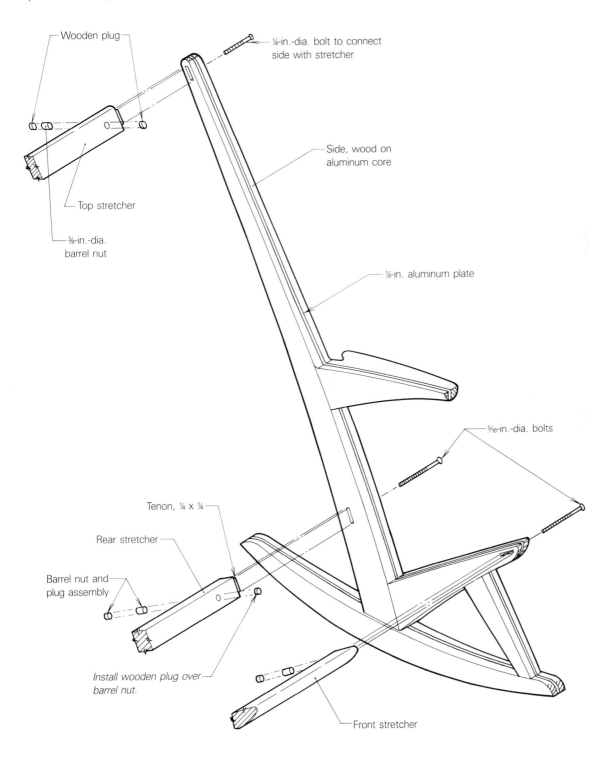

Wooden plug

¼-in.-dia. bolt to connect side with stretcher

Top stretcher

⅜-in.-dia. barrel nut

Side, wood on aluminum core

¼-in. aluminum plate

Tenon, ¼ x ¼

Rear stretcher

Barrel nut and plug assembly

⁵⁄₁₆-in.-dia. bolts

Install wooden plug over barrel nut.

Front stretcher

10

Stringing   The chair is now ready for the nylon cord. To fasten the string at the beginning and at the end, drill a $^{17}/_{64}$-in. hole in each corner of the underside of the rear seat stretcher. Sand one side of a ¼-in. dowel flat, put glue in the starting hole, insert the string and hammer the dowel in.

Stringing the chair takes two people, and it is hard on the fingers because you have to keep tension on the strings at all times.

Wrap the cord around until you come to the last five strings. Put two blocks on the top stretcher **(10)** and clamp them to keep the strings in place. Let your fingers rest a moment.

Wrap the last five strings around without tension **(11)**. Then pull these five strings tight at the same time and retighten the clamp. The strings are all in place and taut, except for the last little dangling end.

To finish, cut the last string to exact length. Put glue in the pre-drilled hole, use an awl to push the end of the string into the hole, and hammer the dowel in **(12)**.

Now trim off the dowel, being careful not to cut the string. Cut the dowel partway through with a saw and then break off the remaining piece with a hammer. Clean up the end of the dowel with sandpaper and the chair is finished.

I was happy that my rocking chair turned out the way it was supposed to. Emma was happy, too—now she can rest her sore hands **(13)**.   □

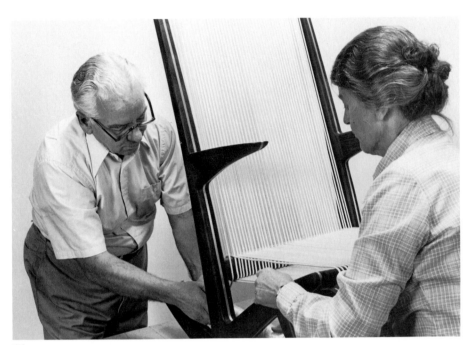

11

12

13

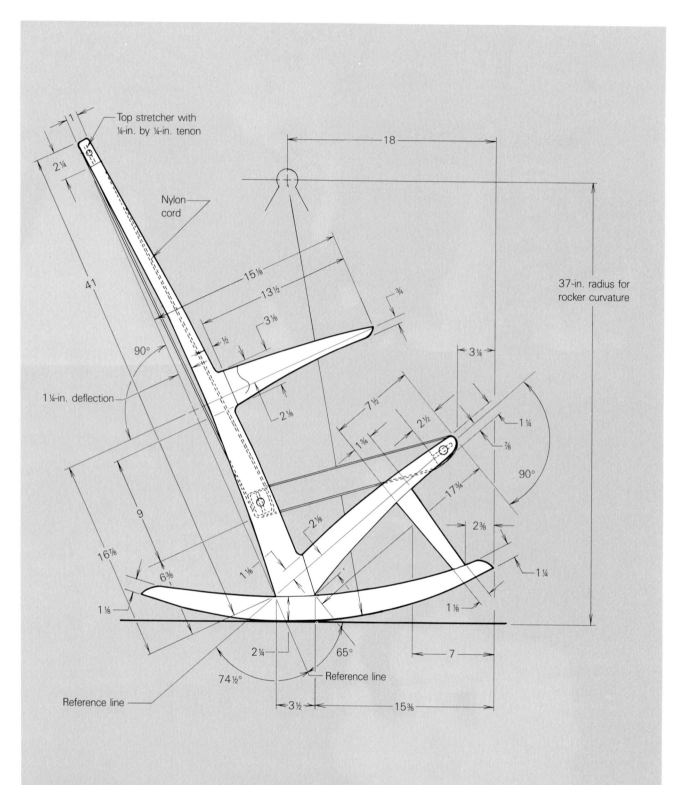

Top stretcher with ¼-in. by ¼-in. tenon

Nylon cord

37-in. radius for rocker curvature

Reference line

Reference line

Reference line

Side View
Scale: ⅛ in. = 1 in.

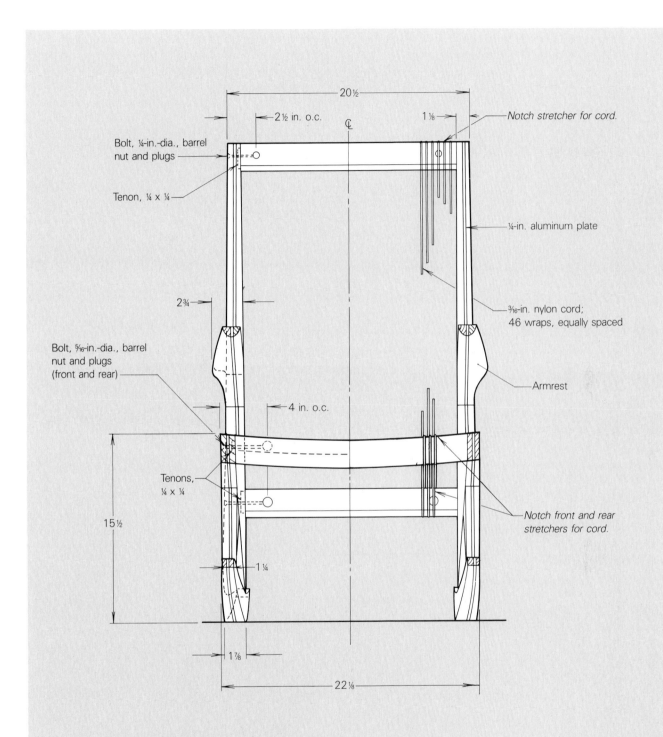

20½

2½ in. o.c.

1⅛

Notch stretcher for cord.

Bolt, ¼-in.-dia., barrel
nut and plugs

Tenon, ¼ x ¼

¼-in. aluminum plate

2¾

Bolt, ⁵⁄₁₆-in.-dia., barrel
nut and plugs
(front and rear)

³⁄₁₆-in. nylon cord;
46 wraps, equally spaced

Armrest

4 in. o.c.

Tenons,
¼ x ¼

*Notch front and rear
stretchers for cord.*

15½

1¼

1⅞

22⅛

Front View
Scale: ⅛ in. = 1 in.

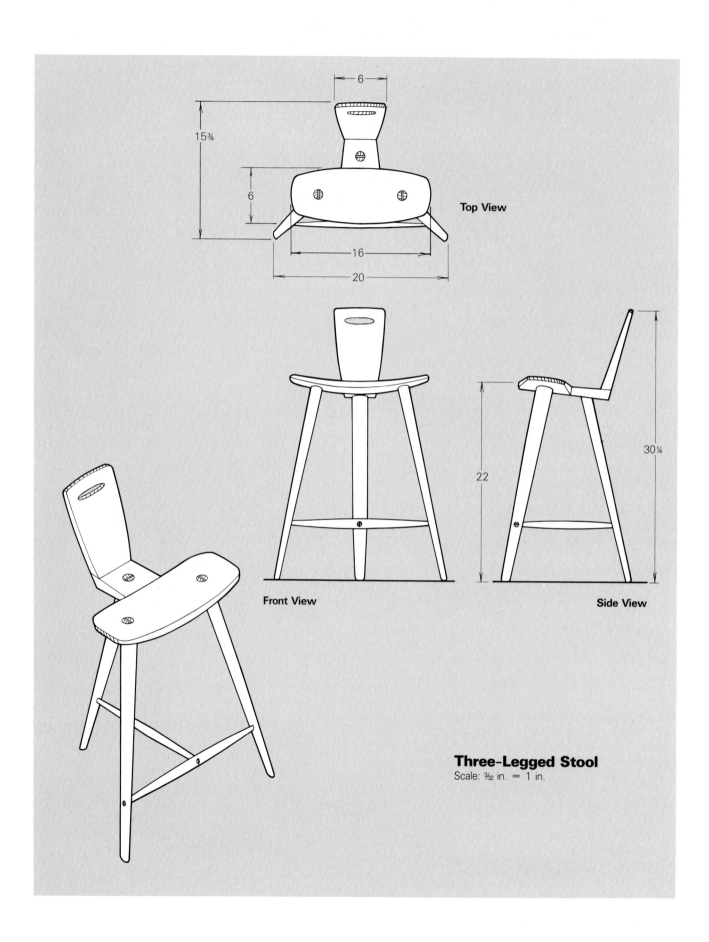

Top View

Front View

Side View

Three-Legged Stool
Scale: ³⁄₃₂ in. = 1 in.

Three-Legged Stool

I hate three-legged chairs, especially those with a full seat and back. They always look ridiculous from behind and are dangerous contraptions to sit in. If a person seated in such a chair leans slightly sideways against the back, the chair will tip over. The person might get hurt, and you might get sued if you are the designer or maker of the chair.

Many people decide to make a three-legged chair just to be different; they wind up constructing around the design. This usually results in some kind of hodge-podge. I have also seen three-legged chairs, usually sculptural, that are so heavy that it is impossible to tip them over. Of course, this doesn't mean they are well designed.

There are, however, some three-legged chairs that are well designed in that the number of legs is a result of the chair's allowed space or function. For example, on some valet chairs the back leg and back are designed primarily to support clothes hanging on top. Comfort for long-term sitting or reclining is not a requirement of such a chair, as it would be for a rocker or even a dining chair.

Three-legged chairs might also be made for a round dining table where it is important to fit as many seats as possible. The natural solution is to shape the chair like a slice of pie and place the single leg in front. This is fine, because the person's two legs will help stabilize the front.

The designer of any seating unit should first decide precisely what its function will be. Then he or she should choose a construction technique and design around that. If the designer has a feeling for form and dimension, the result is usually a good-looking and functional seating unit. The forms must be consistent so that the piece works together and doesn't look like one base with a different top placed on it, or a mixed bag of unrelated parts. I have found proportion—the right relationship between dimensions—the most difficult thing to learn. Many of my students have the same problem. Poor proportions can spoil an otherwise excellent design.

Designing the stool When I started designing this seating unit, I had no intention of making a three-legged stool, but as the design progressed it became the logical choice. I wanted a small seat with a back, and a system where I could use the same seat at three different heights, simply by changing the lengths of the legs. The unit had to be comfortable but of minimum size, and light but as strong as possible.

The whole thing started when my wife and I went to a horse show. We were sitting on a 6-in.-wide rail for several hours, yet we felt quite comfortable. Of course, I am well upholstered; Emma is just right, but she didn't complain either. Suddenly I realized that when you sit on a wooden seat, you sit only on your two cheek bones. The rest of the seat is unnecessary. Obviously, a full seat allows freedom for moving around, unless it is carved to hold you in place, but mainly a small area of seat supports you.

I began experimenting to find the smallest comfortable seat I could get away with. I came up with a piece 6 in. wide and 16 in. long with a gentle curve that deflected ⅝ in. along its length. This piece was very pleasant to sit on and I could bandsaw or rout it out of an ¾ plank. The rough proportions looked good, too.

I wanted to attach a backrest, but without adding much wood to the seat, so I mortise-and-tenoned a small addition to the back of the seat. Now, because this piece behind the seat was small, there was room for only one leg in back. This meant that the backrest had to be narrow and low, which was fine as I only wanted to support the lower part of the spine.

The *T*-shaped seat counteracts the stool's tendency to tip over, because there is no seat area in the back to push against. The weight of the sitter's body is located over the two front legs. The result is a stable, three-legged stool.

I decided to join the backrest to the seat extension with a through dovetail. I needed width at the top of the backrest for support, but not at the bottom. So I removed the excess near the joint and curved the two outside lines, which resulted in a pleasant, oval shape. At the same time, I needed the full wood thickness at the bottom of the backrest for a strong joint, but not at the top. I removed the excess there, but in a straight line because the inside of the back is straight. Trimming the square corners of the seat plank to a rounded line gave me more of an oval. I needed the thickness of the seat at the center for the mortise-and-tenon, but not at the ends, so I removed the excess from the bottom of both ends, which added yet another curved line to the form. Now from the front and top views, everything looked slightly oval. I used this shape in the finger slot at the top of the backrest. I curved the ends of the seat and backrest, and eased the corners so that all the lines would flow together more smoothly. I chamfered the

front edge of the seat for comfort, but gradually brought the line crisply around the top of the back. This detail helps give the piece a handmade feeling. If I had used a router to remove a uniform radius all around, the piece would have had more of a machine-made look.

I turned the legs on the lathe and angled them out to give the stool more stability. After turning the ends of the legs down to a ¾-in. diameter, I through-tenoned and wedged them in the seat. (Whenever you wedge tenons through a solid piece of wood, always position the wedge across the grain of the solid piece to prevent it from splitting.) The stretchers were a simple *T*, also turned and joined to the legs with wedged through tenons.

I made a prototype after making some simple preliminary drawings. I always make a mock-up when I make a new chair, or any other seating unit, to test the comfort and to see how the shapes on the drawings will relate in three dimensions.

In this case, I made my mock-up stool exactly like my preliminary drawings, and found it very comfortable, but it looked awful. I could not put my finger on what was wrong, so I set the stool aside in my shop in a place where I couldn't miss it each time I came in. During the next few weeks, several people came in and sat on it. They found it surprisingly comfortable for its size, but no one was crazy about its looks. One day I was sitting and staring at it and I suddenly realized what was wrong: everything was oval except for the legs and stretchers, which were turned round. It looked like it had a base that had been borrowed from one stool, matched with a top from another. I removed the legs and remade them oval, and then the stool looked like one unit. Testing the prototype a little further, I discovered that if I moved the backrest 1 in. back, there was enough room to comfortably sit backwards on the stool. Now I had the shapes and dimensions more or less finalized and I knew what I was going to make. Although I hadn't started designing with the notion of making a three-legged stool that looked like this **(1)**, the shape resulted naturally from the construction and from the requirements I had originally assigned to the design.

1

I was ready to make final working draw-ings. As I have said before, it is impossi-ble to make a chair or a stool without a full-scale working drawing from which to take all angles and measurements. The drawing must have side, top and front views. (A back view would be useful, too, if there were a lot of carved details or shapes on the back, but I've never used one.) I superimposed the three views, us-ing a different color for each, as de-scribed for the dining chair on p. 125.

After the preliminary drawings, mock-ups and working drawings were done, I made a cutting list. I carefully selected the wood and then milled all parts. When you do this, allow a little extra in the length and width, especially of the legs and stretchers because their ends will be trimmed later, after they have been in-stalled. All the parts are kept square until the joints have been cut; the shaping happens later. With the stock all milled to size, you are ready to begin construction. Here's how to make this stool.

Superimposed Views

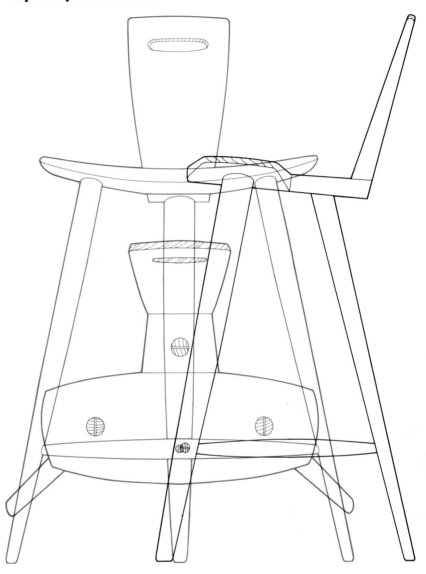

2

3

The seat   While the seat is still square, make the joints. First cut the mortise-and-tenon between the two seat pieces. Make a four-shoulder tenon [*Book 1,* p. 188].

Next drill the round mortises in the seat for the legs. Take the angles of the two front legs from the drawing. Tilt the table of the drill press to get one of the angles **(2)**, and make a jig to get the other one. I've made a simple tilting jig by screwing two long strips of wood to the drill-press table. One acts as a stop and the other raises the opposite edge of the seat to the correct angle **(3)**. Since this is a compound angle, you will have to readjust the table of the drill press to drill the hole at the other end. If you are making more than one stool, set another stop on the jig at one end of the seat as shown in **(3)** and drill the first hole in all the pieces. Then reverse the tilt of the table, change the stop and drill all the other holes. It is always a good idea to check the angles on a scrap piece first to be sure they are right. When you are done with this, follow the same procedure to make the hole in the back extension.

Next dovetail the backrest to the seat extension **(4)**. Notice that this is an angled dovetail. Just cut the ends of the two pieces to the correct angle and make the joint the same way you would make a regular through dovetail. At such a slight degree, the marking gauge works fine.

Now rough-shape the seat (and the backrest, too, while you're at it) before fitting the legs.

Mark the shapes on the pieces to be bandsawn **(5)**. Cut the taper in the thickness, or profile, of the backrest (the piece with the tails) before cutting the outside shape. Do the same thing to the seat. Cut the top and bottom curves before the outsides. It is easier and safer that way because you can work with square edges on the bandsaw table.

Put the two seat pieces together without glue and smooth out the curves. Be sure you don't sand the pins of the dovetails. You don't need to finish-sand the bottom at this stage, but get the final shaping and rough sanding done so that you have something definite to fit the shoulders of the legs to. I used a belt sander for this.

Make the finger slot in the backrest. The smoothest and easiest way to do this is to use a router with a template guide and a jig. When this is done, sand everything with 80-grit paper.

To assemble the seat unit, first glue the mortise-and-tenoned pieces together. When that's dry, glue the dovetailed backrest on. Then sand the joints with 80-grit paper. Set the seat unit aside for a while and turn your attention to the legs.

4

5

6

7

8

9

The legs   Use a plug cutter in the drill press to make the round tenons on the ends of the legs and stretchers. I used a 1-in. cutter for the leg tenons and a ½-in. cutter for the stretcher tenons to match the holes drilled in the seat and the ones I planned to drill in the legs.

Tilt the table on the drill press 90°, so it is parallel to the stand. Clamp a piece of plywood to the drill-press table and attach two parallel pieces of wood for fences that will hold the legs snugly **(6)**. Put a stop between the pieces for the leg bottom. Line up the jig so the tenon will be centered and parallel. Make some tests to be sure it is correct. Set the depth stop on the drill press to the desired length of the tenon, and you are ready to go. Remember, the tenon should be just a little longer than the depth of the mortise, so you can easily trim the end after assembly. After you have drilled the tenons **(7)**, cut the shoulders on the tablesaw.

Cut a slot in the end of each tenon, either by hand or on the bandsaw. The wedge will make the joint tighter when it is put together and the slot will also make the tenon slide in easier when it is being fitted.

Now rough-fit the shoulders of the legs to the bottom of the seat **(8)**. Slide the tenons into place, scribe the shoulders and trim them with a dovetail saw and a chisel. You'll notice that there is no back in these photos. The photographer came early and I hadn't gotten that far. The process can be done either way, but I prefer to cut the dovetail joint and assemble the seat before fitting the legs.

After the shoulders have been rough-fit to the seat, measure from the floor to the edges of the seat to make sure the stool is standing straight **(9)**.

Next measure up from the floor to mark the centers for the front and back stretchers. Mark them ½ in. higher than their final height because you will probably have to trim the bottoms of the legs later to level the stool.

Clamp a straight stick across the front legs. Put the top edge of the stick on the stretcher-center marks and then draw a line on each leg **(10)**.

Set a sliding bevel to the angle between leg and floor **(11)**. Now move it up and draw lines parallel to the floor at the center marks on each of the front legs **(12)**.

To mark the angle on the back leg, hold another stick across the first stick on the front legs and mark the back leg at the correct height **(13)**. Then square the mark across the back leg.

10

11

13

12

14

15

To drill the holes in the legs for the stretchers, tilt the drill-press table to the angle marked on the legs. This angle should still be on the sliding bevel if you haven't changed it. Make another plywood jig to hold the legs, or adapt the one you used for the tenons. When the angle is set correctly, drill the holes in the front legs. Then change the setup and drill the back leg.

When all the holes in the legs have been drilled, mark the tapers and bandsaw them out. Then mark a centerline down the sides as a reference when shaping the legs **(14)**. To make shaping the legs a little easier, I used a router with a chamfer bit to remove the corners. Then I finished the job with a hand plane, a scraper blade and sandpaper.

When that's done, drill the hole in the center of the front stretcher piece on the drill press.

Mark and bandsaw the tapers on the stretchers. After you've sawn the stretchers to the correct profile, again draw a line down the center of the edges **(15)** to use as a reference when shaping. Use a spokeshave to make the stretchers oval and then scrape and sand them. Remember, there aren't any shoulders on the stretcher tenons, so be careful not to sand too much off the ends.

Now that all the joints have been cut and everything has been shaped and sanded, the final fitting of the leg shoulders can begin. The legs have to be positioned correctly.

Assemble the stool without glue. Then fit the upper part of all three legs by scribing the shoulder to the bottom of the seat. Cut and chisel it to shape.

After you have done the fitting, make a sawcut in the ends of the stretchers with a dovetail saw. Be sure to make the cuts so that the wedges will go across the grain of the legs and the front stretcher. Saw the wedges on the bandsaw. Finish-sand all the parts before gluing.

Assembling the stool Now you are ready to glue up the legs and stretchers, but you might want to try this first. Since you have gone to a lot of trouble to make the joints fit snugly, they are going to be real hard to get together as soon as the glue goes on and they begin to swell. If you shrink the wood just before gluing, it will make the joints temporarily looser. Put the legs and stretchers in a 200°F oven for about 1½ hours to remove moisture. They will go together much easier.

If you are warming up the wood, the gluing could be easily done with hot glue, but I suggest letting the wood cool down and then using a slow-setting glue to be safe.

Gluing the stool together can be a little tricky because everything has to be assembled at the same time, so it is a good idea to have an extra pair of hands ready.

Put glue on all the joints, then assemble the parts loosely, working as quickly as possible. As you hammer down on the seat, keep pushing or hammering in on the stretchers so that nothing gets broken or jammed. When all the tenons have been hammered in and the shoulders are tight, glue and tap in the wedges. Be careful to hammer the wedges in straight. Clamps should not be necessary for this job. Also, the legs are drier than the seat, so the joint will get tighter as the tenons swell and the mortises shrink.

When the glue has dried, cut the tenons and wedges flush with the legs and seat and finish-sand them.

The last step before finishing is to level the stool. Measure from the floor to the ends of the seat to see if the whole thing is fairly level and shim the feet if necessary to get it right. Scribe the bottoms of the legs and trim to the lines.

Now the finish can be applied. I put Watco oil on the stools I made because it is simple, durable and easy to repair.

As I mentioned before, the height of the stool can be varied. The seat and backrest remain the same. The only changes are in the angles and lengths of the legs, and the lengths of the stretchers. The legs are a little lighter on the shorter stools, but the stretchers are always the same distance from the floor.

I like these stools about as well as anything I've designed. I've made quite a few of them in three different heights—13 in., 18 in. and 22 in. (The taller stools are the most popular.) Some are in the permanent collection of the Boston Museum of Fine Arts and the Rhode Island School of Design Museum of Art. □

Backrest

Wedge

Seat

Back extension

Wedge

Stretcher

Leg

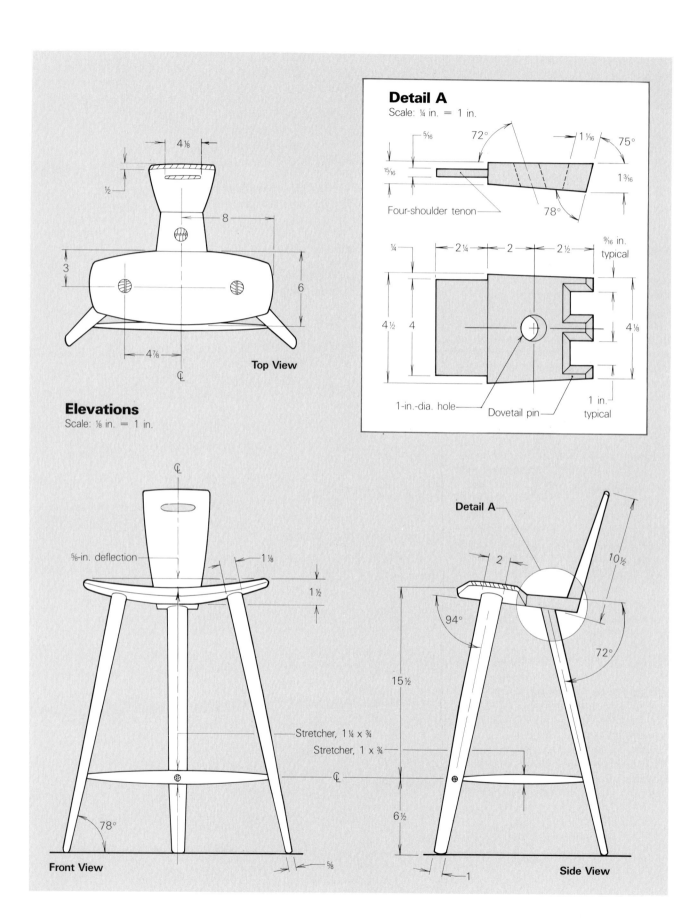

Top View

Elevations
Scale: ⅛ in. = 1 in.

Detail A
Scale: ¼ in. = 1 in.

4⅛
½
8
3
6
4⅞
C̵L

5⁄16
72°
1 1⁄16
75°
15⁄16
1 3⁄16
Four-shoulder tenon
78°

¼
2¼
2
2½
9⁄16 in. typical
4½
4
4⅛
1 in. typical
1-in.-dia. hole
Dovetail pin

Detail A

⅝-in. deflection
1⅛
1½
2
10½
94°
72°
15½
Stretcher, 1¼ x ¾
Stretcher, 1 x ¾
C̵L
6½
78°
⅝
Front View
1
Side View

Casework

Chapter 6

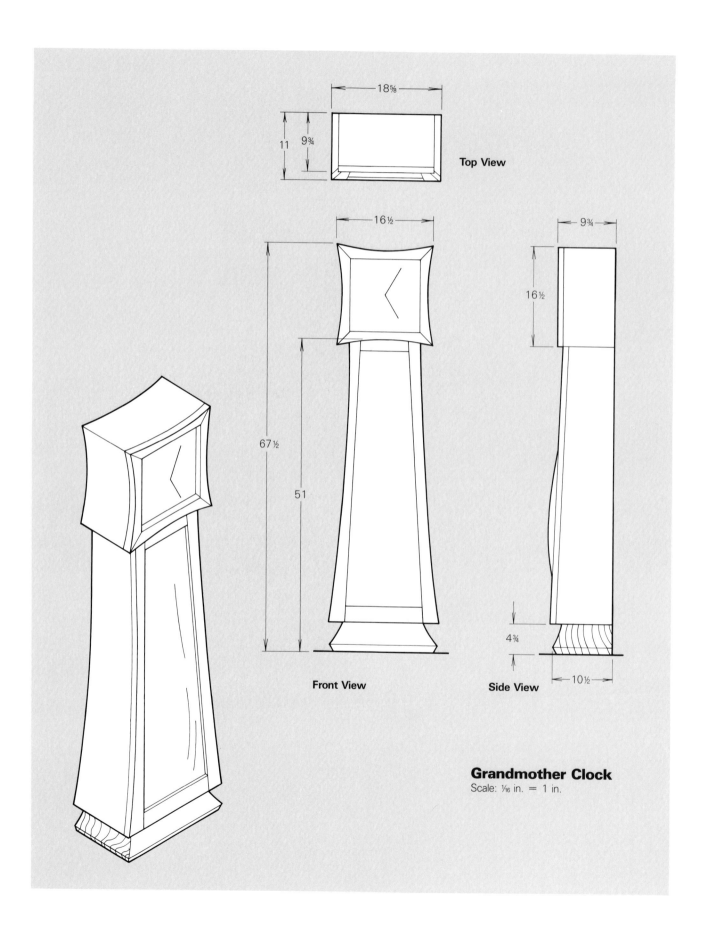

Top View

Front View

Side View

Grandmother Clock
Scale: ¹⁄₁₆ in. = 1 in.

Grandmother Clock

I wanted to make a clock for myself. I like the sounds of ticking and chimes, but not if they're too loud. So I used 1⅝-in.-thick solid walnut for the carcase, which dampens the sound a little and also allowed me to shape the sides. The back is made out of ¼-in. plywood and there's a 1½-in.-dia. hole drilled in the back of the top carcase, which makes the sound just right for me.

I didn't want to see the shiny pendulum and weights, so I designed a door to cover the front of the clock. I used frame-and-panel construction for this; the panel is solid wood and I carved it out with a router. The shape I finally ended up with looks a little like an abstraction of a cat **(1)**.

Both the top carcase and the bottom carcase are joined with full-blind multiple splines [*Book 1*, pp. 110-113]. Because there are only three sides to the bottom carcase, I mortise-and-tenoned a piece of wood at the upper back, between the two long sides. I fastened the two carcases together using T-nuts and dowels (see pp. 16-17).

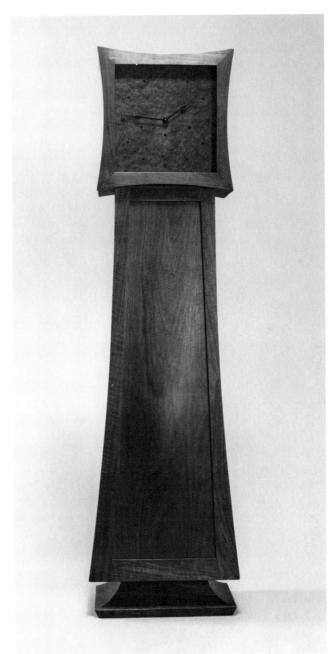

1

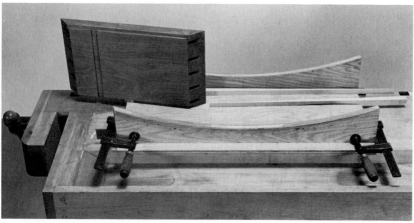

2

3

Shaping the carcase One of the unusual things about making the clock is shaping the sides. To make the pieces of the carcase concave, I made this jig for the router **(2)**.

The two parallel tracks on the outside are cut to the desired curve of the carcase. The work is held in the jig with two pieces of wood, cut at a 45° angle to match the miters on the ends of the carcase piece. The pieces are clamped behind the front track, and two wedges are inserted on the opposite side to hold the work tightly between the two tracks.

The router slides across the work on a sleigh, which is moved along the curved tracks. The guide pieces in the sleigh on which the router slides are straight, but they could be made concave or convex to get a compound curve, if desired.

(3) Here one of the pieces from the top carcase is being routed out, using a ½-in. straight bit with a ½-in. shank. Make several passes, taking no more than ⅜ in. with each cut. Once the panel has been routed, it needs only to be scraped and sanded and it's done. It took me just one hour to make the four identical pieces for the top carcase. The sides of the bottom carcase and the front panel in the bottom frame are done the same way. Because I was making only one clock, I decided not to make a concave sleigh to cut a compound curve for the belly on the front panel. Instead, it was quicker to cut a simple curve and remove the wood on both sides of the belly by hand-carving. The back of the panel is flat.

Clamping up Another unusual thing about making this piece is the way it is clamped together. Clamping 45° miter joints can be tricky, especially if the sides are concave. A simple jig helps. I used four pieces of ¼-in. plywood, each the same size as the carcase sides. I screwed a block of wood with a 45° bevel on both ends of each piece with the beveled edge facing in.

Clamp one piece of the plywood jig to each side first. Then spread glue on the joints, insert the splines and clamp the pieces together **(4)**. The jaws of the clamps fit on the 45° mitered surfaces, which are roughly parallel to each other at the corners. Check for squareness by measuring diagonally from corner to corner. The bottom carcase is clamped together the same way, but the jig can be used only at the bottom end. To prevent the jig from slipping, glue 40-grit sandpaper to the back of the jig. To keep the bottom carcase square, glue in the stretcher at the upper back at the same time. Check squareness by measuring diagonally from corner to corner.

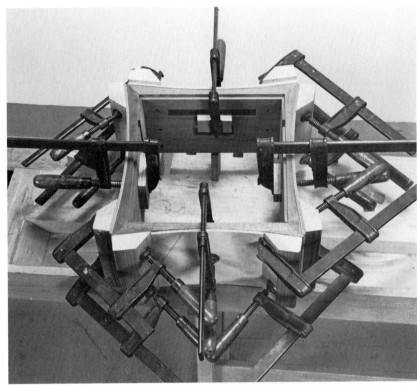

4

Finishing up   The base for this clock is made out of solid wood. Bandsaw the concave curve on the ends and carve out the front. Then screw the base to the underside of the bottom carcase.

I didn't want to have a white clock face staring at me every time I walked into the room, so I made the face out of redwood burl veneer. The inlaid black dots are nylon.

Because of the concave shape of the carcase, I was afraid that hinges on the face frame and the lower frame would not look right, so I used an alternative method of attaching them to the carcase. The frame that holds the glass over the face is held in place with one round, tapered wooden pin on each side and a magnetic catch at top and bottom. The pins bear the weight and the magnets hold the frame against the carcase. (I later removed the glass on my clock because there was too much light reflection due to the dark clock face.)

The bottom frame-and-panel door has two locator pins on top that fit into the bottom of the top carcase.

To carry the weight of the large door, fasten a wooden block to the bottom of the frame. The block rests on the bottom of the carcase when the door is closed. Secure the frame at the bottom with a bullet catch at each corner. Rout a cove cut on the front edge of the carcase bottom for a finger grip, so the door can be easily grabbed for removal. Because the weights are cranked up by means of a key inserted into one of the three holes in the face, the bottom door has to be removed only when you are starting the clock.   □

Top Carcase

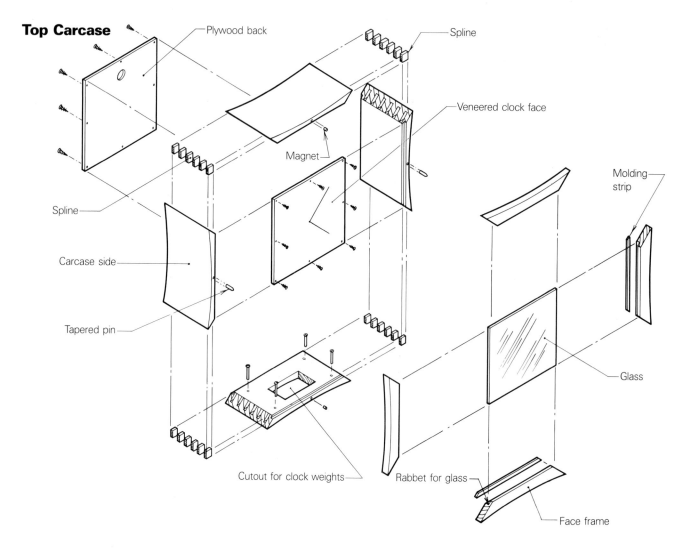

Plywood back

Spline

Veneered clock face

Magnet

Spline

Carcase side

Tapered pin

Molding strip

Glass

Cutout for clock weights

Rabbet for glass

Face frame

Bottom Carcase

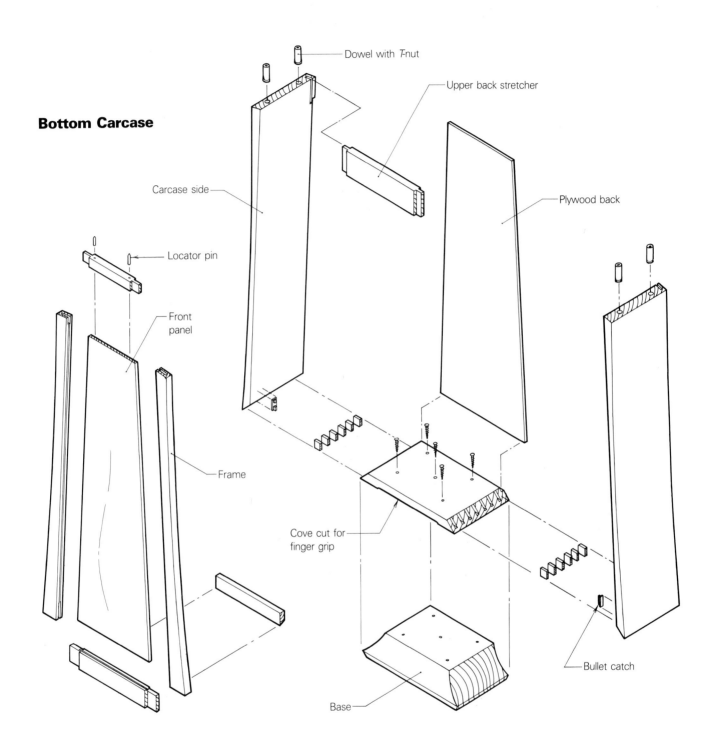

Dowel with *T*-nut

Upper back stretcher

Carcase side

Plywood back

Locator pin

Front panel

Frame

Cove cut for finger grip

Bullet catch

Base

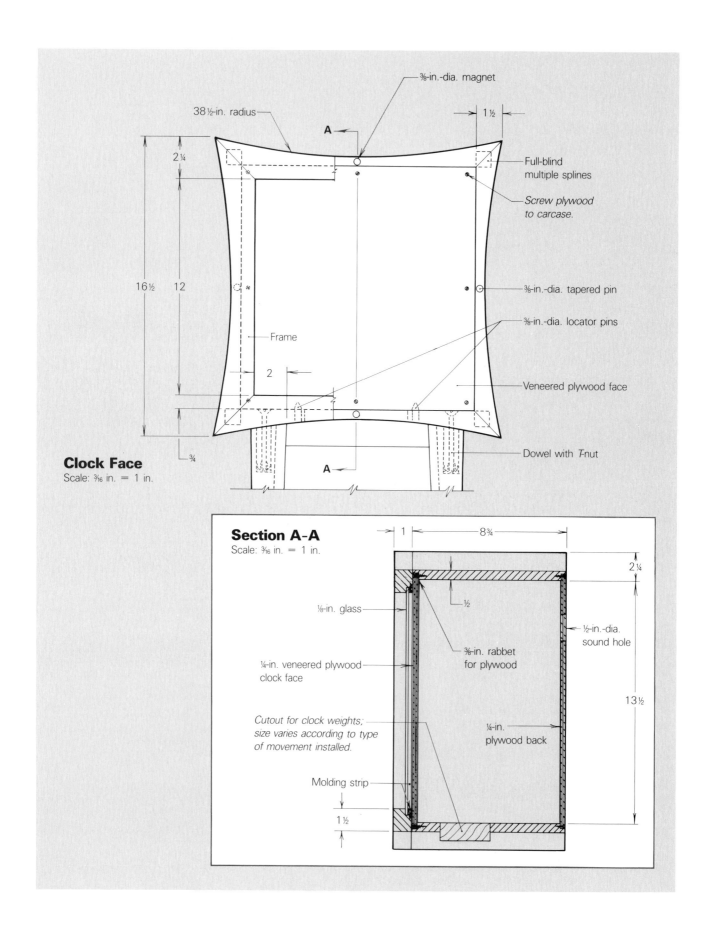

⅜-in.-dia. magnet

38 ½-in. radius

1 ½

A

2 ¼

Full-blind
multiple splines

*Screw plywood
to carcase.*

16 ½   12

⅜-in.-dia. tapered pin

⅜-in.-dia. locator pins

Frame

Veneered plywood face

2

Dowel with *T*-nut

A

Clock Face
Scale: ³⁄₁₆ in. = 1 in.

¾

Section A-A
Scale: ³⁄₁₆ in. = 1 in.

1   8 ¾

2 ¼

⅛-in. glass

½

½-in.-dia.
sound hole

⅜-in. rabbet
for plywood

¼-in. veneered plywood
clock face

*Cutout for clock weights;
size varies according to type
of movement installed.*

13 ½

¼-in.
plywood back

Molding strip

1 ½

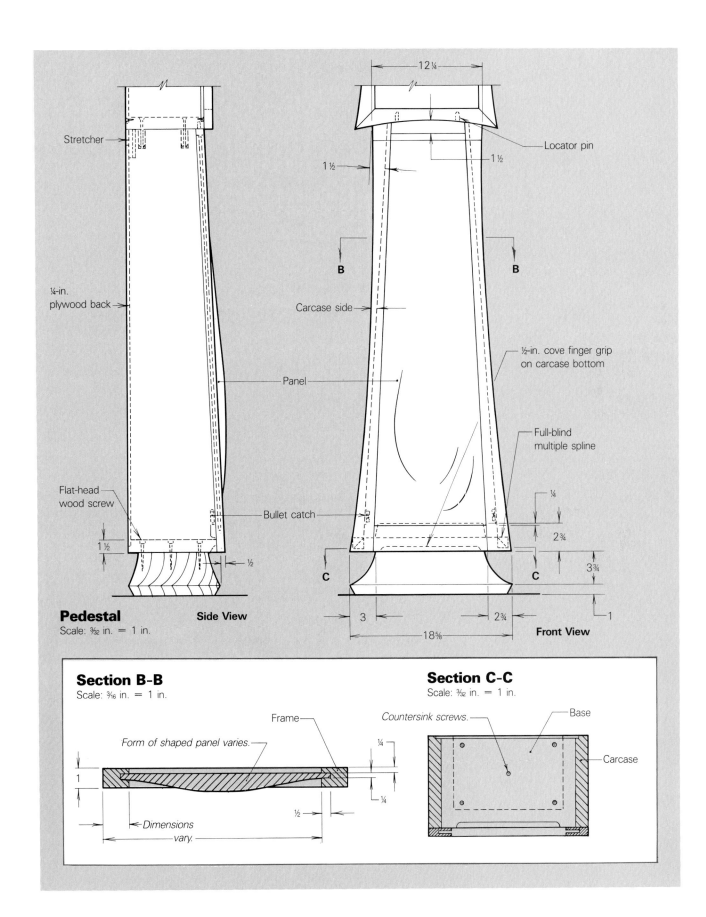

Stretcher

¼-in. plywood back

Flat-head wood screw

1½

½

Pedestal
Scale: ³⁄₃₂ in. = 1 in.

Side View

Panel

Bullet catch

12¼

Locator pin

1½

1½

B   B

Carcase side

½-in. cove finger grip on carcase bottom

Full-blind multiple spline

¼

2¾

3¾

C   C

3   2¾   1

18⅝

Front View

Section B-B
Scale: ³⁄₁₆ in. = 1 in.

Frame

Form of shaped panel varies.

¼

¼

1

½

←*Dimensions vary.*→

Section C-C
Scale: ³⁄₃₂ in. = 1 in.

Countersink screws.

Base

Carcase

Router Jig

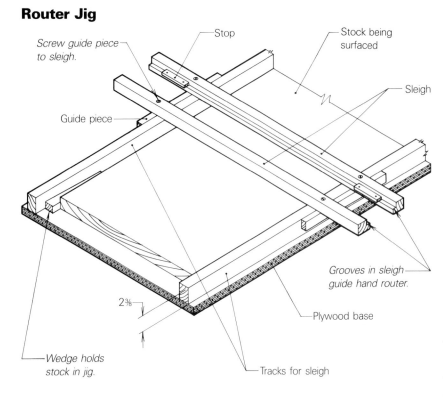

Screw guide piece to sleigh.

Stop

Stock being surfaced

Guide piece

Sleigh

Grooves in sleigh guide hand router.

2⅜

Plywood base

Wedge holds stock in jig.

Tracks for sleigh

Thickness-Planing

A jointer and a thickness planer are two very important machines, but they require a great investment for the small shop. You can make a jig for the router, similar to the one used to make the concave sides of the clock, that can be used to joint and thickness-plane wide boards. In certain woods, like curly maple, it does a smoother job than a jointer or thickness planer.

The drawing shows how to make a simple jig, but it can be adjusted to your needs. For example, you could screw one track permanently to the base and attach the other with bolts riding in slots in the plywood, which would allow you to adjust the jig to the width of the board being worked on. In that case, the guide pieces on the sleigh would have to be adjustable, too. But I have found that it is easier to have two jigs, one for narrow boards and one for wide panels. I use a filler piece if necessary to make up any difference in width.

If a board is twisted, wedges must be put underneath it in opposite corners to level it off when it is being surfaced. When one side is flat, remove the wedges, flip the board over and thickness-plane the other side.

When making such a jig, be sure that the plywood base is perfectly flat and the runners are straight and parallel. Here, the tracks are 2⅜ in. high, so a 2-in.-thick board can be jointed and planed. To joint and plane a 1-in.-thick board in this jig, simply raise the board by putting 1-in. blocks under it. The sleigh is made out of maple. Be sure the two sleigh pieces the router rides on are perfectly straight.

(1,2) Here I am using a 1½-in. straight carbide bit with a ½-in. shank to surface a piece of 25-in. by 78-in. Honduras mahogany. If you use a small router, you will have to use a smaller bit and work more slowly.

Notice how smooth the wood is when it has been jointed and thickness-planed using the router. This plank **(3)** took only ten minutes to do.   □

1

2

3

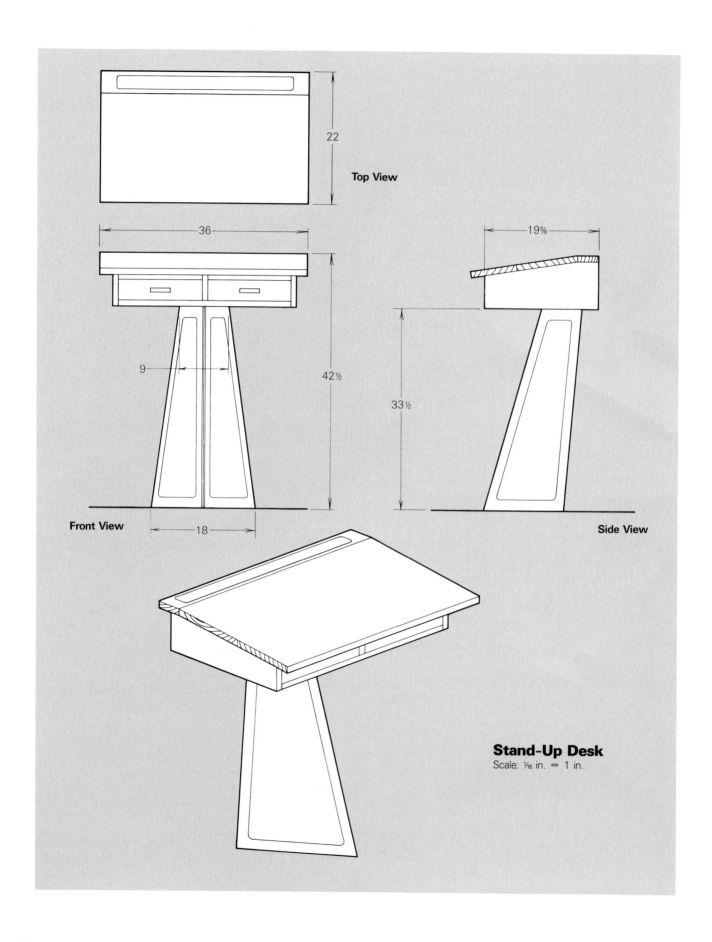

Top View

36

9

42½

Front View

18

19⅝

33½

Side View

Stand-Up Desk
Scale: ⅟₁₆ in. = 1 in.

22

Stand-Up Desk

When I was a child in Denmark, stand-up desks were still common in some of the very old firms, general stores and lumberyards. I can see now that there are some real advantages to them. When I'm writing and get tired of sitting, I'll often stand up for a while at my drawing table to keep on working. It gets the blood circulating and my body feels better than if I had spent all day crammed in a chair. Recently, I designed and made this stand-up desk for myself.

I didn't want legs on the desk because they would have made it look too tall. Also, any leg construction would have had to be quite heavy to be stable when the desk was leaned on, and such heavy legs would have been easy to trip over. So I decided to make the piece with a pedestal base.

Because I would be leaning on the top while writing, the carcase needed strong joints. At the same time, I wanted to take advantage of the solid-wood construction by carving into the sides of the pedestal, the drawer fronts and the pencil tray to give them a decorative three-dimensional texture. With all this carving, I thought that the desk would look too busy if I used exposed joinery for the bottom of the carcase, so I decided to use half-blind dovetails instead [*Book 1*, pp. 72-74]. The top and the pencil tray are joined to the sides with sliding dovetails [*Book 1*, pp. 140-148]. I made the grooves for the drawer runners and the center partition before assembling the carcase, but I slid the runners and the partition in later.

Laying out the pedestal The pedestal is the only unusual part of the construction of this piece. The pedestal is not difficult to make, but because the panels are joined with a compound miter, it's tricky to figure out all the angles exactly on paper. For my purposes, this wasn't necessary. I laid out the pedestal in a couple of simple drawings that I knew would give me the approximate dimensions of the finished piece. It's easy enough to adjust the slope or footprint of the pedestal by recutting the panels after you have assembled the piece.

First make the orthographic top-view, front-view and side-view drawings shown on the facing page. Remember to make the desktop surface higher or lower to suit your own comfortable working height. (The actual width and shape of the pedestal will vary, depending on the compound angle of the miter.)

Next make a full-scale top-view drawing of the pedestal. I prefer to do this on plywood because paper wrinkles and does not always give reliable angles. The width of the pedestal on my desk (9 in. at the top and 18 in. at the bottom) was taken off the front-view drawing. I decided to make each panel 1 ¼ in. thick, 8 in. wide at the top and 16 ½ in. wide at the bottom. These measurements combined to give me the top-view drawing shown below.

Pedestal Layout

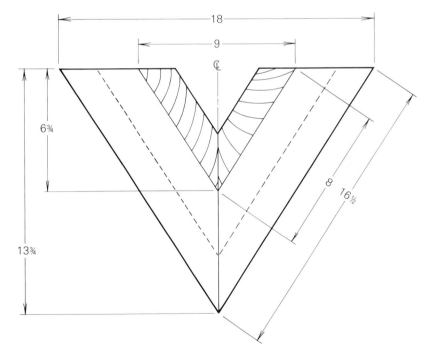

Panel Layout

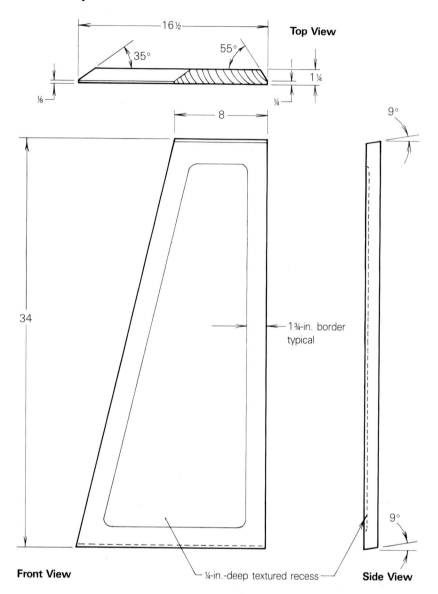

Top View

16½

35°   55°

1¼

⅛   ¼

8

9°

34

1¾-in. border typical

9°

Front View

¼-in.-deep textured recess

Side View

Next lay out the panels. Cut two 1¼-in.-thick by 16½-in.-wide by 34-in.-long rectangular pieces of solid wood. I knew that because of their angle the panels would have to be longer than the 33½-in. height shown in the side-view drawing. Their height will be trimmed later anyway, so you could make them a little longer and trim off the extra after all the pedestal joints have been cut. Taking the same 8-in. and 16½-in. widths used in the top-view drawing, make two marks on the panels, one 8 in. out from what will be the upper back corner of the panel and the other 16½ in. out from the lower back corner. When the miter is cut and the panels are joined, the pedestal will be closer to the wall at the top than at the bottom, as shown in the original side-view drawing, because the base of the pedestal spreads out.

Cutting the miter You'll have to cut the compound miter for this pedestal in two steps because the tablesaw blade won't tilt far enough to do it in one. For the first cut, make a plywood jig for the tablesaw. Place one of the panels on top of a rectangular piece of plywood so that the 8-in. and 16½-in. marks line up on one edge **(1,2)**. Trace the outline of the back and bottom edge of the panel on the plywood and continue the back line out to the front edge. The bottom meets the back of the panel at a right angle, so the angle on the jig that will form the seat of the panel should also be 90° **(3)**. Using a bandsaw, cut away the waste portion to complete the jig **(4)**.

Place the panel in the jig and set the fence so that the saw will begin the cut at the 8-in. mark. With the plywood running against the fence, make the first cut with the blade set at 90° **(5)**, then flip the jig over to cut the other panel. Be sure to place the panels in the jig so their good sides will face out when the pedestal is assembled.

1

2

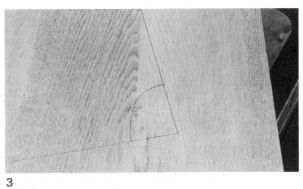

3

4

5

6

7

Now cut the compound angle. You will have to tilt the blade on the tablesaw and position the fence so that the blade tilts away from it. (On my saw, this meant that I had to move the fence to the opposite side of the blade.) Take the angle for the miter from the full-scale top-view drawing of the pedestal and set the blade to that **(6)**. (For this pedestal, I set the blade to about 35°.) If your angles are critical, you can figure them out mathematically, or by drawing a projection of the pedestal from the top view. But I didn't care if the angles on the pedestal were a few degrees smaller or larger than those on the drawing. I rigged up an extra-high fence for this job and made sure it was square to the saw table.

To make this compound cut, hold the outside face of the panel against the fence and run the edge you just cut in the jig over the tilted blade **(7)**. Use a featherboard to hold the panel tight against the fence. Do the same thing to both panels. To make the *V* detail where the two miters meet on the leading edge of the pedestal, simply set the fence about ⅛ in. from the bottom of the blade. This will leave a ⅛-in.-wide surface at a right angle to the outside face of each panel **(8)**, which will form one-half of the *V* when the pedestal is assembled.

When these angles have been cut on both panels, you can run them over the jointer, making a light pass or two to remove the sawmarks or correct the angle if it's a bit off.

8

Joining the panels Now cut the ⅛-in. groove for the spline in each panel by resetting the blade to 90° and running the mitered cut over it. Because I'm right-handed, I moved the fence back to the right side of the blade to make this cut. The spline isn't necessary for a good gluing surface, but it makes it easier to hold the panels in position during glue-up. Test the depth of cut on a scrap of wood first. The mitered surface is about 2 in. wide, so this cut isn't dangerous as long as you hold the miter flat on the table and tight against the fence. To be safe, clamp a board to the fence and another to the saw table, with the end cut to the same angle as the bevel on the panel. These boards will hold the edge of the panel in position, while you push it along the fence **(9)**. This groove **(10)** could also be cut with a router.

When the grooves have been made, assemble the pedestal without glue to determine the angle on the ends of the panels (it will be the same at both the top and bottom) and on the back edges. In this case, the top and bottom angle was about 9° and the back angle was 55° (the complementary angle to the 35° miter). Also measure the inside of the pedestal to find the correct lengths and angles of the top and bottom back stretchers. Then take the pedestal apart and cut the angle on the top and bottom of both panels so that the pedestal will fit flush to the floor and the bottom of the desk carcase. Cut the angle on the back edge of each panel. The mortises for the top and bottom stretchers in the back of the pedestal can be cut with a dado blade.

The textured recess When all the panel joints have been cut, rout out the ¼-in.-deep recess on the outside face. First cut the quarter-round outline of the recessed area, using a fence or a jig to guide the router. (These could be nailed right to the center of the panel where the wood will be removed.) Then fasten the router to a long board with a 2-in. hole for the bit and remove the rest of the wood using a flat cutter. When the recess has been all routed, carve the surface with a gouge, going across the grain **(11)**. Soften the gouge marks by lightly sanding the sharp edges of the high points.

9

10

11

Pedestal

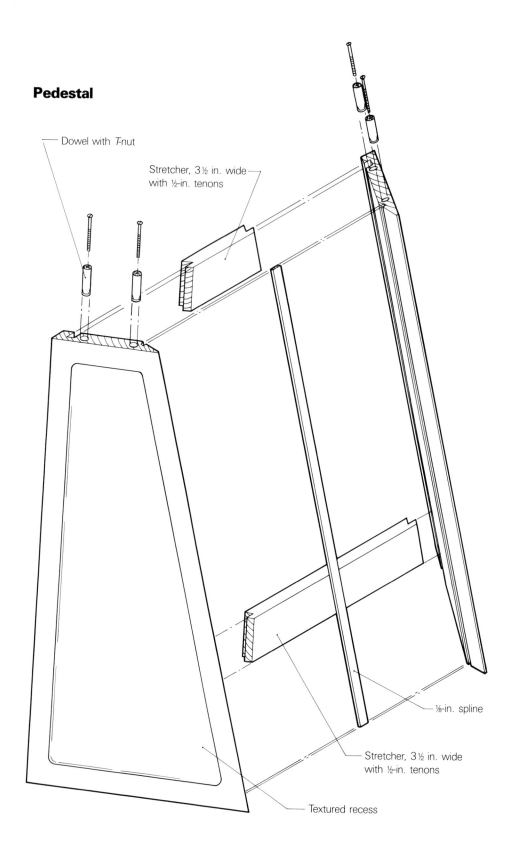

Dowel with *T*-nut

Stretcher, 3½ in. wide with ½-in. tenons

⅛-in. spline

Stretcher, 3½ in. wide with ½-in. tenons

Textured recess

Assembling the desk Now the pedestal can be glued together, with the back stretchers in place.

Use corner blocks attached to plywood to provide a good clamping surface for the mitered joint, as described for the grandmother clock on p. 159.

The pedestal is bolted to the carcase using dowels and T-nuts (see pp. 16-17). The desk is balanced when standing on the pedestal, but for extra stability I secured it to the wall with a beveled cleat. Two pieces of wood with the edges cut at 45° form the cleat. One piece is glued into the back of the cabinet and the other piece is screwed to the wall. The cabinet is lifted up and hung on the wall cleat, although the weight of the desk is carried by the pedestal.   □

Glue face-frame member to underside of top.

Desk Carcase

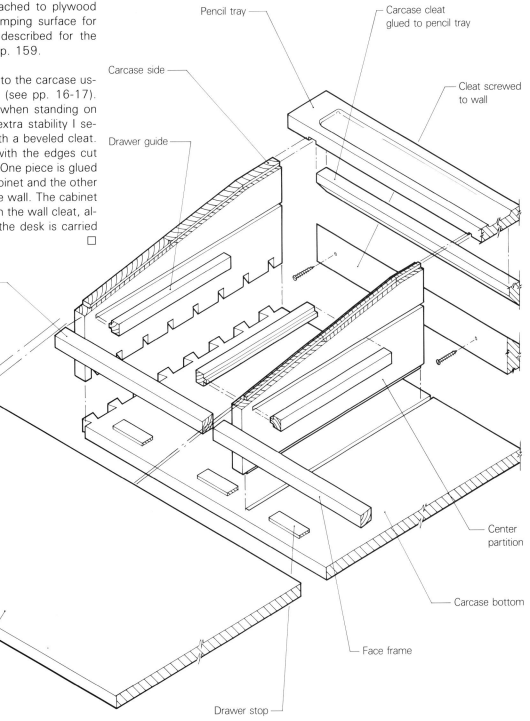

Pencil tray

Carcase cleat glued to pencil tray

Carcase side

Cleat screwed to wall

Drawer guide

Center partition

Carcase bottom

Face frame

Drawer stop

Desktop

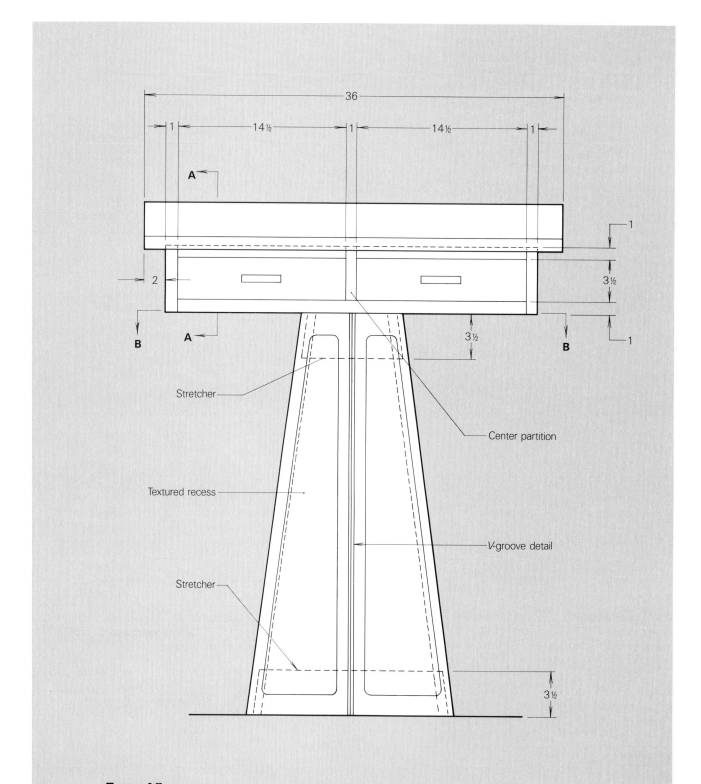

Front View
Scale: ⅛ in. = 1 in.

Section A-A
Scale: ¼ in. = 1 in.

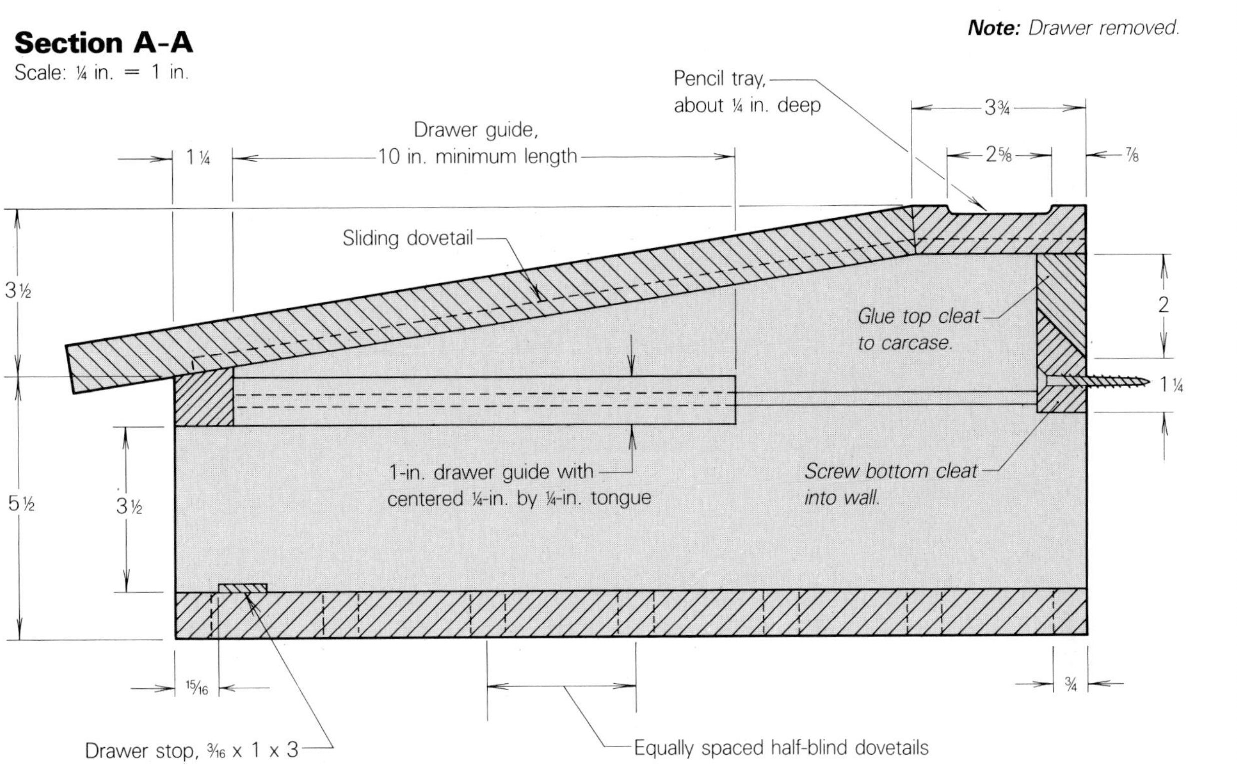
Note: Drawer removed.
Pencil tray, about ¼ in. deep
Drawer guide, 10 in. minimum length
1 ¼
3¾
2⅝
⅞
Sliding dovetail
3½
Glue top cleat to carcase.
2
1 ¼
1-in. drawer guide with centered ¼-in. by ¼-in. tongue
Screw bottom cleat into wall.
5½
3½
15/16
¾
Drawer stop, 3/16 x 1 x 3
Equally spaced half-blind dovetails

Section B-B
Scale: 3/16 in. = 1 in.

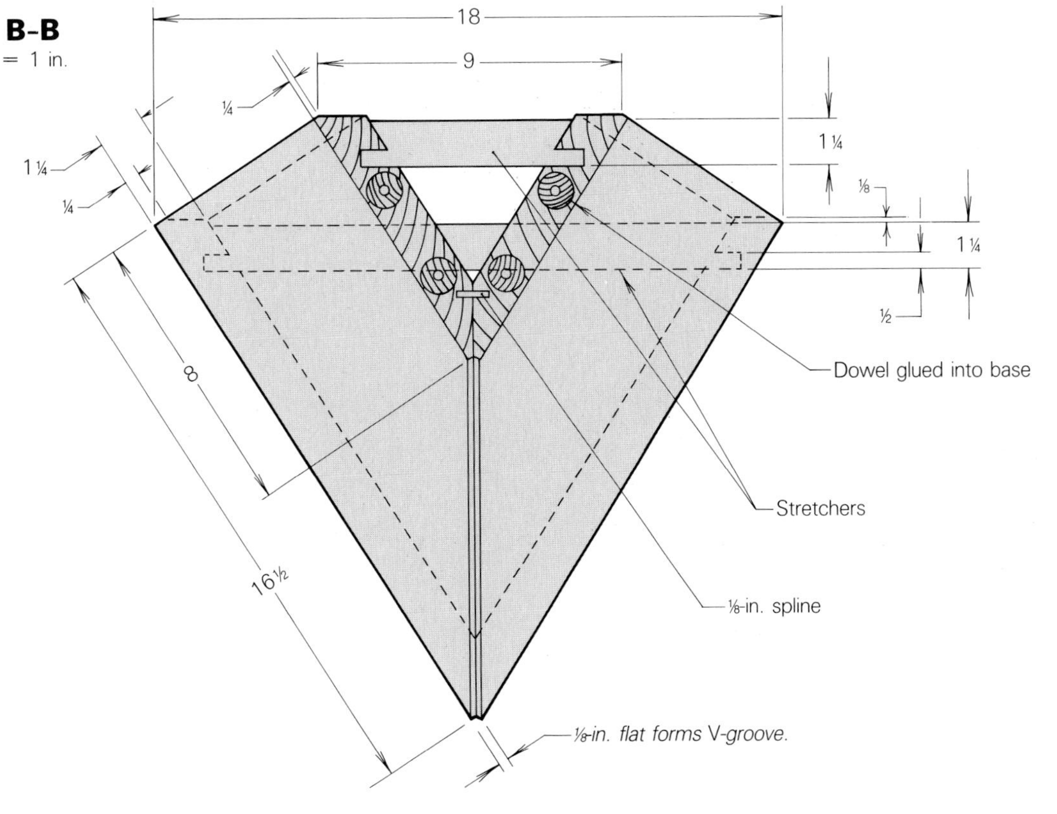
18
9
¼
1 ¼
¼
1 ¼
⅛
1 ¼
½
Dowel glued into base
8
Stretchers
16½
⅛-in. spline
⅛-in. flat forms V-groove.

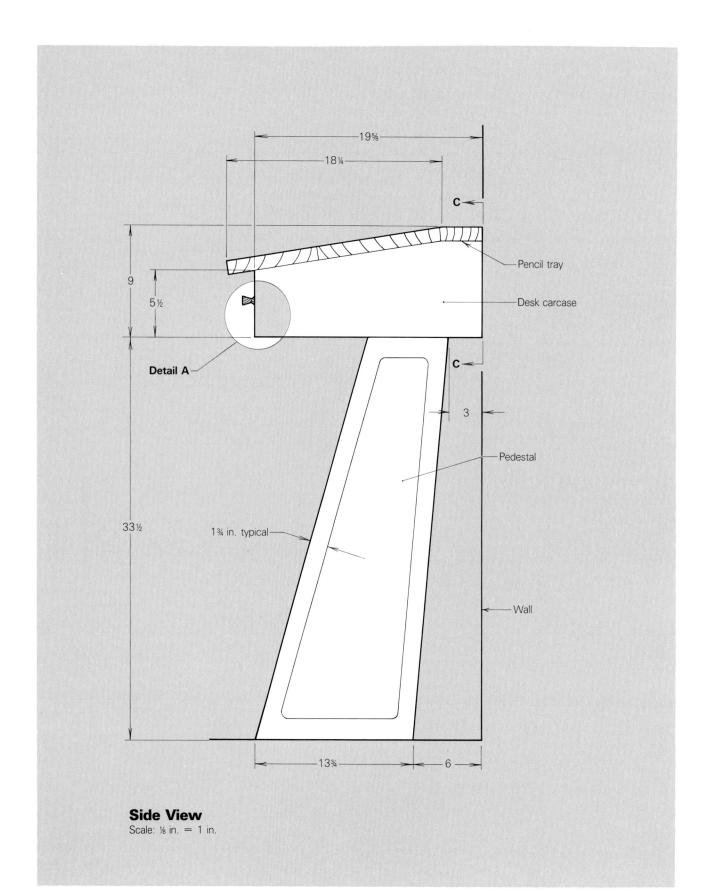

19⅝

18¼

C

Pencil tray

Desk carcase

9

5½

Detail A

C

3

Pedestal

33½

1¾ in. typical

Wall

13¾

6

Side View
Scale: ⅛ in. = 1 in.

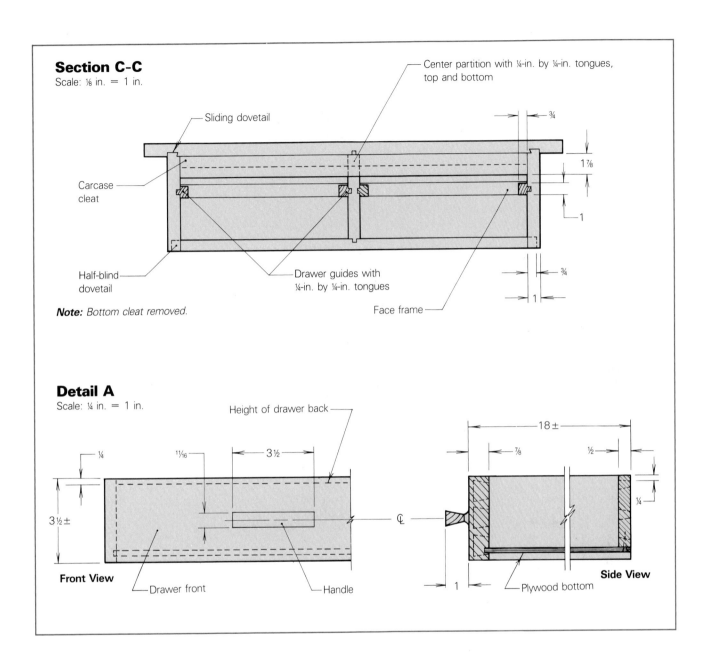

Section C-C
Scale: ⅛ in. = 1 in.

Center partition with ¼-in. by ¼-in. tongues, top and bottom

Sliding dovetail

Carcase cleat

Half-blind dovetail

Drawer guides with ¼-in. by ¼-in. tongues

Face frame

Note: *Bottom cleat removed.*

¾
1⅞
1
¾
1

Detail A
Scale: ¼ in. = 1 in.

Height of drawer back

¼
1¹¹⁄₁₆
3½
3½±

Front View

Drawer front

Handle

18±
⅞
½
¼
1

Side View

Plywood bottom

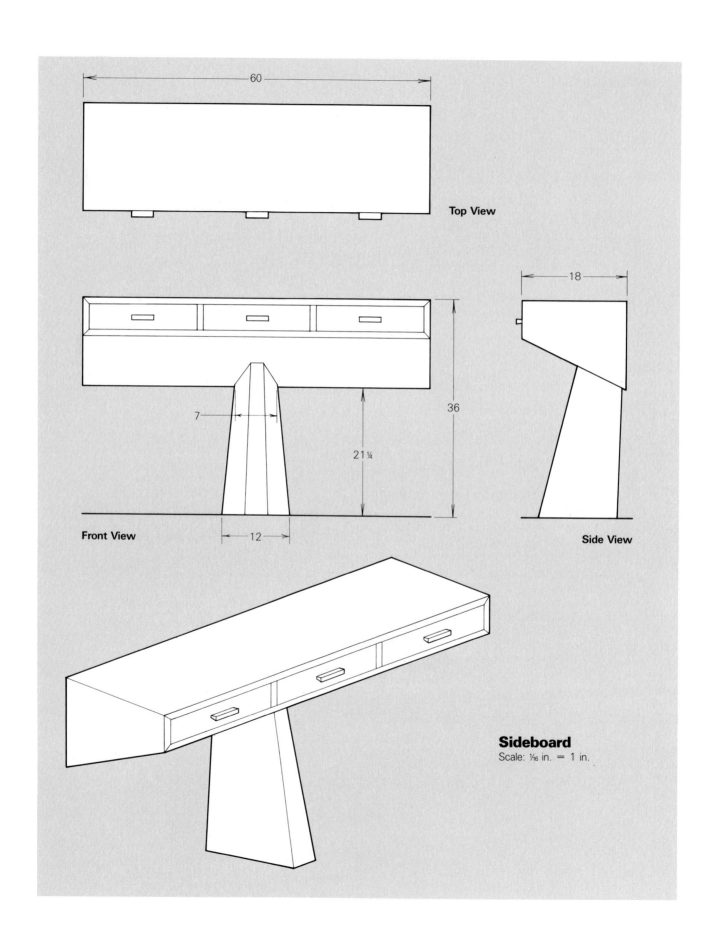

Top View

Front View

Side View

Sideboard
Scale: ⅟₁₆ in. = 1 in.

Sideboard

As I said in chapter 4, the main room in our house is an *L*-shaped combination living and dining room. We use the short part of the *L*, which is 10 ft. by 11 ft., as a small dining area. We needed a sideboard, but a regular, freestanding cabinet with legs would have made the room look even smaller, so I started thinking about designing a piece without legs. I didn't really want a wall-hung cabinet, and I didn't think the wall could carry one anyway, so I decided to make a sideboard on a pedestal **(1)**.

The idea for the pedestal came from an altar I had made for a church many years ago, which was designed to symbolize a cross. The top of the altar was lighter than the sideboard, though, and there were no drawers. I have since made several cabinets on pedestals.

As I mentioned earlier, our house is over 200 years old and has exposed post-and-beam construction. I wanted the sideboard to fit in with the design of the house, as well as with the trestle dining table on p. 44. One day, looking at a door with raised panels that was next to where the sideboard was going to be, it occurred to me that I could make the solid-wood carcase and pedestal resemble raised panels **(2)**.

The side view of the carcase looks like half of a dovetail pin, so I decided that it would be appropriate to join the cabinet together using through dovetails, which would also fit in well with the traditional 18th-century construction of the house. The pedestal and the drawer handles are shaped like a dovetail pin, too.

Because of the tapered shape of the carcase, there is a little wasted space below the drawers. But I did not like the look of a rectangular three-drawer box on a pedestal, so I decided to taper the carcase anyway. After the carcase was built, I realized that you can hide a lot of stuff under the drawers; now I can say I planned it that way.

1

2

3

The sideboard shown here **(3)** and in the drawings in this section has the same dimensions as the one in my house, but was made for a contemporary home.

This one is made of solid walnut, but does not have raised panels like my own sideboard, which would have been inappropriate. It measures 36 in. high, 60 in. long and 18 in. deep, and there are three drawers. The bottom of the pedestal angles forward a little to emphasize the piece's three-dimensional, freestanding quality. Plus, the angle allows the pedestal to clear the baseboard at the bottom of the wall.

I didn't want the joints in this sideboard to show because I wanted it to have clean, crisp lines to match the interior of the house. It also had to fit in with the circular pullout table (p. 96), the serving cart (p. 108) and the dining chair (p. 124), which would be in the same room. So instead of the dovetails I had used in my own sideboard, I joined this carcase with full-blind multiple-spline miters [*Book 1,* pp. 110-113].

The two partitions that separate the drawers are tongue-and-grooved to the top and bottom of the carcase. For strength, I added separate pieces at the front of each partition. These are fitted with double mortise-and-tenon joints on both ends and are glued in when the cabinet is assembled. The partitions are glued into the grooves and to the backs of these front pieces later, after the carcase has been assembled.

The drawer slides are also tongue-and-grooved into the sides of the carcase and the partitions, but are glued only along the front 2 in. to allow the rest of the carcase to move. Remember to make the slides 1 in. shorter than the cabinet is wide because of the inevitable shrinkage. For the same reason, the drawers are stopped in the front to keep their alignment consistent as the cabinet expands and contracts.

Making the pedestal   The process for making the pedestal for this sideboard is very similar to the one described for the stand-up desk pedestal on pp. 167-171, so read that section before you begin making this pedestal.

The drawings of the pedestal and the jig for cutting the long miters can be made the same way as for the desk. In this case, however, you can tilt the blade and make the compound angle in one cut, with the panel in the jig **(4)**. Make a jig for cutting the wide panels, set the sawblade to about 40° and cut the first panel. (Remember that you can vary the width of the pedestal by changing the angles of the miters.) Flip the jig over and cut the other wide panel.

4

Pedestal Layout

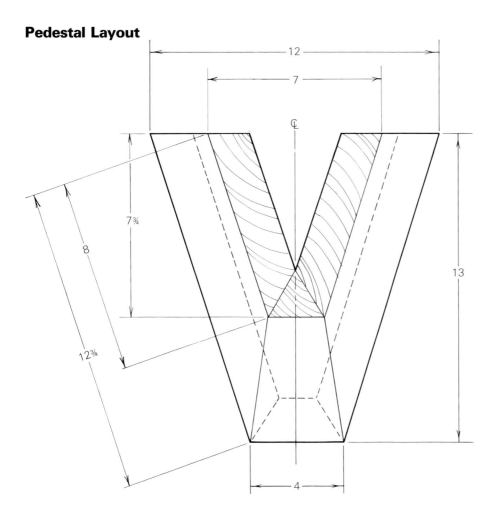

5

Make another jig to cut the compound angle on the narrow front panel, and tilt the sawblade to about 32°. Make the first cut out of a rectangular board **(5)**. (I made this cut with the wide end of the jig forward.) Then tape the waste piece back in place so the board is still rectangular, flip the jig over and cut the other edge of the panel **(6)**.

The long miters between the three panels in the pedestal are splined to make alignment easier during glue-up; without the splines, it would be next to impossible to clamp the assembly together. The grooves for the splines can be cut with the panels held flat on the saw table and the blade tilted **(7)**. Make sure that the groove is at a right angle to the mitered surface of both the wide and the narrow panels, or the splines won't fit right when you put the pedestal together.

6

7

Assembling the pedestal I installed the bottom stretcher in this pedestal using splines, which are easier to fit than a mortise-and-tenon and are just as strong. When all the joints have been cut, glue the pedestal together, using the clamping blocks described for the grandmother clock on p. 159. Then take the angles for the top and bottom of the pedestal from the drawing and mark them out on the glued-up pedestal. You can use either the bandsaw (with the table tilted) or a handsaw to cut them.

At this point you can easily change the angle of the pedestal if you want. Simply lay the back side of the glued-up pedestal and the sideboard carcase on the floor. Push the top of the pedestal against the bottom of the carcase. Insert wedges under the pedestal until it is at the desired angle and then scribe the angle of the carcase bottom to the top of the pedestal. Mark the bottom of the pedestal at a right angle to the floor. Then cut the top and bottom of the pedestal to these angles (using either the bandsaw or a handsaw). If you plan to adjust the angle of the pedestal like this, make sure to allow plenty of extra height in the pedestal, or the sideboard will be too short when you're done.

Pedestal

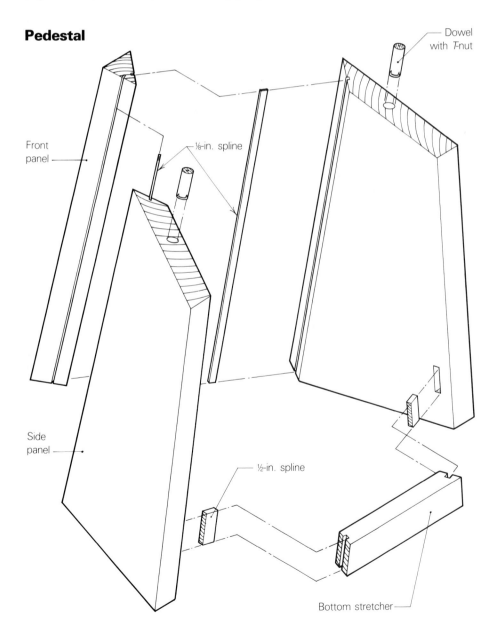

Dowel with T-nut

Front panel

⅛-in. spline

Side panel

½-in. spline

Bottom stretcher

Carcase

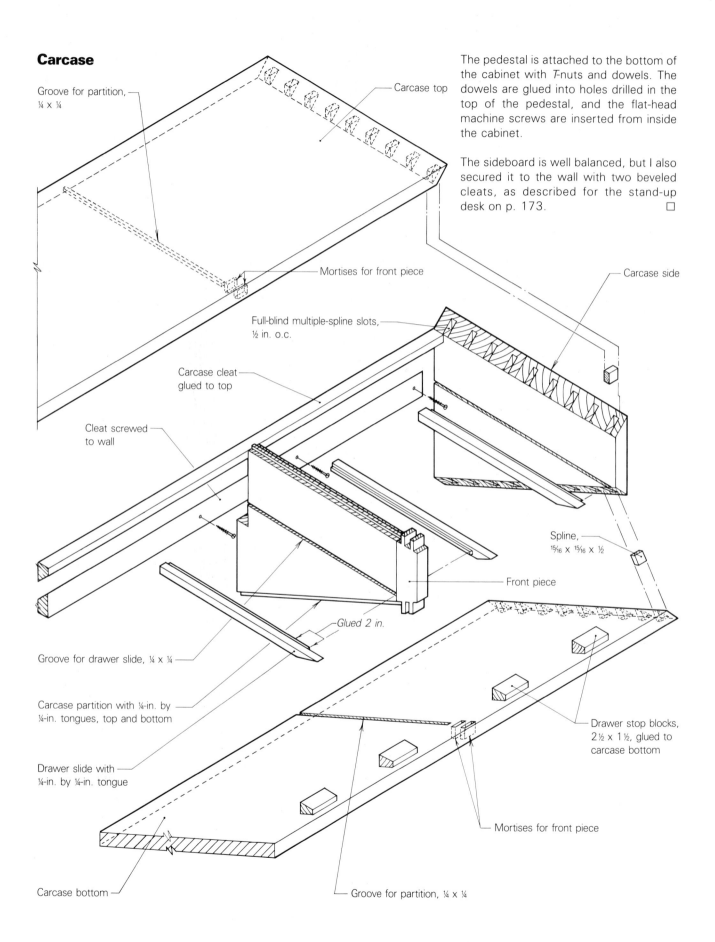

Groove for partition,
¼ x ¼

Carcase top

The pedestal is attached to the bottom of the cabinet with T-nuts and dowels. The dowels are glued into holes drilled in the top of the pedestal, and the flat-head machine screws are inserted from inside the cabinet.

The sideboard is well balanced, but I also secured it to the wall with two beveled cleats, as described for the stand-up desk on p. 173.   □

Mortises for front piece

Carcase side

Full-blind multiple-spline slots,
½ in. o.c.

Carcase cleat
glued to top

Cleat screwed
to wall

Spline,
¹⁵⁄₁₆ X ¹⁵⁄₁₆ X ½

Front piece

Groove for drawer slide, ¼ x ¼

Glued 2 in.

Carcase partition with ¼-in. by
¼-in. tongues, top and bottom

Drawer stop blocks,
2 ½ x 1 ½, glued to
carcase bottom

Drawer slide with
¼-in. by ¼-in. tongue

Mortises for front piece

Carcase bottom

Groove for partition, ¼ x ¼

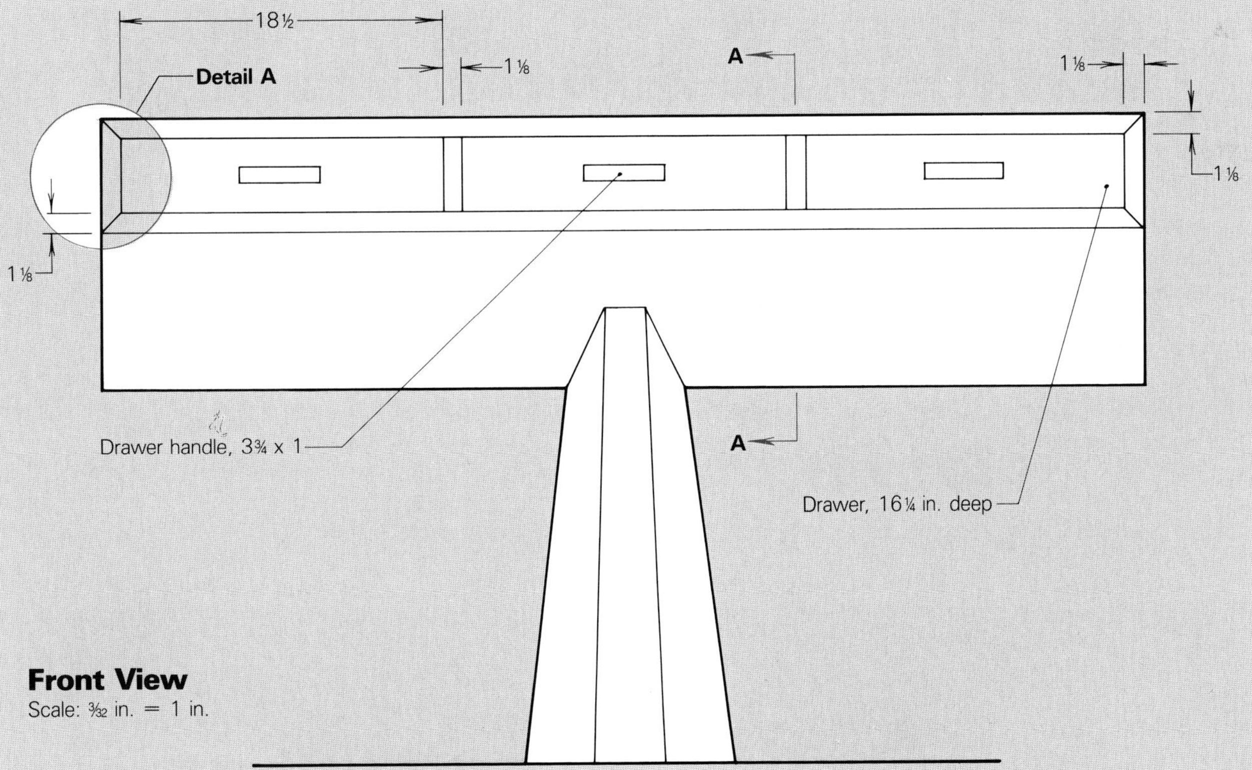
18½
Detail A
1⅛
A
1⅛
1⅛
1⅛
Drawer handle, 3¾ x 1
A
Drawer, 16¼ in. deep

Front View
Scale: 3⁄32 in. = 1 in.

Section A-A
Scale: ⅜ in. = 1 in.

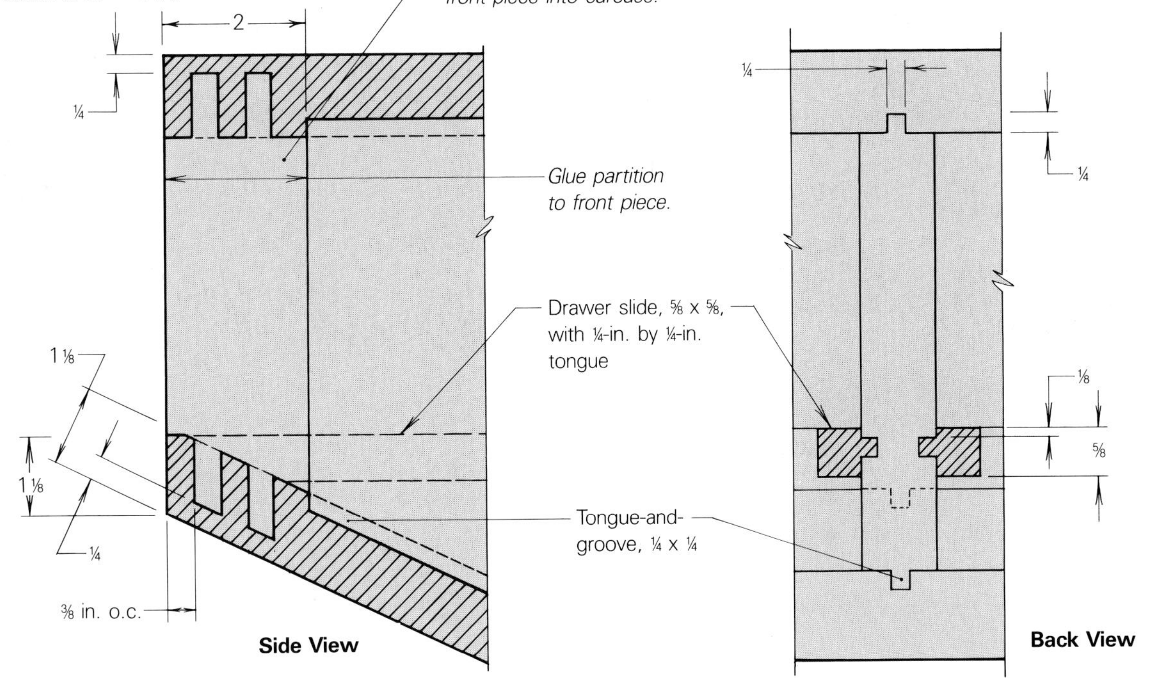
Mortise-and-tenon 2-in.-wide front piece into carcase.
2
¼
Glue partition to front piece.
Drawer slide, ⅝ x ⅝, with ¼-in. by ¼-in. tongue
1⅛
1⅛
¼
⅜ in. o.c.
Tongue-and-groove, ¼ x ¼
¼
¼
⅛
⅝
Side View
Back View

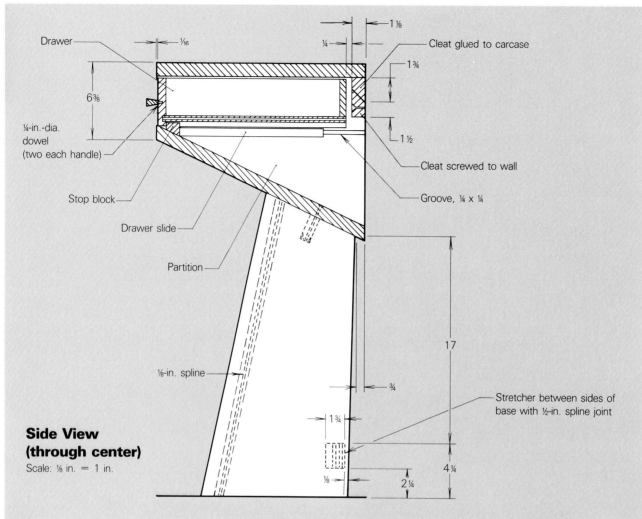

Drawer

1⁄16

1 1⁄8

1⁄4

Cleat glued to carcase

1 3⁄4

6 3⁄8

1⁄4-in.-dia.
dowel
(two each handle)

1 1⁄2

Cleat screwed to wall

Stop block

Drawer slide

Partition

Groove, 1⁄4 x 1⁄4

17

1⁄8-in. spline

3⁄4

**Side View
(through center)**
Scale: 1⁄8 in. = 1 in.

Stretcher between sides of
base with 1⁄2-in. spline joint

1 3⁄4

4 1⁄4

1⁄8

2 1⁄4

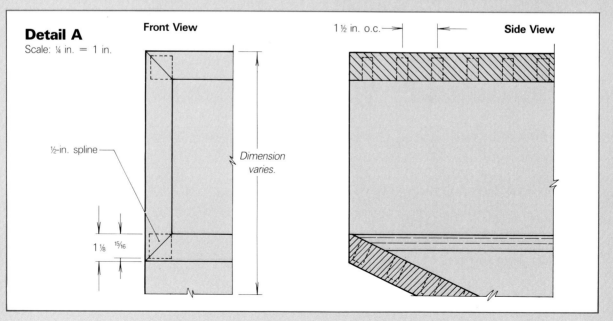

Detail A
Scale: 1⁄4 in. = 1 in.

Front View

1 1⁄2 in. o.c.

Side View

1⁄2-in. spline

*Dimension
varies.*

1 1⁄8   15⁄16

Office and Kitchen

Chapter 7

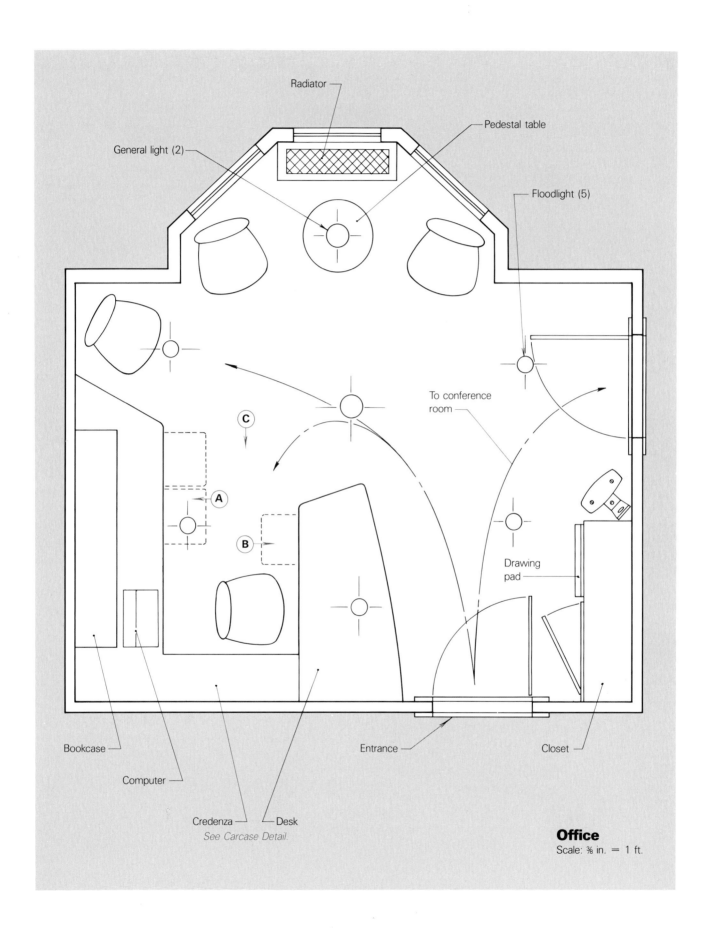

Radiator

Pedestal table

General light (2)

Floodlight (5)

C

A

B

To conference room

Drawing pad

Bookcase

Computer

Entrance

Closet

Credenza — Desk
See Carcase Detail.

Office
Scale: ⅜ in. = 1 ft.

The Office

I designed and made this office furniture for a publisher in Connecticut. The client knew what he wanted. He needed a desk, a bookcase with sliding doors, and a credenza behind him for a computer terminal, which could be easily reached by turning around. He also wanted a couple of file drawers with locks and a few pullout shelves for temporary work surfaces. And he wanted it all made out of American black walnut. One special request was that I try to hide all the wires so the furniture tops didn't look like they had spaghetti on them.

The client also knew where he wanted his desk, and he wanted a separate area with a table and two comfortable occasional chairs on casters. The table only had to be large enough for a phone and for one or two visitors to put coffee cups and papers on because there is a conference room adjacent to the office for larger meetings. I thought a 24-in.-dia. circular pedestal table would satisfy that requirement nicely.

I figured that it would be best to make at least the carcases of the desk, credenza and bookcase out of plywood because it is more economical and easier to work with than solid wood. I decided to use ¾-in. walnut-veneer plywood with a 1-in.-thick solid-walnut top for the desk. For the tops of the credenza and the round table, I sandwiched two thicknesses of plywood (¾-in. and ¼-in.) together to make up the 1-in. thickness.

Since I have already described this kind of plywood carcase construction (see pp. 8-23), I would like to say something here about some of the other aspects of doing a job like this professionally. Here's the way I go about it.

Drawings   For this job, first I did the overall floor plan and placed the furniture so the pathways would be clear, with no sharp corners to bump into. This approach helped in determining the shapes of the individual pieces of furniture, too, especially the desktop. I presented the layout to the client and we further discussed the function of the room, deciding where to put the pullout shelves and other details.

I then did the final drawings to scale with front, side and top views, including all details and lighting specifications.

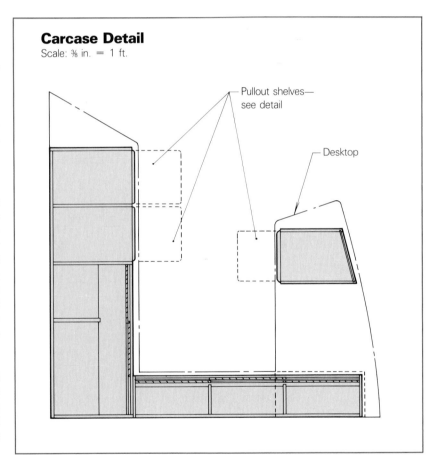

Carcase Detail
Scale: ⅜ in. = 1 ft.

Pullout shelves—
see detail

Desktop

Elevation A   Scale: ½ in. = 1 ft.

Elevation B   Scale: ½ in. = 1 ft.

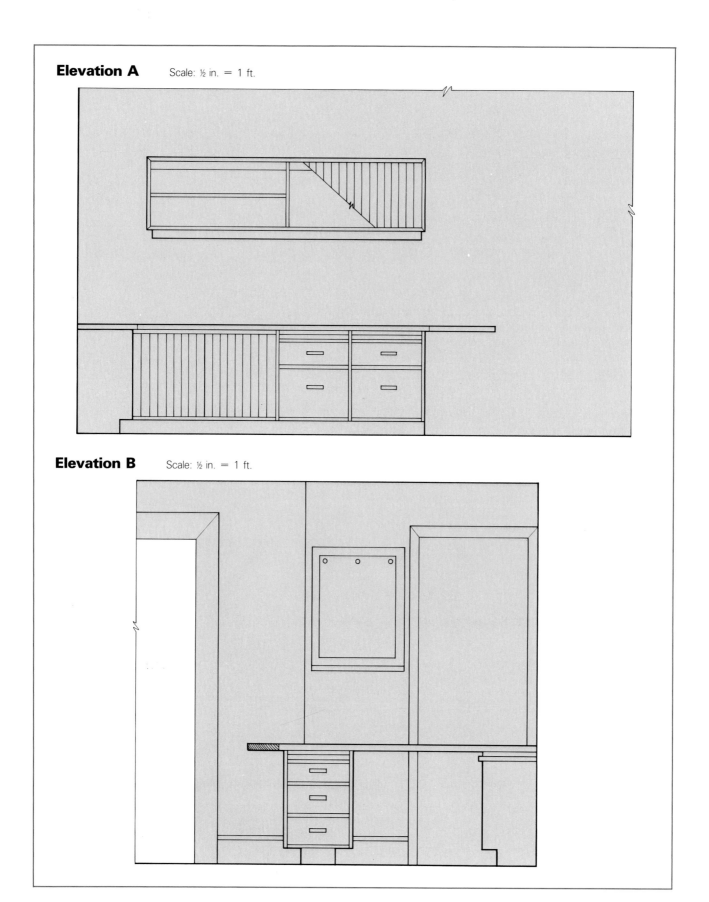

Elevation C   Scale: ½ in. = 1 ft.

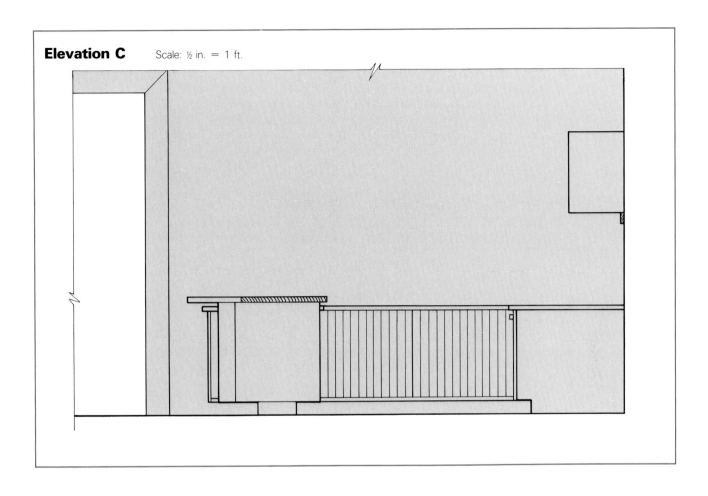

Along with the final drawings, I presented the specifications to the customer for both of us to sign. These spell out the quality of the material, joinery, hardware, finishing, etc., and the payment schedule. Whether I'm making a single piece of furniture or an entire office, I always ask for one-third of the total cost as a down payment, another third when the pieces are ready to be finished, and the final third when everything is delivered and installed.

Sometimes I work with an architect and a client before a house is built. The architect designs the house, then I get the plans and design all the built-ins. I present these to the architect and the client for their approval. Because the house is not yet built, such things as walls, stairs and doors can still be moved, if necessary, to accommodate the furnishings. Once everyone agrees on the design, I lay out all the built-ins on two sets of sticks, one for the contractor and one for myself. When they break ground, I start building the furniture.

In this case, however, the office was already built. When I make furniture that has to fit exactly into an existing space, I also use the stick method to obtain accurate measurements. I still make drawings to work out the design and to show to the customer, but I take all my cutting measurements from the marks on the sticks. Here's how to lay out a roomful of furniture on sticks.

Laying out on sticks I use two 1-in. by 1-in. sticks, each one at least a foot longer than half the length of the longest wall. For this office, the only critical dimension was the distance between the door and the side wall on elevation B, which is about 10 ft., so I used two 6-ft. sticks. Push the sticks between the side walls (or, in this case, between the wall and the door frame) and check to see if the distances are the same top, bottom and center **(1)**. Take note of any discrepancies, and either work from the shortest distance or make allowances in the cabinets' construction so they can be scribed to an exact fit when they are installed. Then screw the sticks together carefully so they can be taken apart and reassembled the same way. I also mark all the electrical and/or plumbing outlets and the extreme dimensions of all doors and windows on the sticks. Don't forget to do the same for the floor-to-ceiling measurements, too **(2)**. I'll put these vertical measurements on another face of the same sticks if the job isn't too big. This process should be repeated on every wall that will receive cabinets.

When I get back to the shop, I reassemble the sticks and transfer all the measurements to a permanent stick the full length of each wall. (These sticks can be made up of smaller boards glued and screwed together.)

On the permanent sticks, I lay out all the parts of the cabinets in full scale. From these marks, I make all the cutting lists and take all exact measurements. This is the safest way to do it. The sticks allow me to translate the scaled drawing into exact full-scale measurements, so there is less room for error.

I learned the hard way to do it right and use the stick method. I used to have a good friend for a partner and we had eight people working for us. One day when I was on my way out to a customer's house to measure for two cabinets that had to fit between a wall and a door jamb, I realized that I'd forgotten my 12-ft. ruler, so I popped back in the door and one of the journeymen lent me his. When I got to the site and took the measurements for the cabinets, I didn't realize that the ruler I had borrowed was only 10 ft. long. Thinking I had measured 12 ft. plus 4 ft., we made the cabinets 16 ft. long. The right length, of course, was 14 ft. You can imagine how I felt when we delivered the cabinets several weeks later and found that they were sticking out 2 ft. beyond the door jamb, almost completely blocking the doorway!

1

2

Cutting List for Desk

Quantity	Description	Finished sizes	Lumber
1	Side 1	¾ x 24 x 24½	Walnut plywood
1	Side 2	¾ x 20½ x 24½	
1	Bottom	¾ x 24 x 17	
1	Back stretcher	¾ x 8 x 17	
1	Pullout	¾ x 20 x 14½	
1	Back	¼ x 17¾ x 23½	
3	Drawer bottom	¼ x 19½ x 15⅜	Oak plywood
4	Front stretcher	¾ x 2 x 17	Solid walnut
1	Drawer front 1	¾ x 8 x 16½	
1	Drawer front 2	¾ x 7 x 16½	
1	Drawer front 3	¾ x 4⅞ x 16½	
1	Top	1⅝	
2	Drawer side 1	⅜ x 8 x 19	Solid oak
2	Drawer side 2	⅜ x 7 x 19	
2	Drawer side 3	⅜ x 4⅞ x 19	
1	Drawer back 1	⅜ x 7¼ x 16½	
1	Drawer back 2	⅜ x 6¼ x 16½	
1	Drawer back 3	⅜ x 4⅛ x 16½	

Note: *Finished sizes are expressed in thickness x width x length.*
Sides 1 and 2 and bottom have ¼-in. front facings and ½-in. back facings (glue on back bottom facing after angle is cut). Back stretcher has a ¼-in. back facing, and pullout has a 1-in. facing on both sides and in front.

The cutting list Once I have all the parts drawn out on the permanent sticks, I'm ready to make the cutting lists. The cutting list for the desk is shown at left.

Because the desktop and the back of the desk cabinet are angled, I made a full-scale top-view drawing of the desk car-case on plywood to find the exact measurements of all the pieces **(3)**. You can take the measurements for the plywood bottom and the stretchers directly from the sticks. To allow for the two ¼-in. by ¼-in. tongues on both ends of the bottom and stretchers, measure the distance between the carcase sides and add ½ in. That gives these pieces an overall length of 17 in., including the two ¼-in. tongues.

In **(3)** I am taking the exact length of the drawer front by measuring between the two inside lines of the carcase sides, which are 16½ in. apart. After this top-view layout has been made on the plywood, it's easy to find the length of the plywood back of the carcase, which is 17¾ in. in this case.

3

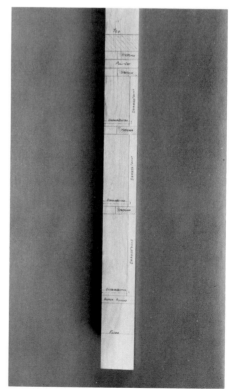

4

This stick **(4)** shows the vertical layout for the front of the desk. Here's how to get the measurements of the width of the drawer fronts and sides for the cutting list **(5)**. The drawers are trimmed and fit to the desk carcase following the same process as for the drawing table on pp. 12-15. Remember to add ¼ in. to the width and 1 in. to the length when roughing out the solid-wood stock.

After the cutting lists were made for each piece, I figured out how best to cut the plywood pieces out of 48-in. by 96-in. sheets of veneer-core plywood. I made scale drawings of all the pieces and found that I needed six sheets of ¾-in. walnut *A-1*, one sheet of ¼-in. walnut *A-1*, one sheet of ¼-in. oak *A-2* and one sheet of ½-in. oak *A-A* [see *Book 2*, p. 116, for a description of plywood grades].

The drawing below shows the layout for two sheets of ¾-in. walnut. The code is as follows: A, B and C refer to the eleva-tion drawings and D refers to the desk. BO means bottom, S side, T top, SH shelf, K kickboard, DRF drawer front and P pullout shelf. It might seem a little confusing at first, but when you get used to such a system, it's very efficient.

With this done, I was able to buy all the materials and cut them up right away with very little waste of time and materials. I labeled each piece so it wouldn't get lost or mixed up.

5

Plywood Layout

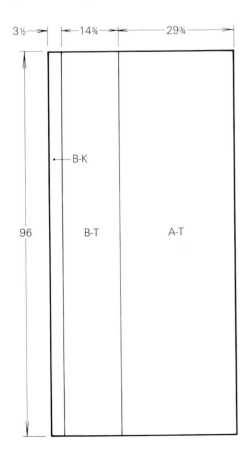

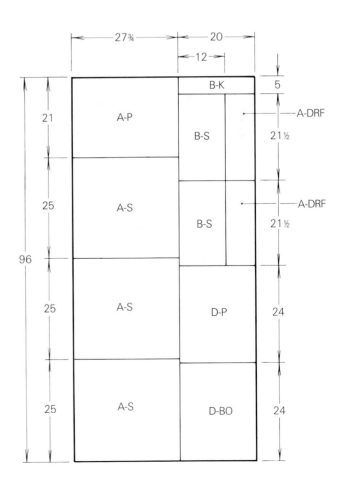

Carcase Joinery

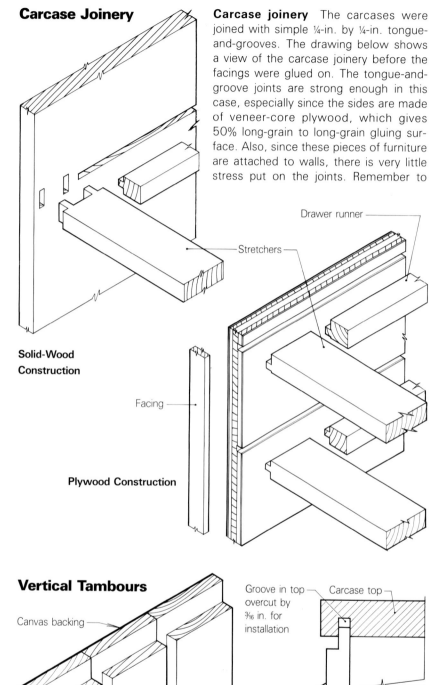

Solid-Wood Construction

Plywood Construction

Facing

Drawer runner

Stretchers

Vertical Tambours

Canvas backing

Groove in top overcut by ³⁄₁₆ in. for installation

Carcase top

Door face

Door face

⁷⁄₁₆-in. rabbet, top and bottom

Carcase bottom

Section

Carcase joinery The carcases were joined with simple ¼-in. by ¼-in. tongue-and-grooves. The drawing below shows a view of the carcase joinery before the facings were glued on. The tongue-and-groove joints are strong enough in this case, especially since the sides are made of veneer-core plywood, which gives 50% long-grain to long-grain gluing surface. Also, since these pieces of furniture are attached to walls, there is very little stress put on the joints. Remember to offset the tongues near the ends of the carcase to avoid splitting out the plywood. The grooves are made before the facings are attached and are run the whole way across. The grooves behind the stretchers are used to attach the drawer runners.

The same system can be used in solid wood, with a couple of exceptions. The stretchers must have two tenons to resist twisting, and only the first 2 in. or so of the runners should be glued in to allow the solid-wood sides to move (see p. 11).

Tambour sliders The doors on the bookcase and credenza are vertical-tambour sliders. If you make sliding doors about 30 in. wide out of ¾-in. plywood, they will eventually warp and become hard to open because of the difference in relative humidity inside and outside the cabinet when the doors are closed. Making tambour sliders eliminates that problem, because the tambours, or slats, make the whole door flexible. Visually, another advantage to using tambours is that they give the doors a three-dimensional feeling.

The procedures for making and installing these doors are very similar to those used for the kitchen cabinets, which are described in detail on pp. 212-221.

Mill all the slats to their final dimensions. I didn't want any handles on these doors, so I cut a ¼-in. by ¼-in. rabbet on one edge of each 1½-in.-wide by ½-in.-thick slat for a small finger groove. Handles would interfere with the sliding, and the groove allows you to grab the doors at any point. After cutting the rabbet on one long edge of each slat, glue the slats to the canvas. The tambours are also rabbeted to ride in grooves top and bottom, and in both sides of the carcase, but these rabbets should be cut after the doors are glued up.

Cut all the grooves in the carcase before assembly using a dado head on a table-saw or a router. Here, the doors just overlap each other and do not disappear into the sides of the carcase, so it was not necessary to build double sides for the cabinet to hide them, as is common with tambour-door construction.

Pullout shelves The pullout shelves in the desk and credenza slide between runners exactly like drawers. The space between the two top stretchers is ⅞ in. The ¹³⁄₁₆-in.-thick strips on the sides and front of the ¾-in. plywood shelves are flush on the top, but stick out ¹⁄₁₆ in. below. I glued a piece of veneer, a little less than ¹⁄₁₆ in. thick, in each back corner on the top side of the shelves to protect the surface. A strip of felt glued on the bottom of the front stretcher above the shelf prevents scratching.

The fronts of the pullout shelves stick out 1 in. beyond the front of the cabinet. I routed a groove underneath so that fingers can easily catch it to pull out the shelf **(6)**.

6

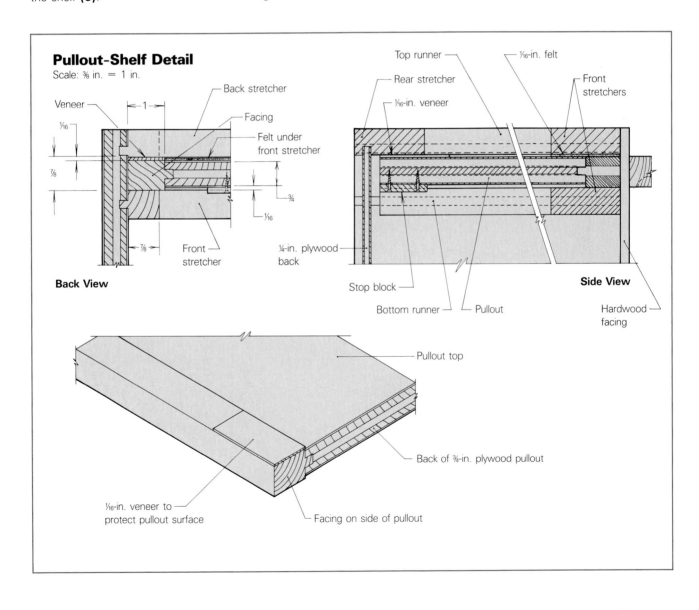

Pullout-Shelf Detail
Scale: ⅜ in. = 1 in.

Veneer

Back stretcher

Facing

Felt under front stretcher

Front stretcher

⅞

Top runner

Rear stretcher

¹⁄₁₆-in. veneer

¹⁄₁₆-in. felt

Front stretchers

¼-in. plywood back

Stop block

Bottom runner — Pullout

Hardwood facing

Back View

Side View

Pullout top

¹⁄₁₆-in. veneer to protect pullout surface

Facing on side of pullout

Back of ¾-in. plywood pullout

7

Round-Table Pedestal

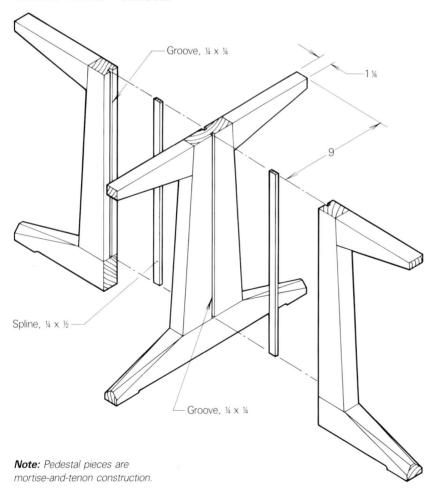

Groove, ¼ x ¼

1 ¼

9

Spline, ¼ x ½

Groove, ¼ x ¼

Note: *Pedestal pieces are mortise-and-tenon construction.*

Finishing up   Here are a couple of additional tips on doing this job.

Because of the size of the credenza top, I could not make the angled cut on the end using the miter gauge. Instead, I made a fence that ran along the edge of the saw table. First I measured the distance from the sawblade to the edge of the table. In this case it was 18 in., but you will have to check your own. Then I clamped a straightedge to the bottom of the top at the desired angle but 18 in. away from the actual cut. I pushed the piece across the saw, keeping the straightedge firmly against the edge of the saw table **(7)**.

To assemble the little round table, I mortise-and-tenoned the separate pedestal pieces together. In the middle of the center piece, I made a ¼-in. by ¼-in. groove on each side and a corresponding groove on the edges of the other pieces. Then I splined and glued the three sections together to make one solid pedestal.

(8) Here's how the office looked when it was completed.

The distance between the desk and the credenza is 48 in., the minimum required for turning around **(9)**. Under the computer terminal are two doors in the credenza that slide to the left and out of the way, to give the maximum amount of knee room when working at the terminal. On the right side of this knee space is another pullout shelf for holding paper **(10)**.

At the end of the credenza the tabletop is angled and overhangs to give the person working there as much knee room as possible **(11)**. There's another pullout shelf there, too.   □

8

10

9

11

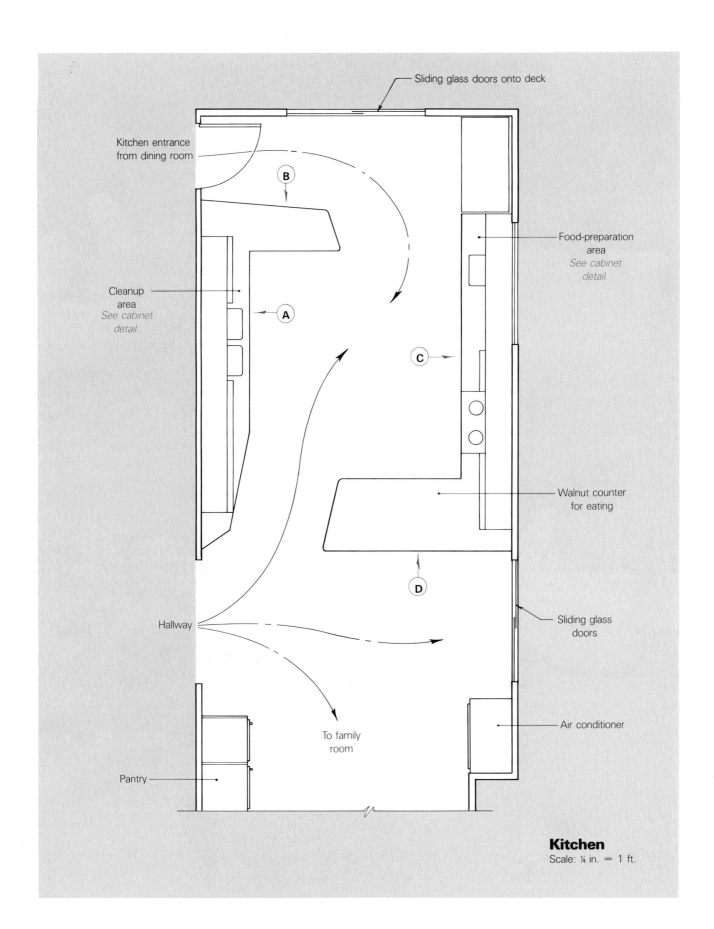

Sliding glass doors onto deck

Kitchen entrance
from dining room

B

Food-preparation
area
*See cabinet
detail.*

Cleanup
area
*See cabinet
detail.*

A

C

Walnut counter
for eating

D

Hallway

Sliding glass
doors

To family
room

Air conditioner

Pantry

Kitchen
Scale: ¼ in. = 1 ft.

The Kitchen

The kitchen is a very important room in any house. It should have a pleasant, warm atmosphere, because the person who does the cooking spends many hours there. Plus, many people take most of their meals in the kitchen, or in an area connected to it. And whenever there is a party, it seems that everybody ends up in the kitchen.

Whenever you design and plan a room, especially a busy kitchen, first lay out the traffic patterns, which are defined by the work areas in the room. As you consider the flow through the kitchen, keep in mind that the entrance should be inviting and not look like a hallway, or be so narrow that it causes a traffic jam. At the same time, be aware of lighting—both natural and artificial. In addition to general room lighting, it is a good idea to have lights over each work area.

The cabinets should be functional, and everything should be organized to save the person(s) working there as many steps as possible. The refrigerator, sink and stove should be close together, and there should be plenty of work space. It is a good idea to separate the food-preparation area from the cleanup area if you have the space. If more than one person will be regularly working in the kitchen at the same time, the room should be laid out so they are not in each other's way. When all of these things have been established, make the detailed top-view, or plan, drawing and then do the side-view elevations.

(1) This is the food-preparation area for a kitchen I designed recently for a family in Connecticut. All of the kitchen was made and installed by Hank Gilpin, except for the upper tambour cabinets, which were made in my own shop (see pp. 212-221).

1

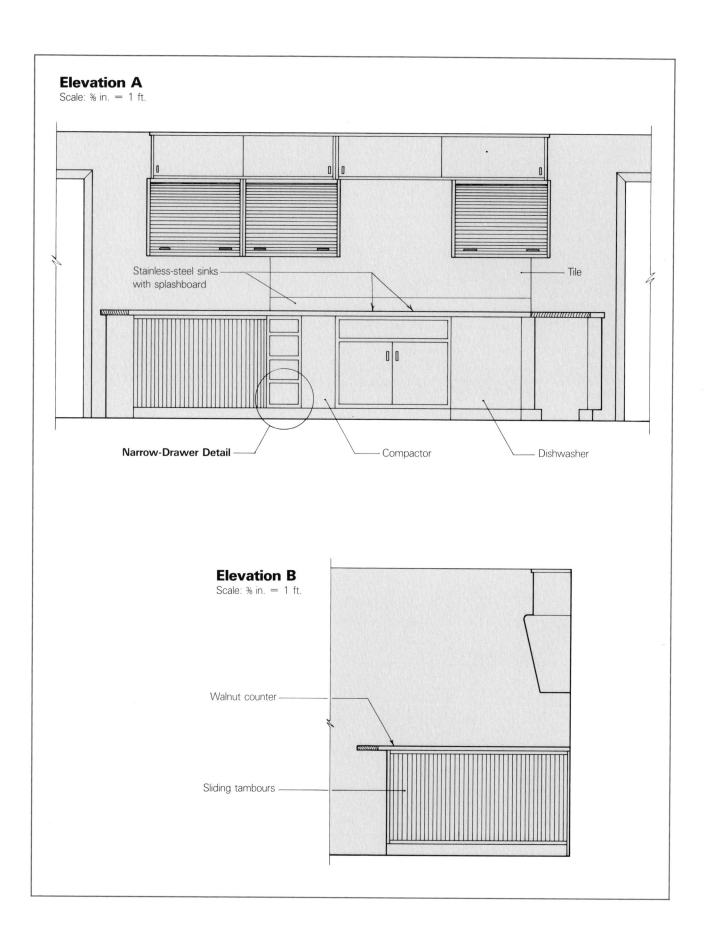

Elevation A
Scale: ⅜ in. = 1 ft.

Stainless-steel sinks
with splashboard

Tile

Narrow-Drawer Detail ⎯ Compactor ⎯ Dishwasher

Elevation B
Scale: ⅜ in. = 1 ft.

Walnut counter

Sliding tambours

Cabinet Detail
Scale: ⅛ in. = 1 ft.

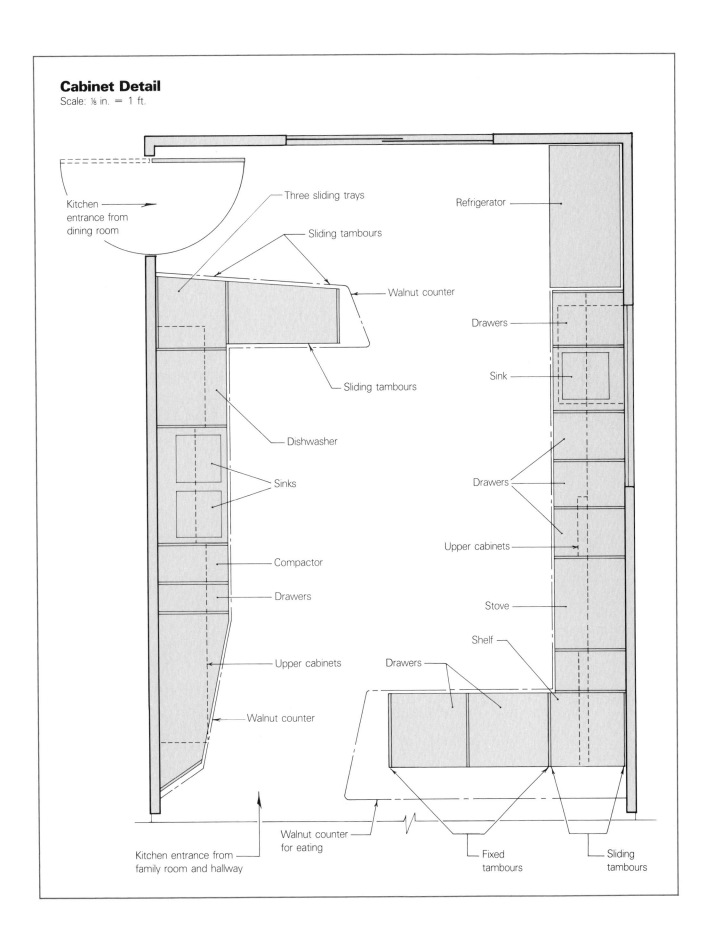

Kitchen entrance from dining room

Three sliding trays

Sliding tambours

Walnut counter

Sliding tambours

Dishwasher

Sinks

Compactor

Drawers

Upper cabinets

Walnut counter

Kitchen entrance from family room and hallway

Walnut counter for eating

Refrigerator

Drawers

Sink

Drawers

Upper cabinets

Stove

Shelf

Drawers

Fixed tambours

Sliding tambours

Elevation C
Scale: ⅜ in. = 1 ft.

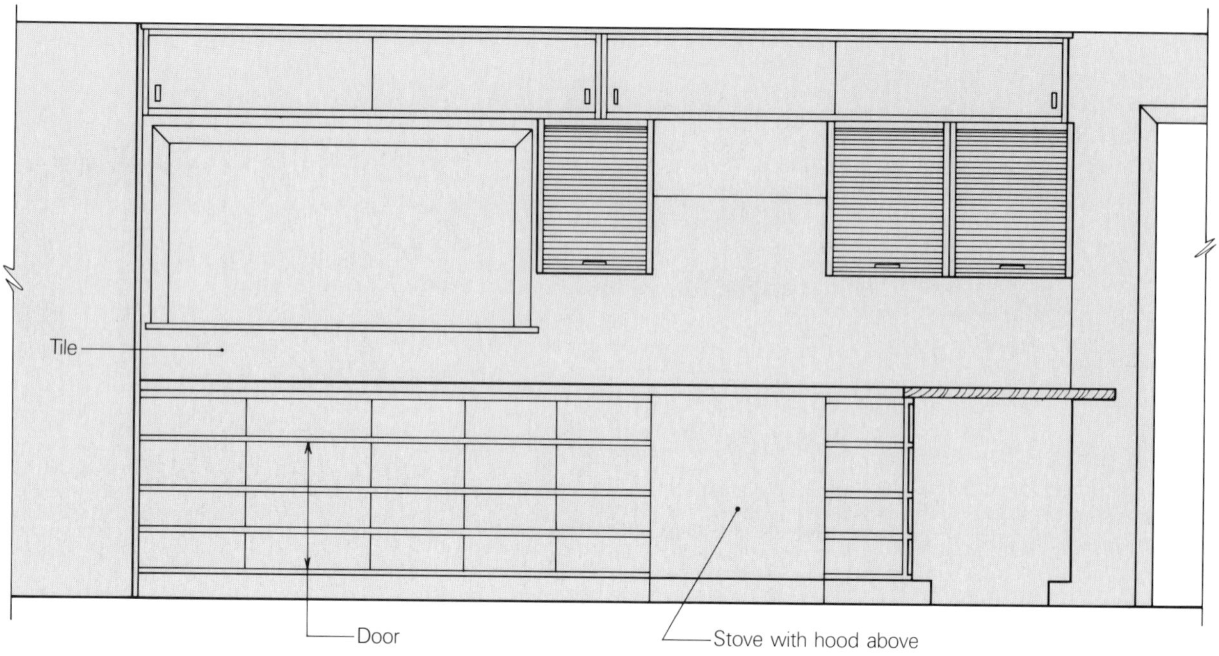

Tile

Door

Stove with hood above

Elevation D
Scale: ⅜ in. = 1 ft.

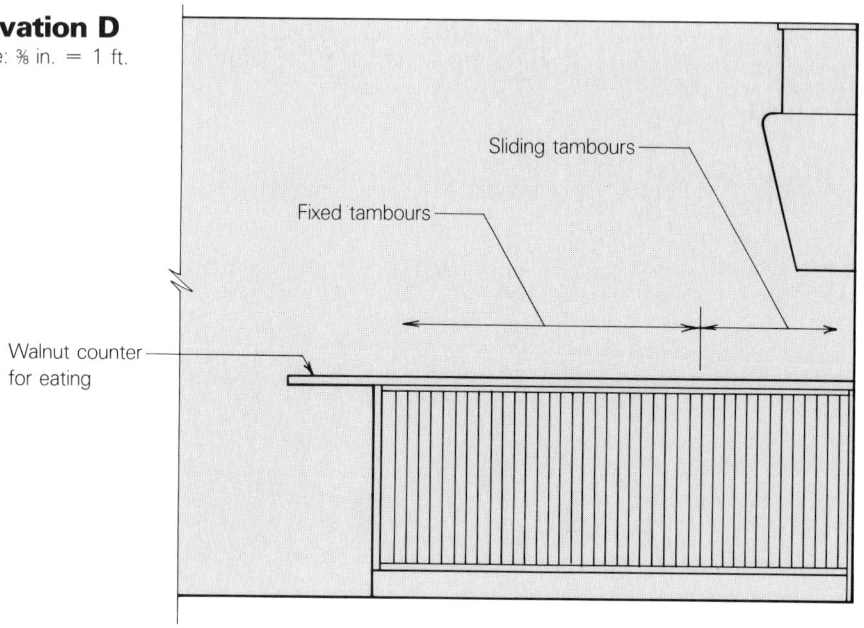

Sliding tambours

Fixed tambours

Walnut counter
for eating

Before the room was finished, the cabinets were laid out on sticks (see pp. 192-193), with one set for Hank and one set for the carpenter, and everything worked out perfectly. Usually this layout is done when the house is just framed; sometimes it is done before the house is even built. But it is especially important that the kitchen be laid out early because of all the crucial plumbing and electrical connections and the critical placement of the windows.

The kitchen cabinets and the cabinets in an adjacent family room area are made out of cherry-veneered plywood and have an oil finish. The countertop and wall in the cooking area are covered with tile, and the single stainless-steel sink is set flush with the tile. Across the room, the back wall in the cleanup area is also tiled. The double stainless-steel sink there is the full width of the countertop and has a stainless-steel splashboard.

Most kitchens are designed with 24-in.-deep lower cabinets that have drawers on the top and doors and shelves on the bottom. Nothing is more frustrating than trying to find something in the back of a deep cabinet. First you have to get down on your knees, remove everything from the front, get out whatever you need, then put everything back. And to put the object away when you are finished, you have to do the same thing all over again. I prefer to have drawers in the lower cabinets and to use drawer runners that extend the full depth of the cabinet so it is easy to reach the things in the back. The hardware and labor involved in making the drawers are more costly than for doors and shelves, but considering the hours spent in the kitchen, I think it is worth it in most cases. The clients for this job agreed, and one of their specifications was to include as many drawers as possible on fully extendable metal slides.

In designing these cabinets, I did not want them to be the same style throughout the kitchen and family room. For visual interest, I wanted the view to be different from various perspectives.

For example, when you enter the kitchen from the hallway or the family area, the view is dominated by the vertical and horizontal tambours **(1)**. If you enter from the dining room, the horizontal lines of the drawer fronts draw your attention **(2)**.

2

3

The drawers are designed so they can be different depths. For example, the drawer for the trays and baking pans has all four drawer fronts attached to make the maximum depth **(3)**. There are single and double drawers, too **(4)**, which are detailed in the drawing on the facing page. And three of the drawer fronts under the single sink are actually fake—they're attached to a door.

I don't like to put attached handles on drawers or cabinets if I can avoid it—they stick out, both physically and visually. So instead, there are finger grips routed in the bottoms of the two upper drawer fronts and on the tops of the two lower drawer fronts.

4

Narrow-Drawer Detail

Scale: ½ in. = 1 in.

Note: *Unless otherwise indicated, drawer construction is similar.*

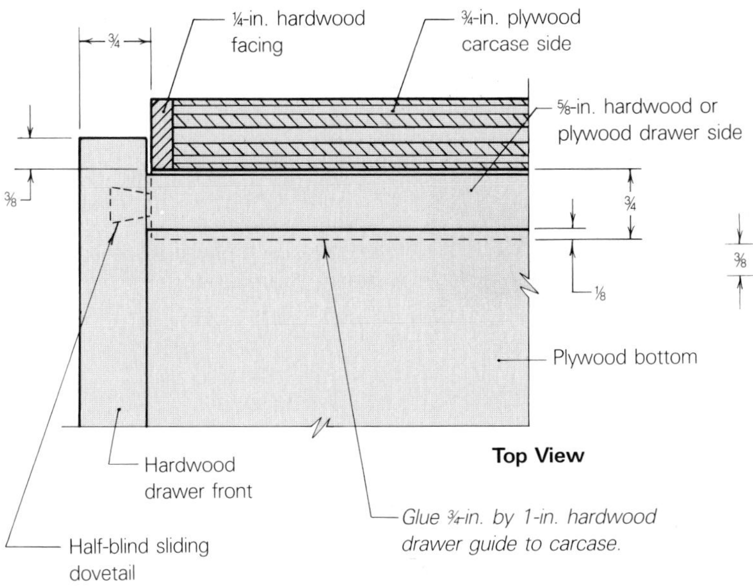
¾
¼-in. hardwood facing
¾-in. plywood carcase side
⅝-in. hardwood or plywood drawer side
⅜
¾
⅛
Plywood bottom
Hardwood drawer front
Half-blind sliding dovetail
Glue ¾-in. by 1-in. hardwood drawer guide to carcase.

Top View

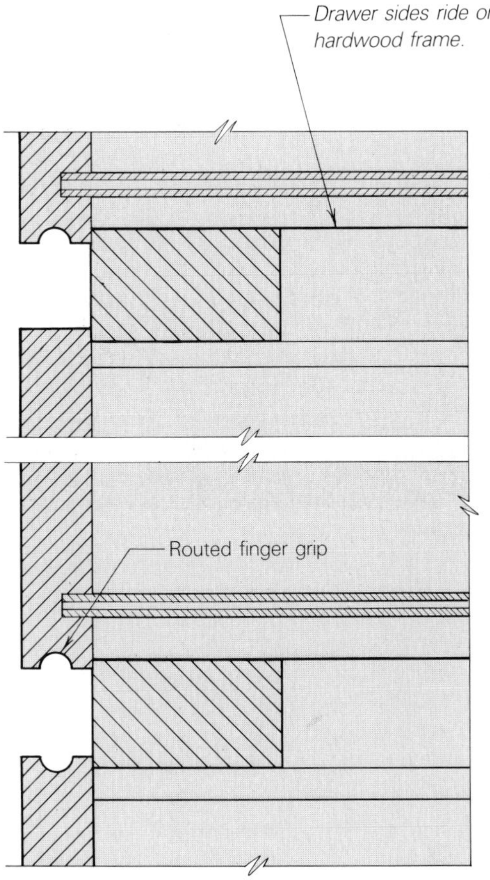
Drawer sides ride on hardwood frame.
Routed finger grip

Side View

Single-Drawer Detail

Scale: ½ in. = 1 in.

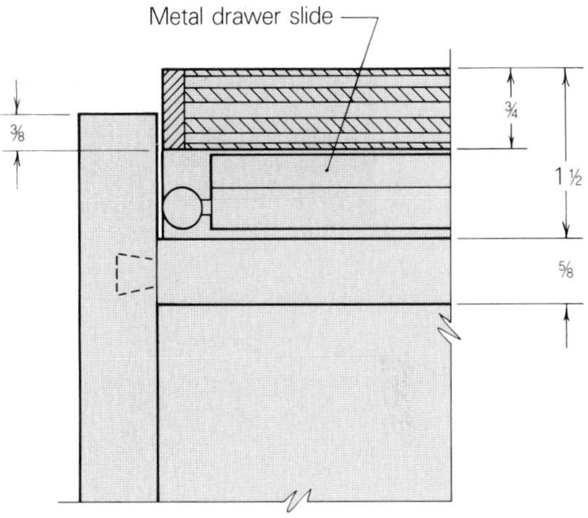
Metal drawer slide
⅜
¾
1½
⅝

Top View

Double-Drawer Detail

Scale: ½ in. = 1 in.

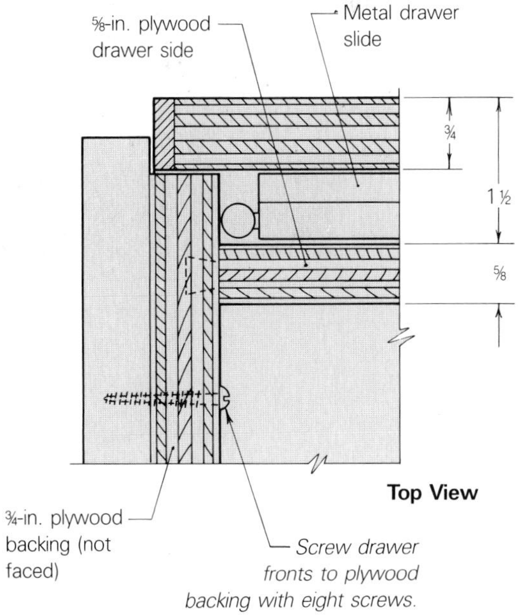
⅝-in. plywood drawer side
Metal drawer slide
¾
1½
⅝
¾-in. plywood backing (not faced)
Screw drawer fronts to plywood backing with eight screws.

Top View

The family wanted a countertop where they could both prepare food and eat, so I decided to use 1⅝-in.-thick solid walnut, which can withstand heavy use. When you make a countertop for eating that has cabinets below, remember that the top has to overhang the cabinets by at least 9 in. for adequate knee room. Here, the end of the countertop is cut at an angle to enhance the traffic flow. The fronts of the cabinets below the countertops in elevations B and C are also angled to make it more inviting to enter the kitchen. (The countertop in elevation B is also 1⅝-in. walnut.)

The cabinet to the right of the dishwasher is for storing dishes after they've been washed **(5)**. It has sliding tambour doors on both sides so that it can be loaded from one side and emptied from the other. On the right side of the cabinet, behind the tambour doors, are three sliding trays. The door behind this area leads to the dining room.

Normally I try to avoid having cabinets go up to the ceiling, because that makes a kitchen look smaller. I like to keep the cabinets about 12 in. below the ceiling so the whole ceiling is visible. Also, the space above is a nice place to display ceramic, wood and copper utensils, which make the kitchen look warm and livable. However, the clients wanted cabinets going all the way to the ceiling for storing dishes not often used, and this kitchen was large enough to handle it.

5

I did not want the upper cabinets to look too tall or bulky, though, so I added a second set on top of the tambour ones. These upper cabinets are 15 in. high and 12 in. deep and have sliding doors. They also provide a convenient place to install lights over the work areas and the fan over the stove. The tambour cabinets are narrower at the bottom than at the top to allow more head room for people working at the counters. Plus, plates and glasses are all different sizes, so the smaller ones can be put in the bottom of the cabinets and the larger ones on top.

Family room Looking at the family room from the kitchen, the top part of the closet on the left next to the sliding glass door is for the air conditioner **(6)**. In the center of the room are two chairs: one for the cat and one for the youngest son to watch T.V. The back end of the room has long windows with a beautiful view of the yard. In front of the windows are a table and chairs for working and eating. The pantry cabinet closest to the kitchen has sliding trays for canned goods and the other three cabinets have adjustable shelves.

6

Family Room
Scale: ¼ in. = 1 ft.

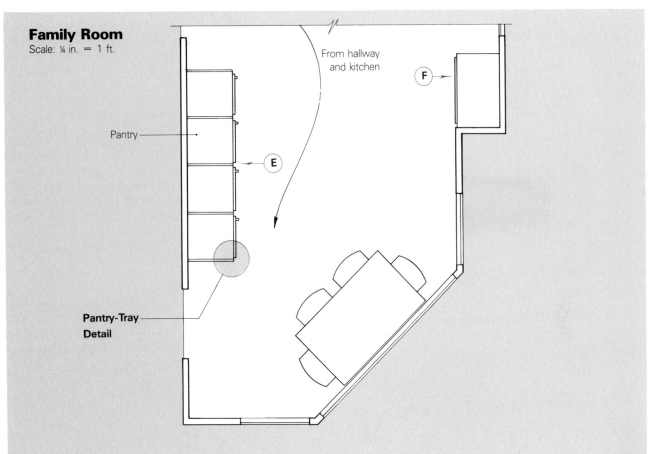

From hallway
and kitchen

F

E

Pantry

Pantry-Tray Detail

Elevation E
Scale: ⅜ in. = 1 ft.

Elevation F
Scale: ⅜ in. = 1 ft.

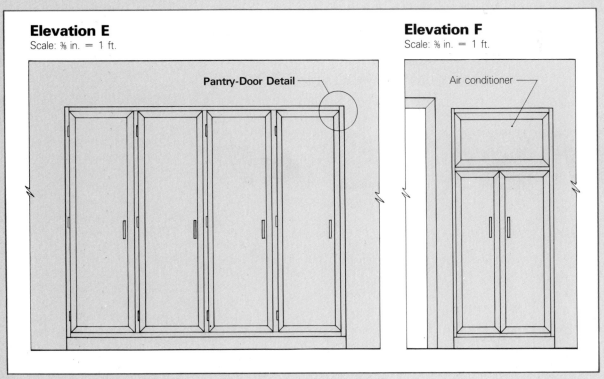

Pantry-Door Detail

Air conditioner

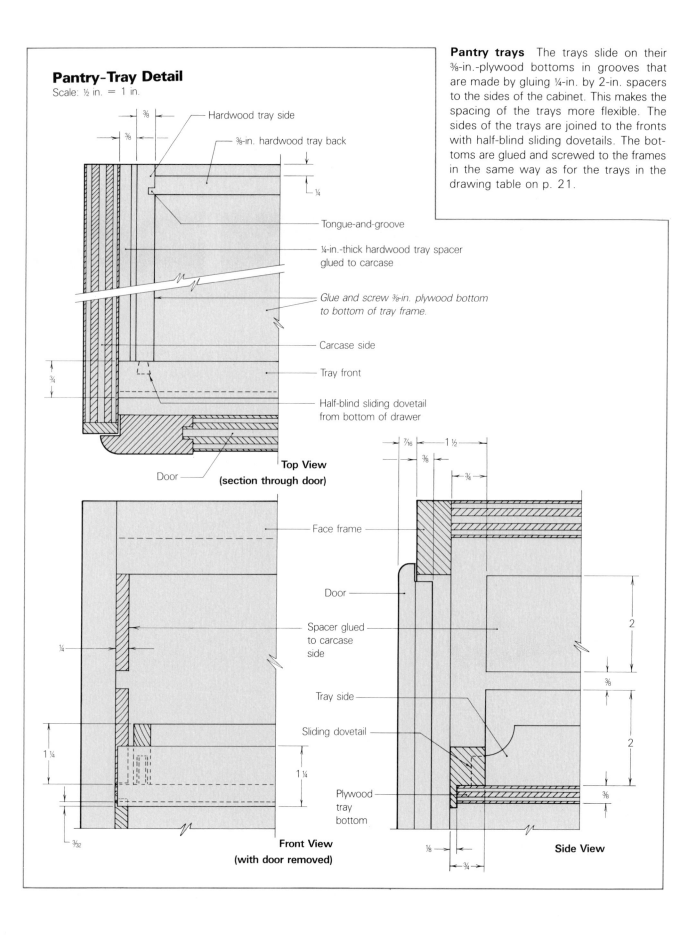

Pantry-Tray Detail
Scale: ½ in. = 1 in.

Pantry trays The trays slide on their ⅜-in.-plywood bottoms in grooves that are made by gluing ¼-in. by 2-in. spacers to the sides of the cabinet. This makes the spacing of the trays more flexible. The sides of the trays are joined to the fronts with half-blind sliding dovetails. The bottoms are glued and screwed to the frames in the same way as for the trays in the drawing table on p. 21.

⅜

⅜

Hardwood tray side

⅜-in. hardwood tray back

¼

Tongue-and-groove

¼-in.-thick hardwood tray spacer glued to carcase

Glue and screw ⅜-in. plywood bottom to bottom of tray frame.

Carcase side

Tray front

¾

Half-blind sliding dovetail from bottom of drawer

Door

Top View
(section through door)

Face frame

Door

Spacer glued to carcase side

¼

Tray side

Sliding dovetail

1 ¼

1 ¼

Plywood tray bottom

³⁄₃₂

Front View
(with door removed)

⁷⁄₁₆

1 ½

⅜

¾

2

⅜

2

⅜

⅛

¾

Side View

Pantry doors The pantry doors are made out of ¾-in.-thick plywood, tongue-and-grooved into mitered frames. The frames are flush with the plywood panels in the back, but are raised ¹⁄₁₆ in. in the front. The door frames have a ³⁄₈-in. by ³⁄₈-in. (depending on the hardware) rabbeted lip running around the edge so they overlap the face frames when the doors are closed.

(7) This photo shows the hinges used. It is very difficult to find good hinges for lipped doors. The hinges used here are from Denmark and are well made (of course), and they are available in the United States. They are a little more difficult to install than ordinary flat hinges, because they have to be inlaid into both the carcase and the door, but it is worth it: The hinges fit the rabbet with very little of the hinge exposed when the doors are closed **(8)**. In addition, the hinges separate, allowing the doors to be lifted right off. □

7

8

9

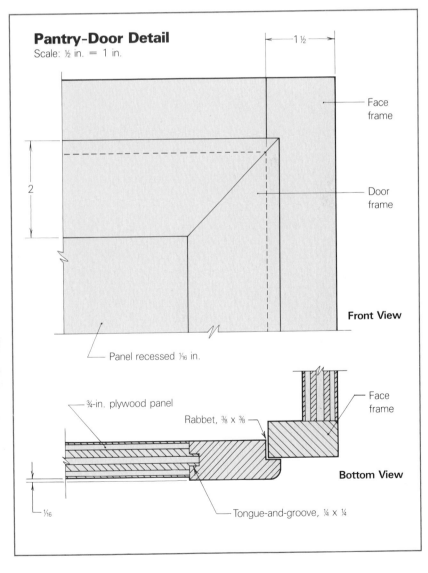

Pantry-Door Detail
Scale: ½ in. = 1 in.

1 ½

2

Face frame

Door frame

Panel recessed ¹⁄₁₆ in.

Front View

¾-in. plywood panel

Rabbet, ³⁄₈ x ³⁄₈

Face frame

¹⁄₁₆

Tongue-and-groove, ¼ x ¼

Bottom View

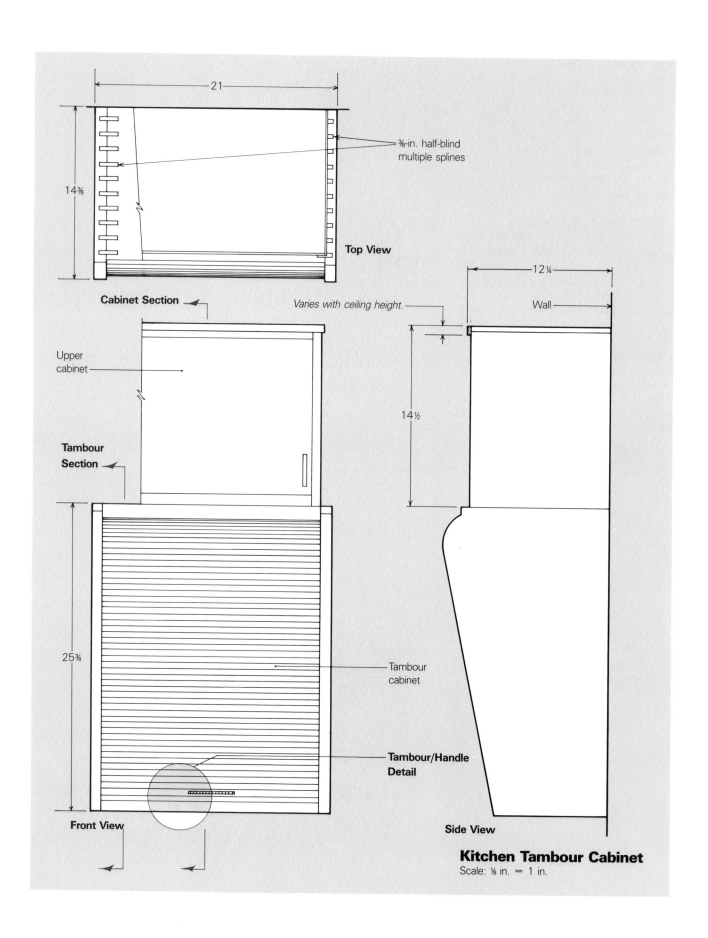

⅜-in. half-blind
multiple splines

14⅜

Top View

Cabinet Section

Varies with ceiling height.

12¼

Wall

Upper
cabinet

**Tambour
Section**

14½

25¾

Tambour
cabinet

**Tambour/Handle
Detail**

Front View

Side View

Kitchen Tambour Cabinet
Scale: ⅛ in. = 1 in.

Tambour Doors

The trickiest construction detail in the office (p. 188) and kitchen (p. 200) is the tambour doors. Tambours are really not difficult to make, but things get more complicated because the cabinet often requires double sides or a double top (depending on whether the doors are vertical or horizontal) and, in some cases, a double back.

The office tambours are simple vertical sliding doors that do not disappear into the cabinet, so they do not require double-wall construction. The wall-mounted kitchen cabinets require a double top, but only a single inside back because the cabinets won't be seen from behind. In this section I will focus mainly on the kitchen tambours **(1)**, which are somewhat more complicated to make than the office doors. The great advantage of these tambour doors is that when opened they disappear, and, because of their flexibility, they can fit almost any shape cabinet you want.

Making the tambours   There are different ways to make tambours, depending on the size, shape and function of the doors. The ones I did for the kitchen are made of ½-in.-wide by ⅜-in.-thick slats, which is a common size for tambour doors. Usually the edges of the slats are beveled so they form a V-joint when the slats are together. That way, if a slat is not perfectly flush, it won't be noticeable. Plus, with the edges removed, the tambours can turn a smaller radius—in this case, 2 in.

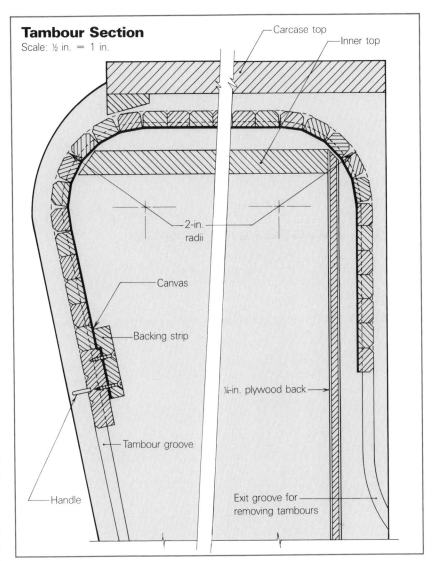

Tambour Section

Scale: ½ in. = 1 in.

- Carcase top
- Inner top
- 2-in. radii
- Canvas
- Backing strip
- ¼-in. plywood back
- Tambour groove
- Handle
- Exit groove for removing tambours

2

To bevel both edges on the slats, I fastened the router upside down in a router table and attached a fence with a rabbet for the ⅜-in. slat thickness. I clamped two featherboards to the plywood to push the slats into the rabbet **(2)**. The slats should fit tight, but still move freely.

After you have beveled all the slats, make a jig to hold them in place while the canvas is glued on. Nail a straightedge on a piece of plywood and nail down another straight piece at a right angle to the first one **(3)**.

3

Now place all the slats for one door face down and tight against the two straight pieces. Nail on a third piece, also at a right angle to the first straightedge, to push the slats together **(4)**. The slats should be held tight, but not pushed too hard, because as the glued-on canvas dries, it will shrink a little and could make the door concave.

Before gluing the canvas on, check that the tambour measurement across the slats is the same at both ends **(5)**. I used ordinary untreated painters' canvas for these tambour doors, but if the back of the door will be exposed, thin leather could be used.

4

5

Mark the width of the canvas on the slats **(6)** and you are ready to put the glue on.

The best glue to use is hot hide glue—it sticks well to the canvas the minute it cools. In a double boiler, heat the glue to the consistency of honey [*Book 1*, p. 94]. Then brush it on, always going with the grain of the tambours **(7)**; if you sweep the brush across the slats, the glue might be forced into the cracks, gluing the slats together. Spread the glue evenly, and go beyond the pencil lines to be sure that the edges of the canvas will be stuck down.

When positioning the slats inside the jig, I placed an extra slat on each end. This slat **(8)** doesn't get glued; it is there to prevent the canvas from being glued to the jig. Take your time putting on the glue, since it will be cold before the canvas goes on anyway.

6

7

8

9

10

Fold the canvas as shown **(9)** to make it easier to lay it down without air pockets. Remember to leave about 6 in. extra at what will be the bottom of the door, where the handle is to be attached. This will be screwed down and trimmed later.

When the canvas has been laid down, get all the air out and flatten the material with your hands. Starting from one edge of the canvas and in the middle **(10)**, push across the door in the same direction as the tambours. If you push across the tambours, you will stretch the canvas and make the door concave. Work your way out from the middle toward both edges until all the air pockets have been removed.

Now reheat the glue with a warm iron **(11)**. Do one small area at a time, again moving along the tambours. Watch that the hot glue doesn't come through the canvas, or the canvas will become brittle and break when the glue is dry. (If the glue just comes through in a few small places, that won't hurt it.)

While the glue is still hot from the iron, push the canvas down using a veneer hammer or a block with rounded edges **(12)**. As always, be sure to go with the tambours and work from the middle outward. About a half hour after you're done, remove the door from the jig to check if any slats have been glued together and, if so, scrape off the glue between them.

11

12

Cutting the rabbets When the glue is dry, cut the door to size on the tablesaw **(13)**. Keep the side that was against the first straightedge on the jig against the fence on the saw. Cut the uneven end, leaving the door a little wide. Then reset the fence to the exact width of the door and cut the other end.

Because the tambours are ⅜ in. thick but the grooves they run in are only ¼ in. by ¼ in., the tambours have to be rabbeted and fit to the groove on both ends. I usually cut the rabbets on the back side of the door and always make them a little longer than the grooves are deep, as shown at top right. If the wood in the cabinet moves, the door will still slide freely.

If the rabbet were cut to fit tightly in the groove, as shown in the lower drawing at right, the slightest movement of the wood in the carcase would make it impossible to move the door.

To cut the rabbets, clamp a straightedge on the door as a router fence. Here I'm cutting the rabbet on the back side of the door **(14)**.

Tambour Rabbets

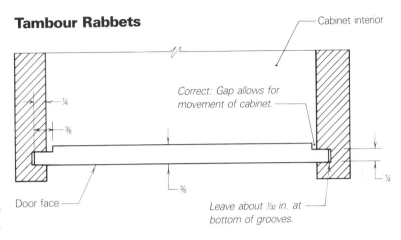

Cabinet interior

Correct: Gap allows for movement of cabinet.

Door face

Leave about 1/32 in. at bottom of grooves.

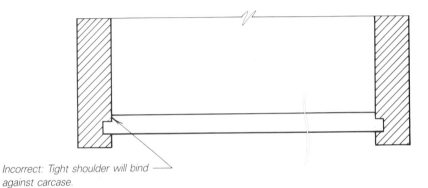

Incorrect: Tight shoulder will bind against carcase.

13

14

15

Handles I decided to add separate handles to these doors because of the weight of the horizontal tambours and the fact that they would be mounted high on the wall above the countertop. But whenever you work with tambour doors, the handles have to be removable so the tambours can be taken out and repaired if anything goes wrong. This is easily done by placing the handles in a bottom slat, which is attached after the tambours have been installed.

When the rabbets have been cut in the tambours, make the bottom slat the width of three tambours, and fit the handles to it. I wanted the bottom slat to look the same as the rest of the tambours, so I cut two beveled grooves in it. I ran the slat across the tablesaw, with the blade tilted to a 45° angle. Once the bottom slat is made, rout ⅛-in. grooves in it for the handles. Then glue in the ⅛-in.-thick handles, with the end grain exposed, as shown here **(15)**. This makes the handles stronger than if the grain ran in the same direction as the grain in the slats. With use, the end grain will become darker than the rest of the cabinet, which I think makes a nice detail.

Now fit the bottom slat and the backing strip that holds the canvas in place **(16)**. (These are only positioned, fit and drilled now; they will be screwed on after the door is installed.)

16

Tambour/Handle Detail
Scale: ½ in. = 1 in.

¼

Groove in carcase for rabbet

½-in.-wide tambour slats with beveled edges

Solid-tambour bottom slat

Carcase bottom

Front View

Note: *This view shows handle position for wide kitchen tambour doors.*

⅜

⅜

Canvas

¾-in. #8 flat-head screw

Backing strip

Trim canvas here.

Handle

½

1⅝

³⁄₁₆

½

Side View

The carcase Once the tambours doors and the bottom handle slats are done, you are ready to make the carcase. Here is how to make the upper tambour cabinets for this kitchen.

First shape the sides out of solid wood and then cut the joints. (I usually avoid installing tambour doors in a plywood carcase because the end grain of the plywood will wear out the softer long grain of the tambours.) I put the carcase together with half-blind multiple-spline joints, using a router with a template guide and a ¼-in. plywood jig to make the groove for the tambour door and the mortise for the back cleat. (For these cabinets, I made an exit groove in the back of the cabinet for installing and removing the doors.) I nailed the jig right to the side, but placed the nail where the holes for the adjustable shelf brackets would be drilled later.

After I removed the jig, I made the grooves for the plywood back and the solid-wood inside top **(17)** using the router and a fence.

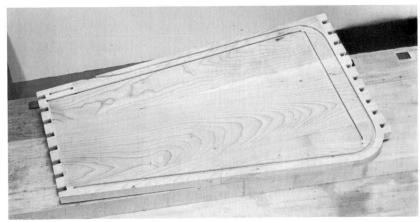

17

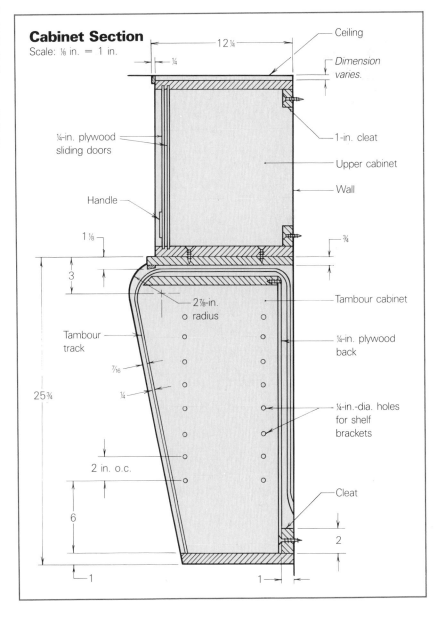

Cabinet Section
Scale: ⅛ in. = 1 in.

12¼

¼

Ceiling

Dimension varies.

¼-in. plywood sliding doors

1-in. cleat

Upper cabinet

Wall

Handle

1⅛

¾

3

2⅞-in. o radius

Tambour cabinet

Tambour track

¼-in. plywood back

⁷⁄₁₆

¼

25¾

¼-in.-dia. holes for shelf brackets

2 in. o.c.

6

Cleat

2

1

1

18

(18) Here is the cabinet lying on its side, with the inside top and back in position, ready to be glued together. Once the cabinet is assembled and glued, it can be sanded and oiled. It is a good idea to rub the groove in the carcase (and the ends of the tambours) with paraffin so the door slides more easily. Install the tambour door through the exit groove and screw on the bottom slat and the backing strip. Then trim off the excess canvas.

(19) Here is the finished cabinet closed. To install these tambour cabinets, I screwed the upper cabinet to the wall first. Then I screwed the top of the tambour cabinets and the bottom of the upper cabinets together. Next I screwed the tambour cabinets to the wall through the bottom cleat.

19

Vertical tambours If the slats in your tambour doors are vertical, such as the tambour sliders in the office (pp. 188-199), you can simply make the top groove in the cabinet ⅜ in. deep and the bottom one ³⁄₁₆ in. deep, as shown at bottom right. Then you can push the door up into the top groove and drop it down into the bottom one. Note that the tambours in the office are rabbeted on the outside to provide finger grips.

If you are making vertical tambours that have to turn a corner and retract into the cabinet, however, you must screw an extra piece in for a handle on one end of the door. In that case, the handle piece should be ³⁄₁₆ in. longer than the rest of the tambours in the door to keep it from jumping out of the grooves.

Rolltop tambours If very long tambours are used, as for example in a rolltop desk where they may be 4 ft. to 5 ft. long, they have to be treated differently. The slats should be joined together so they don't separate when pressure is put on the tambours. The drawing at top right shows three different ways of joining them. The first is a matching cove and bead routed into the edges of the slats. The second is a shiplap joint. The third involves drilling holes through the tambours and inserting three or four flexible wires to keep them together. The first two methods would be used with a canvas backing; the third would not.

On rolltop desks, the wood for the rabbet that rides in the groove has to be removed from the front, because the slats are thicker and they would not otherwise be able to make the sharp turns at the corners. In that case I would cut a large rabbet so that there would be enough play. I would also incorporate the rabbet as a design detail, perhaps by running it down one edge of each tambour, as I did for the vertical tambours in the office. □

Tambour Sections

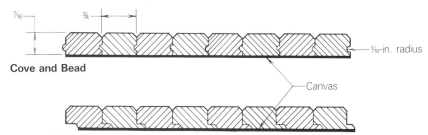

Cove and Bead

Shiplap Joint

Flexible wire in drilled holes

Wired Tambour

Vertical and Rolltop Tambours

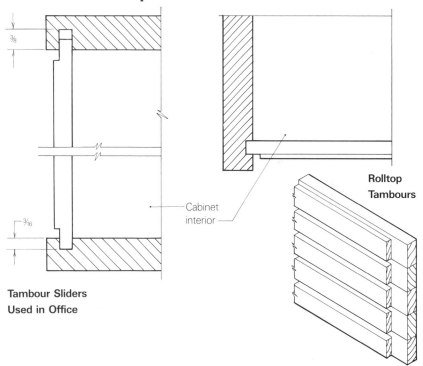

Tambour Sliders
Used in Office

Rolltop Tambours

Gallery
Chapter 8

Oval bar with tambour doors; walnut; 64 in. high; 1984. *Photo by Steven Sloman.*

Above and at left: Bar; rosewood. Above: Corner chair; mahogany. Corner lamp; walnut with rice-paper backing. Coffee table; walnut with rose-metal inlay. Bowl; elm. Knox Gallery, Buffalo, N.Y., 1961.

Kitchen; walnut cabinets, slate countertops; Rochester, N.Y., 1954.

Wall-hung sideboard; walnut with tambour doors; 36 in. high by 9 ft. long by 36 in. wide; 1955. Sideboard hangs about 10 in. above the floor. *Photo by Linn Duncan.*

Pedestal linen cabinet; walnut; 32 in. high by 48 in. long by 18 in. wide; 1980. Sides, top and doors are shaped to resemble raised-panel construction. *Photo by Roger Birn.*

Chest of drawers; Japanese ash plywood carcase with walnut drawers and frame; 1950s. Middle drawer flips down and shelf pulls out for writing surface. Design was inspired by the rafters in a cottage ceiling.

Flip-top writing desk; walnut;
48 in. long; 1950s.

Dining/boardroom table; walnut; 6 ft.
long; 1954. *Photo by Linn Duncan.*

Dining room and stairway; walnut cabinets, stairway and railing; Rochester, N.Y., 1955.

Turning flip-top table; mahogany base with fiddleback-mahogany-veneer plywood top; 1983. Side chair (on left); walnut; 1957. Side chair (on right); walnut; 1983. *Photo by Steven Sloman.*

Cabinet; mahogany; 62 in. high; 1983. Doors and back are frame-and-panel construction. Sides are solid wood, like top and bottom, and are relieved for the panel detail. *Photo by Steven Sloman.*

Coffee table; walnut with rose-metal inlay; 1983. *Photo by Steven Sloman.*

Three-legged stools; walnut; 13 in., 18 in. and 22 in. high; 1983. *Photo by Steven Sloman.*

Publisher, Books: Leslie Carola
Associate Editors: Scott Landis, Christine Timmons
Design Director: Roger Barnes
Associate Art Director: Heather Brine Lambert
Copy/Production Editor: Nancy Stabile
Editorial Consultant: John Dunnigan
Illustrations: Charles E. Lockhart, Seth Stem
Cover Illustration: Paola Lazzaro
Photography: Roger Birn
Manager of Production Services: Gary Mancini
Coordinator of Production Services: Dave DeFeo
Production Manager: Mary Galpin
System Operators: Claudia Blake Applegate, Nancy-Lou Knapp
Darkroom: Deborah Cooper, Mary Ann Snieckus
Pasteup: Ruth Eaton, Karen Pease Marino

Typeface: Univers II Light 8.9 point
Paper: Warren Patina, 70 lb., Neutral pH
Printer and Binder: Kingsport Press, Kingsport, Tenn.